In Memory Of

Facing Facts

Facing Facts

Stephen Neale

CLARENDON PRESS · OXFORD

OXFORD
UNIVERSITY PRESS

Great Clarendon Street, Oxford OX2 6DP

Oxford University Press is a department of the University of Oxford.
It furthers the University's objective of excellence in research, scholarship,
and education by publishing worldwide in

Oxford New York

Athens Auckland Bangkok Bogotá Buenos Aires Cape Town
Chennai Dar es Salaam Delhi Florence Hong Kong Istanbul Karachi
Kolkata Kuala Lumpur Madrid Melbourne Mexico City Mumbai Nairobi
Paris São Paulo Shanghai Singapore Taipei Tokyo Toronto Warsaw
and associated companies in Berlin Ibadan

Oxford is a registered trade mark of Oxford University Press
in the UK and in certain other countries

Published in the United States
by Oxford University Press Inc., New York

British Library Cataloguing in Publication Data

Data available

Library of Congress Cataloging in Publication Data
Neale, Stephen.
Facing facts/Stephen Neale.
p. cm.
Includes bibliographical references and index.
1. Facts (Philosophy) 2. Philosophy, Modern—20th century. I. Title.
B105.F3 N43 2001   111—dc21   2001036729
ISBN 0-19-924715-3

1 3 5 7 9 10 8 6 4 2

Typeset in Sabon by
Cambrian Typesetters, Frimley, Surrey
Printed in Great Britain
on acid-free paper by
Biddles Ltd
Guildford & King's Lynn

Don't say "face facts" to me. . . . Everybody keeps saying it just now; but the fact is, it's impossible to face facts. They're like the walls of a room, all around you. If you face one wall, you must have your back to the other three.

(E. M. Forster)

Thus the theory of description matters most.
It is the theory of the word for those
For whom the word is the making of the world,
The buzzing world and lisping firmament.

(Wallace Stevens)

For Haidy

Preface

At the 1995 meeting of Logic and Language, held at the University of London, I gave a talk on something I had been discussing in seminars at Birkbeck College that spring and at the University of California, Berkeley, the previous year: Kurt Gödel's "slingshot" argument and its philosophical implications. I had received so much stimulating and challenging feedback from Herman Cappelen, William Craig, Tim Crane, Donald Davidson, Josh Dever, Eli Dresner, Marcus Giaquinto, Jim Hopkins, Martin Jones, Ariela Lazar, Jonathan Lebowitsch, Michael Martin, Benson Mates, John Searle, Hans Sluga, Barry Smith, Scott Sturgeon, Bruce Vermazen, and Jamie Whyte that I was not at all confident I could get across my points convincingly in a one-hour lecture at the conference. My presentation was inevitably compressed, but the main ideas seemed to go over well, mainly because the audience was so well versed in the relevant subject matter. The editor of *Mind* was present and, perhaps aware of my constitutional inability to send anything to a journal without semi-official encouragement, asked if I would consider writing up my talk for submission, on the off-chance that *Mind* decided to publish selected proceedings of the conference. I was torn, as I felt I could not do justice to the issues in a journal article and had viewed myself as in the process of writing a book. Several weeks later I aired the main ideas again in lectures at the Universities of Oslo, Stockholm, and Stuttgart, where Jens-Erik Fenstad, Olav Gjelsvik, Sören Häggkvist, Matthias Högström, Hans Kamp, Jonathan Knowles, Per-Martin Löf, Jan-Tore Lønning, Paul Needham, Peter Pagin, Dag Prawitz, Bjørn Ramberg, and Dag Westerståhl left no symbol unturned. For the following five or six weeks I had the privilege of a residential fellowship at the Rockefeller Foundation's Villa Serbelloni in Bellagio, where I was able to devote my time to preparing the article. Trying to explain myself to poets, potters, and virologists was not always easy; but the experience as a whole was invaluable, and the setting ideal for concentrated work.

The editor of *Mind* was not amused by the length of the Bellagio paper and rightly ordered me to shorten it. After much haggling, I delivered a pruned version in time for the October 1995 issue, where it appeared under the prosaic title "The Philosophical Significance of Gödel's Slingshot". I stand by the main points of that paper and a follow-up, "Slingshots and Boomerangs", that Josh Dever and I wrote for the January 1997 issue. But a growing correspondence about corners I had cut to produce a journal-length piece, the exchange in *Mind*, a reply by W. V. Quine to my discussion of his "slingshot" arguments, further discussions with Davidson and Searle, and the growing realization that a more detailed exposition of my 1995 proof and its philosophical morals still constituted a considerable project led me to complete the book I had originally intended—minus chapters on necessity, analyticity, and apriority which mushroomed into a sequel entitled *Possibilities*.

For the past six years I have been bombarded with questions and advice. Audiences at Rutgers University, the University of California at Berkeley, the University of California at San Diego, Stanford University, the University of Oslo, the University of Stockholm, the University of Stuttgart, Birkbeck College, the University of London, Oxford University, Cambridge University, the Federal University of Pernambuco, Brazil, the University of Konstanz, the Karlovy Vary Colloquium, the University of Delaware, the University of Barcelona, the University of Haifa, and the University of Iceland helped me to sharpen many points (and dispense with others). Besides the people already mentioned, I would like to thank Varol Akman, Kent Bach, John Blair, Michael Brody, Liz Camp, Ramon Cirera, Alan Code, Sarah Cole, Yvette Derksen, Max Deutsch, Michael Devitt, Wayne Dodd, Dagfinn Føllesdal, Rick Gaitskell, Delia Graff, B. Gudmundsdottir, Carolin Hahnemann, Peter Hanks, Richard Hanley, Gilbert Harman, Jennifer Hornsby, Paul Horwich, Jennifer Hudin, Meleana Isaacs, David Israel, Bibi Jacob, Ruth Kempson, Philip Kitcher, Hilary Koprowski, Saul Kripke, Ernie LePore, Bernard Linsky, Brian Loar, Peter Ludlow, Trip McCrossin, Colin McGinn, Josep Macià, John

Madsen, Paolo Mancosu, Genoveva Marti, Maryam Modjaz, Gary Ostertag, John Perry, Ruy de Queiroz, the late W. V. Quine, the late Jane Rabnett, Greg Ray, François Récanati, Stephen Reed, Teresa Robertson, Mark Sainsbury, Nathan Salmon, Stephen Schiffer, Gabriel Segal, Andrew Solomon, David Sosa, Patricia Spengler, Tim Stowell, Matthew Whelpton, and Zsofia Zvolenszky for many helpful observations, suggestions, or questions. Very special thanks must go to Akman, Davidson, Dever, LePore, Sainsbury, Searle, and Zvolenszky for detailed comments over the years, many stimulating discussions, and excellent advice. Akman, Sainsbury, and Zvolenszky read through the penultimate draft of the entire manuscript and picked up scores of things I had missed.

I gratefully acknowledge the support of the University of California (1994–5), the Rockefeller Foundation (Spring 1995), the National Endowment for the Humanities (Spring 1998), Rutgers University (Spring 2000), the British School at Athens (1999–2001), and the Universities of Stockholm and London for various short-term visiting professorships during which I was able to present much of the work and pick some great minds. Thanks are also due to my patient editors, Peter Momtchiloff and Charlotte Jenkins of Oxford University Press, my copy-editor Laurien Berkeley, my former student and co-author Josh Dever, and successive research assistants from 1994 onwards: Meleana Isaacs, Liz Camp, and Zsofia Zvolenszky. Without these people, my fellow inmates at Le Gamin, Space Untitled, Patisserie Valerie, and Café Naxos, and the support and encouragement of family and friends, instead of a book I would have a thousand pages of notes for yet another distant book.

My biggest debt is to my wife, Haidy, who makes all things possible. To her this book is lovingly dedicated.

Naxos   S.R.A.N.
June 2001

Contents

I

The End of Representation?

The idea that one thing might represent another is a cornerstone of modern philosophy: thoughts, utterances, and inscriptions are said to have content in virtue of their power to represent reality; those that do the job accurately are true, they correspond to the facts or mirror reality (nature, the world). This idea is not without its critics. Donald Davidson and Richard Rorty, for example, have rejected talk of representations, which they see as bound up with unfortunate talk of facts, states of affairs, situations, counterfactual circumstances, and correspondence theories of truth, talk that lures philosophers into empty debates about scepticism, realism, subjectivity, representational and computational theories of mind, other possible worlds, and divergent conceptual schemes that represent reality in different ways to different persons, periods, or cultures.[1] The time has come, Davidson and Rorty claim, to see only folly in the idea of mental and linguistic representations of reality. With this realization philosophy will be transformed as many of its staple problems, posits, and procedures evaporate; "traditional" philosophical problems will now defy coherent articulation as they presuppose an untenable dualism of *facts* and their *representational surrogates*. If there are neither facts nor things that represent them—the legitimacy of each is said to depend upon the legitimacy of the other—attempts to frame problems about, for example, realism, relativism, scepticism, and objectivity are doomed.

How much substance is there to this startling line of thought? I shall provide a precise, albeit complex answer based on a watertight deductive proof, a looser form of which has been used by Davidson himself to cast doubt on an ontology of facts. The

---

[1] See in particular Davidson (1984, 1989, 1990, 1996) and Rorty (1979, 1991, 1992).

content of the proof I construct is due in no small measure to Kurt Gödel (1944); but the *form* in which I present it originates with W. V. Quine (1953*c*, 1960). Gödel and Quine were both unclear at key points, but with some work a thoroughly transparent proof of great philosophical significance can be constructed using Gödel's hints and Quine's framework. The proof demonstrates conclusively (i) that any supposedly non-truth-functional operation must satisfy an exacting logical condition in order to avoid collapsing into a truth-function, and (ii) that any theory of facts, states of affairs, situations, or propositions must satisfy a corresponding condition if such entities are not to collapse into a unity. No great technical expertise is needed to understand the proof—from a mathematical perspective it is remarkably simple. But a lot of work is involved in finding exactly the right pieces, in assembling them systematically, in rendering the proof's logico-semantic presuppositions transparent and uncontroversial, in working out how to apply them in concrete cases, and in seeing how to draw definite philosophical implications.

1.1 FACTS AND REPRESENTATIONS

A proper examination of the case against representations made by Davidson and Rorty must include an analysis of Davidson's notorious argument against *facts*, for the position he and Rorty espouse boils down to this: in order to give any substance to the idea of representations of reality, reciprocal substance must be given to the idea that there are facts which true statements and beliefs represent. But the requisite substance cannot be provided, Davidson claims, because a modicum of logic and semantics can be invoked to show that any attempt to spell out a satisfactory theory of facts will lead to a formal collapse. Doubts have been expressed about the importance of Davidson's rejection of facts to his assault on representationalism. But the rejection is vital, and Davidson has confirmed as much in recent work: "my rejection of facts as entities correspondence to which can explain truth is central to my views of truth and meaning, to my rejection of the scheme–content distinction, representationalism, and much more" (1999*e*: 667).

What is involved in rejecting facts? The answer can be understood only in the context of a specific aim of much twentieth-

The End of Representation

3

century philosophy: to characterize the contents of our thoughts, utterances, and inscriptions in a systematic and compositional fashion. There is no prospect of doing this, many have thought, without articulating theories of facts, states, or propositions to serve as the items that are represented. Facts are usually seen as non-linguistic entities to which accurate representations *correspond*. But the representational power of false beliefs, utterances, and inscriptions cannot be neglected, and so theories of facts have been supplemented (or supplanted) by theories of states of affairs, and propositions. Finally, with a view to explicating modal and counterfactual discourse, maximal—or at least very big—collections of, for instance, states, situations, or propositions have been taken by some philosophers to constitute alternatives to the way things have actually turned out, so-called possible worlds. In short, great efforts have gone into articulating theories of entities like facts, situations, states, propositions, and worlds, and it is widely held that this has been a good thing because questions about, for example, meaning, reference, truth, causation, explanation, time, change, necessity, action, knowledge, perception, and obligation can be tackled more fruitfully with theories of such entities at hand.[2]

But according to Davidson there are no individual facts; there is at most a *factual entirety*, an objective world largely not of our own making. Like Strawson (1950a), Quine (1960), and Geach (1972), Davidson maintains that positing facts achieves nothing; but he also provides two more direct reasons for resisting facts: (i) facts are not postulated by our most plausible theories of meaning, and consequently there is no sensible way of motivating their existence; (ii) there is a formal argument, a *collapsing argument*, that effectively undermines any appeal to individual facts, "a persuasive

---

[2] Early in the twentieth century Russell (1918), Wittgenstein (1921), C. I. Lewis (1923) and others made use of facts. Ontologies of facts, states of affairs, and situations were later proposed or discussed by e.g. Alston (1996), Armstrong (1993, 1997), Austin (1950, 1954), Barwise and Etchemendy (1989), Barwise and Perry (1980, 1981, 1983), Baylis (1948, 1968), Bennett and Baylis (1939), Bennett (1988), Bergmann (1960, 1992), Clark (1975), Ducasse (1940, 1942), Fine (1982), Grossman (1983, 1992), C. I. Lewis (1944), Mellor (1991, 1995), Olson (1987), Perry (1996), Pollock (1984), Prior (1948, 1967), Ramsey (1927), Reichenbach (1947), Searle (1995, 1998), Skyrms (1981), Sommers (1993), Taylor (1976, 1985), Tooley (1997), van Fraassen (1969, 1973), Vendler (1967a,b), Wells (1949), and N. L. Wilson (1959b, 1974). Possible worlds (in distinct varieties) have been employed by e.g. Carnap (1947), Hintikka (1963), Kanger (1957), Kripke (1963a,b, 1980), C. I. Lewis (1923, 1944), D. K. Lewis (1973, 1985), and Montague (1963).

argument, usually traced to Frege (in one form) or Kurt Gödel (in another), to the effect that there can be at most one fact" (1996: 266). And a single "Great Fact", as Davidson laughingly calls it, is insufficient to underpin representational philosophy.

With the case against facts made, Davidson believes that the case against representations—and with it the case against correspondence theories of truth—comes more or less for free:

> The correct objection to correspondence theories [of truth] is . . . that such theories fail to provide entities to which truth vehicles (whether we take these to be statements, sentences, or utterances) can be said to correspond. If this is right, and I am convinced it is, we ought also to question the popular assumption that sentences, or their spoken tokens, or sentence-like entities or configurations in our brains, can properly be called "representations", since there is nothing for them to represent. If we give up facts as entities that make sentences true, we ought to give up representations at the same time, for the legitimacy of each depends on the legitimacy of the other. (1990: 304)

Once we give up representations, we lose our grip on a number of traditional philosophical problems and notions, for example those surrounding talk of conceptual relativism:

> Beliefs are true or false, but they represent nothing. It is good to be rid of representations, and with them the correspondence theory of truth, for it is thinking that there are representations that engenders thoughts of relativism (1989: 162–3).

The intelligibility of relativism presupposes an untenable dualism between "conceptual scheme" and "empirical content", between representations and things represented. And as Davidson (1984: 193–4, 1999e: 667) recognizes, a key premiss in his central argument against this dualism is that there are no (distinct) *facts* to which true utterances (or thoughts) correspond. In summary, the success of Davidson's central arguments against the scheme–content distinction, representations, and correspondence theories of truth depends upon the prior success of his arguments against *facts*.

1.2 ANTI-REPRESENTATIONALISM

I am not wholly unsympathetic to the view that much of Rorty's (1979, 1991, 1992) critique of representational philosophy is bluster.

But there is an aspect that should be taken seriously, at least prima facie: the attempt to push Davidson's dismissal of the scheme–content distinction to its limit. According to Rorty, modern philosophy is exhausted by debates about the relation between mind and reality, or language and reality; and the only useful application of the phrase "the problems of philosophy" is to "the set of interlinked problems posed by representationalist theories of knowledge ... problems about the relation between mind and reality, or language and reality, viewed as the relation between a medium of representation and what is purportedly represented" (1992: 371). For Rorty, the problems of post-Cartesian philosophy amount to the problems of representation. For roughly the first three-quarters of the twentieth century these problems amounted to problems of linguistic representation; during the last quarter they shifted back to problems of mental representation. By undermining the scheme–content distinction, Davidson has made it all but impossible to formulate many of the traditional philosophical problems:

If one gives up thinking that there are representations, then one will have little interest in the relation between mind and the world or language and the world. So one will lack interest in either the old disputes between realists and idealists or the contemporary quarrels within analytic philosophy about "realism" and "antirealism". For the latter quarrels presuppose that bits of the world "make sentences true", and that these sentences in turn represent those bits. Without these presuppositions, we would not be interested in trying to distinguish between those true sentences which correspond to "facts of the matter" and those which do not (the distinction around which the realist-vs.-antirealist controversies revolve). (1992: 372)

Once we give up *tertia*, we give up (or trivialise) the notions of representation and correspondence, and thereby give up the possibility of epistemological scepticism. (1991: 139)

It is a virtue of Davidson's work, says Rorty, that it shows us "how to give up" truth-makers and representations. Davidson, as portrayed by Rorty, is an "anti-representationalist" philosopher in a tradition said to include Dewey, Heidegger, Wittgenstein, Quine, and Sellars. The attack on the distinction between scheme and content "summarizes and synthesizes Wittgenstein's mockery of his own *Tractatus*, Quine's criticism of

Carnap, and Sellars's attack on the empiricist 'Myth of the Given' " (1991: 5). These philosophers, says Rorty, are linked by a rejection of the "reciprocal relations" of *making true* and *representing* that are central to so-called "representationalism". But there is more to anti-representationalism than this; it is "the attempt to eschew discussion of realism by denying that the notion of 'representation', or that of 'fact of the matter', has any useful role in philosophy" (1991: 2). Davidson is an anti-representationalist because he is said to be committed to the thesis that "there is no point to debates between realism and antirealism, for such debates presuppose the empty and misleading idea of beliefs 'being made true' " (1991: 128). And it is precisely the idea that sentences are "made true" by non-linguistic entities, i.e. *facts*, that Davidson is meant to have discredited, and that has led to the rejection of the scheme–content distinction and thereby the evaporation of controversies about, for example, "realism" and "scepticism".

There is a revolutionary tone to Rorty's claims: once we accept that we must give up representations, we will realize that we are no longer confronted with the standard problems of philosophy. The demise of representations renders the stock problems "obsolete" and presents a challenge for philosophers to find a new place for themselves within the academy. Debates between "realists" and "antirealists" and between "sceptics" and "antisceptics", to name just two, are "pointless . . . the results of being held captive by a picture, a picture from which we should by now have wriggled free" (1991: 2–3).

Although Rorty's rhetoric is simultaneously flamboyant and imprecise, it is clear from some of the remarks I have quoted that his attack on representationalism trades heavily on Davidson's rejection of facts and conceptual schemes. At the same time Rorty's conclusions seem more radical. According to Davidson, the demise of representations ushers in an era in which we can eliminate some philosophical questions, eliminate popular answers to other more recalcitrant questions, and mercifully close off certain barren avenues of research. Rorty goes further: he sees the demise as presenting an opportunity to "shrug off" the traditional philosophical questions as "pointless" or "obsolete", to turn our backs on those who bring them up; the traditional problems evaporate with representations of reality; and once the word is out, philosophers will have to find other things to do if they are to earn their keep. Presumably, there will also be trouble in the territories philosophy shares with cognitive science and linguistics, for these areas are just as representational as those at the centre of philosophy. Cognitive science is standardly taken to be the study of the mind undertaken through the philosophical and empirical study of mental representations—of many stripes, to be sure. And theoretical linguistics, on its dominant construal at least, is the development and investigation of systems of rules or principles that generate representations of linguistic structure, the meanings of which are a function of the ways in which their components hook up to the world. If there are no representations, a good deal of work that passes for serious research in philosophy, in cognitive psychology, in linguistics, and even in philosophical logic is going to be worthless.

As I mentioned at the outset, one aim of the present work is to ascertain how much there is to the critique of representationalism. On the surface, my strategy is simple: I shall subject Davidson's arguments against facts to agonizing scrutiny. However, so many interlocking logical and semantic issues are raised by these arguments that a successful examination requires the clarification of a number of foundational issues concerning the nature of compositionality, extensionality, inference principles, and the semantics of definite descriptions and class abstracts. Rorty is surely right that most philosophical problems will not be dissolved by a critique of language. But—and this is where he blunders—it is quite wrong to conclude from this that a careful (and perhaps formal) examination of sectors of our language will not be philosophically fruitful, for it is by such examination that a great deal of nonsense is exposed. And there can be no reason to stipulate in advance of such investigations that claims made about facts or representations are magically exempt from critical scrutiny. To declare in advance that such examinations are "pointless" or "obsolete" or "unintelligible" is to commit the worst kind of intellectual sin: to declare off limits any form of enquiry that subjects a favoured position to careful scrutiny. Such a sin cannot be tolerated in medicine, science, banking, gardening, or cooking, and it cannot be tolerated in philosophy. Nor can the claim that careful examination itself presupposes the viability of representationalism.

1.3 COLLAPSING ARGUMENTS

The critique of the fact–representation distinction constitutes a direct challenge to the presuppositions of much work in modern philosophy, a challenge that can be met straightforwardly by the construction of a viable theory of facts. But according to Davidson, a superficially simple, formal argument shows that no such theory can be constructed.

The type of argument in question was for a while called the *Frege Argument* because Alonzo Church (1943*a*) and Kurt Gödel (1944) had claimed to discern it in the work of Gottlob Frege, who argued that a sentence's truth-value is its reference (*Bedeutung*). Frege appears to have reached this conclusion, at least in part, by way of the conviction that if sentences have references, then in order to preserve a valuable and intuitively plausible Principle of Composition, exactly two entities must be postulated to serve as their references, one to which every true sentence refers, the other to which every false sentence refers. In view of the evident difficulty involved in attributing to Frege precisely the form of argument used by Church and Gödel, I shall not call it the Frege Argument— I will, however, try to establish just what sort of argument *can* be extracted from Frege's writings and determine how close that argument comes to those Church and Gödel present. I shall use the label introduced by Jon Barwise and John Perry (1981, 1983): in deference to the minimal machinery and presuppositions of the type of argument, and its giant-slaying potential, Barwise and Perry dubbed it the "slingshot"; but, as we shall see, the form of slingshot used by Gödel has a feature that makes it more useful than the form used by Church and those he has influenced, so really there are at least two versions of the slingshot, as Davidson notes.[3]

---

[3] Reed (1993) goes out of his way to argue that Church was the originator of slingshot arguments—mistakenly reading Wallace (1969) as claiming it was Gödel—on the grounds that (*a*) Church's review of Carnap's (1942) book *Introduction to Semantics* appeared in the May 1943 issue of the *Philosophical Review*, (*b*) Gödel submitted his (1944) paper "Russell's Mathematical Logic" for publication in the collection on Russell only on May 17 1943, and (*c*) Gödel thanks Church for assistance with English expression at the end of his paper. Caution is in order here. First, dates decorating journals are notoriously unreliable; witness the spurious publication date of Reed's own paper: the volume of *Logique et Analyse* in which it appears is dated September–December 1993, but Reed mentions in his paper a typescript of mine dated 2 May 1994, and Diderik

A slingshot is a *collapsing argument*, an argument purporting to show that there are fewer items of a given kind than might be supposed previously. Such arguments have been used by Church, Quine, and Davidson in attempts to undermine a tightly connected batch of philosophical and linguistic theses, most notably (i) the thesis that there are individual *facts* to which true sentences correspond, (ii) the closely related thesis that declarative sentences—relativized to particular utterances or inscriptions—refer to *propositions, states of affairs,* or *situations,* (iii) the seemingly unrelated thesis that expressions such as "necessarily", "possibly", "probably", "provably", "before", "after", and "because" are (on at least some of their uses) semantically equivalent to non-extensional sentence connectives, and (iv) the thesis that languages may mechanically yet fruitfully combine quantifiers and modal operators. In each of these cases there is meant to be a collapse of some sort: (i) the class of facts collapses into a singleton, the "Great Fact"; (ii) the class of items capable of serving as the references of sentences collapses into a class of just two entities which, following Frege, we might as well take to be Truth and Falsity; (iii) the class of sentence connectives satisfying an elementary logical condition collapses into the boring class of truth-functional connectives; and (iv) modal distinctions collapse—i.e. $\phi \equiv \Box\phi$ is valid—in languages that attempt to combine modality and quantification.

Such collapses, if they could be demonstrated conclusively, would certainly embarrass approaches to the semantics of natural language seeking to get work out of facts, situations, states of affairs, propositions, or non-truth-functional sentence connectives. But for reasons already mentioned this seems to be just the beginning. If there are no facts to which true sentences correspond, it is far from obvious how facts can function as "truth-makers", causal relata, or objects of knowledge; if sentences do not stand for states-of-affairs or situations, then it is unclear how such entities can be

---

Batens's editorial preface states that Reed's paper *was* presented on the afternoon of Friday 16 December 1994 at a conference on philosophical logic held at the University of Ghent, and that the volume forms part of *after-the-fact* conference proceedings. (The "September–December 1993" volume of *Logique et Analyse* was actually published in 1995.) Secondly, it is unclear how long Gödel had been working on his long piece for the collection on Russell or how long Church had been working on his brief review of Carnap's 1942 book (see n. 6). As I point out in Ch. 9, there is some evidence that a proto-slingshot was also forming in Quine's mind around 1941.

characterized in ways that make them the sorts of things that can be perceived, desired, deplored, brought about, or prevented by our actions (and inactions); and if words like "necessarily", "possibly", "probably", "provably", "before", "after", and "because" cannot be treated as non-truth-functional sentence connectives, and if there is no prospect of combining modality with quantification, then philosophy's favourite non-truth-functional logics are of little value when it comes to addressing problems in metaphysics, action theory, ethics, and the philosophy of mind. Finally, as I have already made clear, if Davidson and Rorty are right, then if there are no facts, there are no representations; and if there are no representations, there would appear to be precious little chance of formulating many of the traditional "problems of philosophy".

There is an extensive literature on slingshot arguments, but to my mind almost all of it is confused or inconclusive: friends and foes alike seem to commit themselves to needlessly strong, often unmotivated, and occasionally outlandish theses concerning well-formedness, variable-binding, transparency, extensionality, substitutivity, identity, rigidity, direct reference, semantic innocence, aboutness, analyticity, causation, intensional entities, domain purification, class membership, the semantics–pragmatics distinction, the semantics of definite descriptions and class abstracts, logical equivalence, logical consequence, logical truth, and logical constants. I propose to answer the important logical questions raised by slingshot arguments by reflecting carefully upon (i) the proposed inferential properties of sentence connectives, (ii) the most plausible semantic treatments of descriptions and abstracts, and (iii) the elegant slingshot suggested by Gödel (1944) which, until recently, had received much less attention than those presented by Church, Quine, and Davidson.[4]

---

[4] Discussions of the slingshot arguments by Church, Quine, and Davidson include those by Altman *et al.* (1979), Anscombe (1969), Barwise and Perry (1980, 1981, 1983), Bennett (1988), Burge (1986*a*), Cummins and Gottlieb (1972), Dale (1978), Davies (1978, 1981), Evnine (1991), Føllesdal (1965, 1966, 1983), Gottlieb and Davis (1974), Harré and Madden (1975), Hochberg (1978, 1984), Horgan (1978, 1982), Kaplan (1964), Levin (1976), Lindström (1991), B. Linsky (1992*a*), Lycan (1974), McGinn (1976), Mackie (1974), Manning (1998), Mellor (1991, 1995), Morton (1969), Neale (1993*b*, 1995), Neale and Dever (1997), Oliver (1998), Olson (1987), Perry (1996), Quesada (1993), Reed (1993), Rodriguez-Pereyra (1998*a*), Rosenberg and Martin (1979), Sainsbury (1990), Searle (1995), Sharvy (1970, 1972, 1973), Sleigh (1966), Taylor (1976, 1985), Travis (1973),

According to Gödel, any theory that posits facts to which true sentences correspond must, if it is to avoid the "Eleatic" conclusion that all true sentences stand for the same fact, give up either the intuitive Fregean Principle of Composition or else the intuitive Fregean idea that definite descriptions are referential devices. (Russell, as Gödel notes, gives up the latter in his Theory of Descriptions.) In a compressed footnote Gödel provides assumptions from which he claims this might be "proved rigorously". Reconstructing the argument Gödel must have had in mind pays handsomely. First, once polished Gödel's assumptions are weaker than those of Church, Quine, and Davidson. Secondly, Gödel sees very clearly that the philosophical utility of any slingshot turns crucially on the semantics any would-be giant-slayer is going to ascribe to devices of description (or abstraction).[5] Thirdly, the argument can be converted into a deductive proof demonstrating that anyone wishing to posit facts, situations, states of affairs, or propositions—*whether or not such items are to serve as the references of sentences*—and anyone wishing to posit non-extensional sentence connectives must take a stand on the semantics of definite descriptions. Fourthly, a careful examination of the proof yields virtually everything that is needed to settle a number of vexed questions in philosophical logic and expose much nonsense in discussions of non-truth-functional languages. Finally, the proof can be converted into an elegant test for examining certain philosophical claims and the logical properties of philosophically important linguistic contexts.

Although the supply of technical questions one can ask about inference principles, reference, description, identity, logical equivalence, and variable-binding seems to have no clear limit, by the end

Trenholme (1975), Wagner (1986), Wallace (1969), Wedberg (1966, 1984), Widerker (1973, 1985), Williamson (1976), N. L. Wilson (1974), and Yourgrau (1987).
  There are fewer discussions of Gödel's slingshot, the premisses of which are importantly weaker. It is discussed explicitly by Bernays (1946), Donaho (1998), Neale (1995, 2000*a*), Neale and Dever (1997), Olson (1987), Oppy (1997), Parsons (1990), Omelyanchyk (forthcoming), Perry (1996), Quine (2000), Wallace (1969), and Wedberg (1966, 1984). Aspects of the argument are noted by Burge (1986*a*), B. Linsky (1992*a*), and Parsons (1990); and it is mentioned in passing by Anscombe (1969), Davidson (1996, 1999*e*, 2000), Morton (1969), Quesada (1993), Salmon (1981), Widerker (1983), and Yourgrau (1987).
  [5] This is something that Church (1943*a*, 1956) also seems to see, but the picture is much sharper in Gödel's discussion.

of this book we will be in a position to answer most questions of a technical nature raised by slingshot arguments, and to persuade philosophers of the need to face the genuine philosophical questions that Gödel's version poses: (i) Which rules of inference that can be applied validly to sentences occurring in extensional contexts can also be applied validly to sentences occurring within, say, modal, causal, and what I shall call *factual* contexts? (ii) Is it possible to have useful ontologies of propositions, states of affairs, situations, or facts, and if so what conditions must theories of such entities satisfy? (iii) What are the consequences for theories of facts, states, situations, propositions, and modalities of accepting or rejecting Russell's Theory of Descriptions? (iv) What are the prospects for "representational" philosophy?

The answers I provide are intertwined, complex, but clear. Representational philosophy survives the Davidson–Rorty onslaught because non-truth-functional logics and ontologies of facts, states of affairs, situations, and propositions survive not only the *actual* arguments deployed against them but also the most precise and powerful slingshot arguments that *can be* constructed. But this does not mean that all is well. The most precise and powerful slingshot arguments demonstrate conclusively that the logical and ontological theories originally targeted must satisfy non-trivial conditions if they are to avoid logical or ontological collapse. And showing that any *particular* theory satisfies the relevant conditions involves articulating the theory in such a way that non-trivial semantic choices must be made, primarily choices about the semantics of descriptions. In short, a watertight, deductive proof based on Gödel's slingshot yields an exacting, non-trivial, formal constraint— the *Descriptive Constraint*—that must be satisfied by *any* theory of facts, situations, states, circumstances, or propositions and by *any* non-truth-functional logic, connective, or operator.

There is a good deal of work to be done before all of this will become clear. First, a number of issues in the philosophy of language must be examined. To the extent that facts, states, situations, and propositions are to be associated with *sentences* (relativized to utterances or occasions of use), and to the extent that the nature of such an association must have something to do with the *meaning* of the sentence (and thereby the meanings of its parts), some semantic work needs to be done, mostly clarificatory work on compositionality, semantic innocence, direct reference, truth, contextual definition, description, abstraction, substitution, variable-binding, scope, and extensionality. Unfortunately, there is still a widespread confusion about these notions in the literature, and it is necessary to eliminate it before getting to more complex issues. Once the logical terrain has been cleared, the full force of a simple proof can be appreciated, a proof that by way of first placing a stricture on non-truth-functional discourse delimits the territory within which theories of facts, states, situations, and propositions—if there are such things—must lie if they are to do the sort of work that many philosophers typically expect of them. The Descriptive Constraint is basically a filter on theories, one that not every extant theory succeeds in passing. Gödel was right to this extent: choices made about the semantics of descriptions and the metaphysics of facts place non-trivial constraints upon one another.

Importantly, the Descriptive Constraint can be derived as a secure formal result without assuming that a semantic theory must treat sentences as having references, without assuming semantic innocence (or guilt), direct (or indirect) reference, or anything contentious about the semantics of singular terms, and without assuming very much at all about the semantics of definite descriptions. But at the same time it places a formal demand upon anyone who posits facts, states, situations, propositions, possible worlds, or non-truth-functional sentence connectives to say something very much more precise (if only disjunctively) about the semantics of definite descriptions. (It also seems to provide indirect support for Russell's Theory of Descriptions, or at least its contemporary incarnation within a general account of natural language quantification.)

For the most part, the formal discussion will be conducted at an abstract level as I will be less concerned with the mechanics of this or that theory of, say, facts, than with a precise constraint that *any* theory of such entities must satisfy if it is to avoid an embarrassing collapse. However, most of the relevant prior discussion has centred on facts, and in view of the claims made by Davidson and Rorty about the need for facts to sustain much of what passes for modern philosophy, it is in connection with facts that the main theses of the present work have most bite. Once the main logico-semantic work has been accomplished, I examine some representative theories of facts, showing where they are apt to run into trouble.

1.4 STRUCTURE

A few words about the structure of the book are needed as the (non-chronological) order of presentation might baffle readers not already steeped in the philosophy of language. In Chapter 2 I examine Davidson's semantic programme, the relation between semantics and ontology that he champions, his arguments against facts and the scheme–content distinction, and the ways in which he and Rorty assail the notion of representation. Chapters 3 and 4 take us back to Frege and Russell, respectively. Investigations are needed of Frege's idea that a sentence refers to a truth-value, his Principle of Composition, and his abandonment of what Davidson calls "semantic innocence" before examining Russell's idea that true sentences stand for facts (rather than truth-values) and the philosophical and formal details of his Theory of Facts and Theory of Descriptions (which are poorly understood to this day). With these pieces on the table I proceed to set out, in Chapter 5, Gödel's slingshot argument. The original argument—or, at least, the premisses of the argument I attribute to Gödel—can be found in a fleeting footnote to a discussion of the relationship between the Theory of Descriptions and the Theory of Facts. Usually each theory is viewed as quite independent of the other. Gödel argues otherwise, that the viability of the latter depends upon the viability of the former (or at least upon the viability of *some* non-referential theory of descriptions). This was a novel claim, and there appears to be no record of Russell's reaction to it.[6]

In Chapters 6 and 7 I carefully set out and clean the formal tools that are needed in the remaining chapters, clarifying what is meant by such terms as "extensional" and "scope", and separating various inference principles. Drawing upon a strategy first used by Quine (1953e), in Chapters 8 and 9 I convert the two basic forms of slingshot argument—one used by Church, Quine, and Davidson, the other by Gödel—into knock-down deductive proofs that are agnostic on key semantic issues. In particular, *the proofs assume no*

---

[6] As I mentioned in n. 3, Gödel appears to have submitted his paper in May 1943. In a note appended to Russell's (1944: 741) "Reply to Criticisms", dated July 1943, Russell states that "Dr Gödel's most interesting paper on my mathematical logic came into my hands after my replies had been completed, and at a time when I had no leisure to work on it."

particular account of reference and do not even assume that sentences have references. Using this procedure, I show in Chapter 8 that cleaned-up versions of the slingshots used by Davidson and Quine demonstrate theses weaker than those their authors were seeking—the impossibility of facts and non-truth-functional (e.g. modal and causal) connectives. This is primarily because the arguments depend upon (*a*) logical equivalences and (*b*) theories of definite descriptions (or class abstracts) that must satisfy certain semantic conditions if the aforementioned logical equivalences are to obtain.

Using the same procedure, I show in Chapter 9 that a slingshot engendered by Gödel's suggestions can be converted into a proof which delivers an exacting constraint on non-extensional discourse—the Descriptive Constraint—and which is more general than anything Gödel appears to have had in mind. Importantly, the proof of this constraint is constructed without appeal to logical equivalences, without assuming that a semantic theory must treat sentences as having references, without presupposing anything contentious about the semantics of singular terms, and without commitment to any particular semantics for definite descriptions. A constraint on facts, situations, states of affairs, and propositions—indeed on anything that is expressed or represented sententially—drops out as a trivial consequence of a constraint on non-extensional discourse.

Chapter 10 revolves around the matter of whether the stronger results that Quine and Davidson were attempting to derive from slingshot arguments might be forthcoming if other theories of descriptions were assumed. This also provides an opportunity to evaluate various theories as potential competitors to Russell's theory.

With the Descriptive Constraint at hand, in Chapter 11 I examine diverse theories of facts with a view to establishing how viable they are, and then turn to claims about the semantics of causal statements that have been used to motivate ontologies of facts and events. There is considerable confusion in the literature on the matter of whether causal statements are extensional; once the clarifications effected in earlier chapters are brought to bear, almost all of the confusion can be eradicated and decisive results obtained. There are certainly some extensional causal statements, and they can be delimited on the basis of their superficial grammatical forms; but there are other causal statements for which it is, as far as I can ascertain, still an open question whether extensional or non-extensional treatments are to be preferred, much turning on one's position on the overall shape of a semantic theory. If non-extensional treatments prove appealing, the resulting theories will have to satisfy the strictures imposed by the Descriptive Constraint.

In my earlier book *Descriptions* (1990) I argued at length that Russell's Theory of Descriptions is a far more powerful and plausible theory than people tend to think, and I dealt with a range of formal and philosophical objections to the theory. Several new objections to the theory—or at least new twists on old objections—have appeared in intervening years along with objections to certain aspects of my defence, implementation, or expansion of the theory. I have found no reason to soften my position in the light of the objections. Indeed, most of them seem to be based on oversight or a failure to take into account independent features of a semantic theory (quantification, variable-binding, scope, compositional structure, and so on). Those objections that appear to have generated most concern are addressed in a second edition of *Descriptions* I am preparing for Oxford University Press. Perhaps the most important semantic lesson of the present work is that anyone proposing formal or argumentative manoeuvres within non-truth-functional contexts must face up to questions about the logical behaviour of definite descriptions raised by the Descriptive Constraint. To this extent, Russell was surely right when he claimed, nearly a century ago, that without a proper account of how descriptions function, many purportedly philosophical theses lack clear sense.

2

Davidson:
Truth and Correspondence

2.1 INTRODUCTORY REMARKS

Philosophers are fond of deploying formal or semi-formal arguments that revolve around substituting one piece of language for another deemed to be "equivalent" in some important semantic respect. Referential equivalence (co-reference), material equivalence (equivalence of truth-value), necessary equivalence (equivalence of truth-value across possible worlds), and logical equivalence (equivalence of truth-value across models) are some of the forms of equivalence that will concern us here, notions at the core of a strain of substitution arguments lightly sketched and heavily deployed by Church (1943a, 1956), Gödel (1944), Quine (1953c,e 1960), and Davidson (1980, 1984, 1990, 1996, 2000), arguments that appear to have their origins in Frege's (1892) talk of a sentence having a truth-value as its referent.

Where Frege took all true sentences to stand for the True (see Chapter 3), Russell (1918) and Wittgenstein (1921) took them to stand for individual *facts* (see Chapter 4); and it is in connection with this idea that Gödel (1944) hinted at a proof (see Chapter 5) which, relative to certain not wholly unreasonable assumptions, seems to demonstrate that if a compositional semantic theory treats true sentences as standing for facts, then all true sentences must stand for the same fact, the Eleatic "One" (Gödel) or "Great Fact" (Davidson).

An argument similar in structure to the one Gödel hinted at was set out by Church (1943a), who took issue with Carnap's (1942) claim that sentences stand for *propositions*, and then sketched a proof which, relative to certain assumptions likely to be granted by Carnap, showed that if a compositional semantic theory treats

sentences as standing for entities, then it must treat all true
sentences as standing for the same entity (e.g. the True) and all of
the false ones as standing for a distinct single entity (e.g. the False).
From the perspective of someone trying to construct a systematic and comprehensive semantic theory for a natural language, it
is not an intuitive or obvious requirement that a final theory must
appeal to the idea that sentences have *references*. Our ordinary uses
of 'refer', 'reference', and so on suggest it would be unnatural to
view sentences (or even sentences-relative-to-contexts) as referring
to things (except in the sense in which we often say, when examining a text, that a particular sentence or verse refers to, say, the Viet-
nam War or man's despair). But of course the theoretical
semanticist who appeals to the idea that sentences have references
need not be entirely shackled by ordinary usage. Certainly we do
well to begin with ordinary usage and depart from it grudgingly;
but it is well attested that although (many of) our theoretical terms
(in both the sciences and the humanities) derive from ordinary
usage, as theorizing becomes more complex, such terms may begin
to diverge in meaning from their ordinary language counterparts, a
normal pattern of linguistic development in any discipline that is
advancing.

It is natural to ask whether it might not be possible to construct
an adequate semantic theory that is not based upon the idea that
sentences stand for things. At what points in our semantic theorizing do we encounter strong pressures to associate entities with
expressions as their meanings? A full-blown entity-theoretic
approach to meaning proceeds by assigning to each meaningful
expression some entity, beginning with individual words (or more
plausibly morphemes) and working upwards in a compositional
manner through phrases all the way to sentences. The theories of
Frege (Chapter 3) and Russell (Chapter 4) do this. But there are
other ways one might proceed: most notable is the truth-theoretic
approach pioneered by Davidson (1984, 1990, 2000), according to
which the starting point of a semantic theory is *truth*, seen not as
an entity but as "a concept . . . intelligibly attributed to things like
sentences, utterances, beliefs, and propositions, entities which have
a propositional content" (2000: 65). Ontological issues arise only
in so far as certain entities must be posited in the provision of such
a theory. It is an interesting question, according to the truth-theo-
rist, whether there are expressions that must be seen as standing for

entities, a question that can be answered only by attempting to construct semantic theories.

It is Davidson's (1980, 1984, 1990) contention (i) that we can go about constructing theories of meaning that do not assign entities to anything other than our standard referential devices (singular terms, including variables under assignment); (ii) that such theories will take *objects* and *events*, construed as particulars, to be the sorts of thing to which singular terms refer; (iii) that as far as the theory of meaning is concerned, we can free ourselves of the idea that predicates refer to *properties* (or anything else) and the idea that individual sentences refer to, stand for, represent, correspond to, or are made true by particular *facts* (or by particular *states of affairs*, *situations*, or *circumstances* that obtain); (iv) that even if we wanted facts to serve as the references of true sentences, we could not have them because a slingshot argument demonstrates that such entities would collapse into one Great Fact; (v) that if there are no facts, then we cannot make sense of "correspondence" theories of truth, for such theories are built upon the idea that a sentence is true if and only if there is some fact to which it corresponds; and (vi) that if there are no facts to which true sentences correspond, we cannot make sense of a distinction between "conceptual scheme" and "empirical content" and so must give up attempts to render intelligible talk of alternative conceptual schemes, representations of reality, relativism, and scepticism; traditional philosophical problems surrounding these notions simply evaporate for lack of genuine subject matter.

2.2 MEANING AND TRUTH

The truth-theoretic approach to meaning forms the basis of a respected research programme in the semantics of natural language and is the best example, to date, of a systematic approach to meaning that seeks to do its job without appealing to universals, properties, functions, or even classes as the semantic values of predicates, or to propositions, situations, states of affairs, or facts as the semantic values of sentences. I want to present it in its best light here, in a form free of certain defects commentators claim to see in it—the theory is frequently maligned through ignorance, which is not to say it is without interesting problems.[1] I should stress immediately that a good portion of this chapter will involve exegesis, and to that extent it may irritate readers unsympathetic to Davidson's programme. I do not need to endorse the programme in order to make any of the main points of this book—nor do I need to reject it or endorse the tenets of some competing theory—but I do need Davidson's theory on the table *dialectically*. First, understanding his case against representations requires understanding his case against facts; understanding his case against facts requires understanding his views on reference and substitution; understanding his views on reference and substitution requires understanding how reference axioms are meant to form part of a theory of truth; and understanding what constitutes an acceptable theory of truth requires understanding what it means for such a theory to "do duty as" a theory of meaning. By getting clear about what an acceptable theory of truth is supposed to do and look like, we can set out all of the machinery needed to see how Davidson's formal argument against facts is supposed to work, and how his theory of meaning is meant to fit into his larger philosophical scheme, which repudiates facts and draws powerful conclusions from their departure. Secondly, working through Davidson's theory forces to a head a number of neglected or overlooked questions in semantic theory, questions about the nature of theorems and axioms—particularly in so far as they concern reference and description—about the delimitation of so-called logical constants, and about the distinction between semantics and analysis.

It is frequently said that a semantic theory for a language should specify what each of its sentences means. It is sometimes added that in order to achieve this a semantic theory must deliver *theorems*, one for each sentence, specifying what that sentence means. And this is often said to amount to the following (I think erroneously, but let that pass): putting to one side the complications raised by the existence of indexical, demonstrative, and other context-sensitive expressions, a theory of meaning for a language L is a theory that delivers, for each sentence S of L, a theorem of the following form:

---

[1] This discussion should be seen as supplanting my all too brief discussions in "On Representing" (1999a) and "From Semantics to Ontology" (1999b), which I now see as flawed in several ways, mostly dialectically.

(M) S^* means (in L) that p,

where instances of (M) are sentences in a metalanguage L^* rich enough to talk about sentences of the object-language L in which the expression replacing "S^*" is an expression of L^* that uniquely describes S in terms of its structure—a so-called structural description of S—and the sentence replacing "p" is a sentence of L^*.[2] On this definition, a theory of meaning for French (L), stated in English (L^*), must deliver (1)—or something very like (1)—as a theorem:

(1) "La neige est blanche" means (in French) that snow is white.

The structural description functioning as the subject of 'means' in (1) is an expression of English created by putting quotation marks round a sentence of French. In a more precise statement, something like the following structural description might be used to describe the French sentence in question:

(2) $[_S[_{NP}[_D$ la$][_N$ neige$]][_{VP}[_V$ est$][_A$ blanche$]]]$.

A definition of meaning in terms of theorems of form (M) is *not* Davidson's starting point. Nor is his point of departure one that overtly invokes the concept of *truth*. Davidson's main ideas can be set out as a series of six definitions and theses. The first of these is what he offers in place of the popular definition just given:

(i) A theory of *meaning* for a language L is a theory with the following feature: knowing what the theory states would suffice for understanding (utterances of sentences of) L.

There is no overt talk here of theorems satisfying schema (M), indeed no overt talk of theorems at all. It is, of course, open to someone to say that the way to *construct* a theory of meaning in Davidson's sense is to construct a theory that issues in theorems satisfying schema (M). But this is not what Davidson does. He starts on a seemingly new topic: *truth*. Drawing inspiration from Tarski's (1956) celebrated definition of truth for well-behaved formal languages, Davidson offers us a second definition:

(ii) Ignoring, for a moment, the complications raised by the existence of indexical and other context-sensitive expressions, a

[2] There are, I believe, serious worries about instances of (M); as they are not pertinent to my main theme, I do not take them up here.

theory of *truth* for a language L is any theory that yields, for each sentence S of L, a theorem of the form

(T) S^* is true (in L) $\equiv p$,

where instances of (T) are sentences in a metalanguage L^* used to talk about sentences of the object-language L, "S^*" is a structural description (in L^*) of S, "p" is a sentence of L^*, and $\equiv$ (read "if and only if") is the material biconditional.

For example, if the object-language (L) is French and the meta-language (L^*) is English, then the following would both be instances of schema (T):

(3) "La neige est blanche" is true (in French) $\equiv$ snow is white
(4) "La neige est rouge" is true (in French) $\equiv$ snow is red.

Instances of schema (T) Davidson calls *T-sentences* or *T-theorems*. Like any other theory, in the first instance a theory of truth will be judged by whether its theorems are true. In order for an instance of (T) to be true, it suffices that the sentences replacing "S^* is true (in L)" and "p" have the same truth-value (and hence, given our understanding of "is true (in L)", that the sentence of L described by the structural description replacing "S^*" have the same truth-value as the sentence replacing "p"). No stronger connection is needed because $\equiv$ is (only) the material biconditional.[3] Thus (3) and (4) are both true: in the former $\equiv$ stands between two true sentences; in the latter it stands between two false ones.

Notice that no direct connection between a theory of *truth* and a theory of *meaning* is stated by (i) or (ii). However, (i) tells us what conditions a theory—*any* theory—must satisfy in order to be a theory of meaning, and since a theory of truth is a *theory*, we can infer (iii):

(iii) A theory of truth (henceforth a *T-theory*) θ for a language L would be (qualify as, serve as, do duty as) a theory of meaning for L if knowledge of what θ stated sufficed for understanding L.

Davidson strikes out beyond definition with the following bold claim:

---

[3] Tarski takes the undefined semantic notion of *translation* (hence *meaning*) for granted and uses it to place constraints on what counts as an adequate definition of *truth* for a language; by contrast Davidson uses a primitive notion of *truth* in order to characterize what he takes to be the most plausible way of constructing a theory of meaning. For discussion, see Davidson (1990) and Soames (1994, 1999).

(iv) For any natural language L there is at least one T-theory for L that qualifies as a theory of meaning for L.

And he goes further with the following claims:

(v) As a matter of empirical fact, any T-theory for L qualifying as a theory of meaning for L has the following property: knowing what is stated by its *T-theorems alone* suffices for understanding L (knowledge of what its *axioms* state is not necessary).[4]

(vi) The background logic used to derive T-theorems from the axioms of a T-theory is standard, extensional, first-order logic with identity.

There are a number of notoriously difficult issues involved in trying to establish whether the optimism expressed in (iv), (v), and (vi) is well-founded.[5] My purpose here is not to settle the case one way or the other but to indicate clearly the character of certain perceived difficulties that bear on my main themes.

Let us say that a T-theory for L is *acceptable* if knowledge of what is stated by its T-theorems suffices for understanding L. The challenge for the Davidsonian is to explain how an acceptable T-theory can be constructed.

(*a*) It is usually agreed that not *every* T-theory is acceptable. Suppose there is a T-theory θ_I for French that delivers the following T-theorem for the sentence "La neige est blanche":

(5) "La neige est blanche" is true (in French) $\equiv$ JFK was assassinated.[6]

Since the left- and right-hand sides of this material biconditional

---

[4] This is something Davidson (1999*b*) states explicitly in response to Segal (1999). Still more recently he has argued in private that even knowledge of what is stated by the theorems may go beyond what is strictly necessary.

[5] These have been examined by Davidson (1984, 1990, 1999*b*), Evans and McDowell (1976), Fodor and LePore (1992), Foster (1976), Higginbotham (1992), Larson and Segal (1995), LePore and Loewer (1990), Loar (1976), Quine (1977), Segal (1999), and Soames (1992, 1994). I draw liberally on the work of these authors and on discussions with Davidson over the years in sketching some potential objections and rejoinders. I present the main points in a dialectical rather than chronological order.

[6] If the background logic is unconstrained, extensional, first-order logic with identity, θ_I will not deliver *just* (5) for "la neige est blanche": it will deliver, for this sentence, a collection of T-sentences whose right-hand sides are logically equivalent to the right-hand side of (5). In principle, requiring the derivation of T-theorems to conform to the canons of a canonical proof procedure will pare down the collection. See below.

are both true, it is a true instance of schema (T). But knowing what is stated by *this* T-theorem would not suffice for understanding "la neige est blanche". And from this definite fact, it might be inferred that knowing what is stated by *all of the* T-theorems of θ_I would not suffice for understanding "la neige est blanche" (or, quite probably, for understanding many other sentences of French, particularly those containing the words "neige" or "blanche"). The additional assumptions needed to draw the general conclusion are far from obvious—indeed the general conclusion may well be false—but let us suppose they are compelling: although delivering a true theorem of the form (T) for every sentence of French (including the sentence "la neige est blanche"), θ_I cannot do duty as a theory of meaning for French—it is impeccable as a theory of *truth* for French but inadequate as a theory of *meaning*. Something seems to be missing. Or so it might be argued.

(*b*) If θ_I is not acceptable (i.e. if it does not qualify as a theory of meaning for French), then one task facing the Davidsonian semanticist is the specification of conditions a T-theory must satisfy to be acceptable, conditions that do not invoke the concept of understanding or related semantic concepts such as meaning, synonymy, or translation. It might be suggested that general considerations governing, or at least informing, the interpretation of empirical theories should be brought to bear: a theory of meaning for French is an empirical theory, so its theorems should be lawlike and support counterfactuals.[7] As proof of the failure of (4)—and thereby of θ_I—to support counterfactuals, the apparent falsity of (5′) might be contrasted with the apparent truth of (3′):

(5′) If JFK had not been assassinated, "la neige est blanche" would not be true (in French).

(3′) If snow were not white, "la neige est blanche" would not be true (in French).

Some hard questions must be faced by anyone wishing to pronounce on the utility of the apparent contrast. Are sentences to be individuated, in part, by their semantic features? Or will that threaten the whole project? Does the parenthetical appendage "in French" occurring in the T-theorems I have been using signal a willingness to see the same structural description existing and meaning

---

7 See Davidson (1984, pp. xiv, xviii, 26 n. 11, and 174).

something in more than one language? Do (5') and (3') exhibit ambiguities of scope that may be interfering with judgments of truth and falsity, ambiguities attributable to the fact that the structural descriptions are Russellian definite descriptions? (For example, might not (2) above be read as "the sentence formed by concatentating the noun phrase formed by concatenating ..."?) What are the truth-conditions of counterfactuals in any case?

I do not have the stomach to tackle these questions here. To keep things moving, let us simply stipulate (i) that structural descriptions are indeed Russellian descriptions (rather than names), (ii) that structural descriptions are language-relative, and (iii) that (5') is false and (3') true whatever the scopes of the structural descriptions they contain. The first stipulation certainly has some independent plausibility (see Chapter 4). The second and third are controversial but will play no crucial role once we get past counterfactuals; they just simplify exposition. The second stipulation (which would probably be required to justify the third) allows us to drop the annoying appendage '(in French)' from T-theorems for French sentences, which henceforth can be read as exemplifying the form (T'):

(T') the L sentence S^* is true $\equiv p$.

(Prefixes such as "the French sentence" will be omitted where no confusion will arise.)

By the third stipulation, θ_1 can be discarded on the grounds that its theorems are not lawlike. But it might be argued that a T-theory θ_2 delivering (6) is not yet eliminated, witness the alleged truth of (6'):

(6) "La neige est blanche" is true $\equiv$ snow is a form of frozen water.

(6') If snow were not a form of frozen water, "la neige est blanche" would not be true.[8]

If this is right, a criterion that goes beyond the nomological is required to deflect unacceptable T-theories.

---

[8] A better pair might be the following, due to Segal (1999):

(i) "Copper conducts heat" is true (in English) $\equiv$ copper conducts electricity
(i') If copper did not conduct electricity, "copper conducts heat" would not be true (in English).

(c) It might seem obvious *what* is missing from θ_1 and θ_2: the English (metalanguage) sentences "JFK was assassinated" and "snow is a form of frozen water" do not *mean* the same thing as the French (object-language) sentence "la neige est blanche". And so it might be supposed that a T-theory θ_3 for French with the following property will be acceptable: in every theorem of form (T), the metalanguage sentence replacing "*p*" *means the same as* (or *translates*) the French sentence described by the expression replacing "*S*". To borrow a label from the literature, in order to be acceptable a theory of meaning θ_3 must be *interpretive*: a T-theory is interpretive just in case all of its T-theorems are interpretive; a T-theorem is interpretive just in case the metalanguage sentence replacing "*p*" on the right-hand side of (T) means the same as (or translates) the object-language sentence described by the expression replacing "*S*" on the left-hand side.

An interpretive T-theory for L would be equivalent to what Tarski (1956) called a (materially adequate) *truth definition* for L (a definition of "true-in-L"). Tarski could help himself freely to notions like synonymy or translation: his objective was to define (i.e. characterize) *truth* (in L), not meaning. But appeals to synonymy or translation are not available to Davidson, nor does he claim they are: the challenge, which Davidson and others have taken up, is to specify a set of conditions which hold only of interpretive T-theories but which do not invoke any threatening semantic concepts.[9]

---

[9] See e.g. Larson and Segal (1995) and Segal (1999). It is sometimes claimed—although not by Davidson, Larson, or Segal—that in order to be acceptable, a T-theory must "ultimately" yield theorems of the form (M):

(M) *S** means (in L) that *p*.

Someone insisting on this will then say that a T-theory is acceptable only if each of its T-theorems can be "interpreted as", "mapped onto", or "converted into" the corresponding M-theorem. An M-theorem, it will be claimed, is "more informative" than its corresponding T-theorem: the former (which is non-extensional) entails the latter (which is extensional), but not vice versa. Occasionally, Davidson (1984: 60, 175) allows statements of form (M) to pass unchallenged, but nowhere does he claim they form the backbone of a theory of meaning.

It is sometimes said that Davidson is proposing a "truth-conditional" theory of meaning which identifies the meaning of a sentence with its truth-conditions—casual remarks in some of Davidson's articles have surely encouraged such claims but they are confused on two counts. First, a specification of the truth-conditions of a sentence is a specification of the conditions necessary and sufficient for its truth. Since the connective ≡ in a T-theorem is the *material* biconditional, it is no part of (*d*) One way to avoid appealing to semantic notions would be to invoke only *formal* conditions. Some non-interpretive T-theories could be discarded by restricting attention to those producing their theorems in a *compositional* and *systematic* fashion, on the basis of the structurally significant parts of sentences. Any T-theory that delivers

(7) "Santorin est volcanique" is true ≡ Santorini is volcanic

via the following axioms for "Santorin" and "est volcanique" might be regarded as satisfying this requirement (at least as far as "Santorin est volcanique" is concerned):

(Ax. 1) the referent of "Santorin" = Santorini
(Ax. 2) (∀α) (⌜α est volcanique⌝ is true ≡ the referent of α is volcanic).

Notes: (i) "α" ranges over proper names. (ii) There is no attempt to quantify into quotation in (Ax. 2). The expression

(8) ⌜α est volcanique⌝

is just shorthand for the definite description

(9) α ∩ "is volcanic"

what it is to be a T-theory that the sentence replacing '*p*' in a true theorem of form (T) specify the truth-conditions of the sentence described by the expression replacing '*S**'. The connective would have to be at least as strong as the *strict* (modal) biconditional ⥽ to ensure a specification of truth-conditions.

Secondly, the unadorned thesis that the meaning of a sentence is identical to its truth-conditions is easily refuted: (*a*) to specify the truth-conditions of a sentence is to specify conditions necessary and sufficient for its truth; (*b*) a necessary truth is true under all conditions; (*c*) so all necessary truths have the same truth-conditions; (*d*) so (i) and (ii) have the same truth-conditions:

(i) snow is white
(ii) snow is white and 2 + 2 = 4;

(*e*) if the truth-conditions of a sentence are identical to its meaning, then knowing its truth-conditions is the same thing as knowing its meaning (this would seem to be the place to mount a challenge to the argument); (*f*) but knowing the meaning of (i) is not the same thing as knowing the meaning of (ii); (*g*) so the meaning of a sentence is not the same thing as it truth conditions. A further problem for the unadorned thesis is raised by expressions that give rise to what Frege calls *colouring* and Grice calls *conventional implicature*. Examples include "but", "although", "yet", "furthermore", and "nonetheless", which seem to contribute to meaning without contributing to truth-conditions. For discussion, see Neale (1999c).

read as "the expression produced by concatenating α and 'est volcanique' ". (iii) For simplicity I have ignored the internal struc-ture of the object-language predicate.

Using extensional, first-order logic with identity, (7) can be derived (i.e. *proved*) from our axioms using the Principle of Universal Instantiation (UI) and the Principle of Substitutivity for Singular Terms (PSST).[10]

[1] "Santorin est volcanique" is true ≡ the referent of "Santorin"
                                              is volcanic (from (Ax. 2)
                                              using UI)

[2] "Santorin est volcanique" is true ≡ Santorini   is   volcanic
                                              (from [1] and (Ax. 1)
                                              using PSST)

(For detailed discussion of inference principles, see Chapter 7.)

The idea here, then, is to restrict attention to T-theories respect-ing the syntactic structure of sentences. Axioms for singular terms might look like (Ax. 1), those for one-place predicates like (Ax. 2), those for two-place predicates like (Ax. 3), those for two-place connectives like (Ax. 4), and so on:

---

[10] I have made the simplification—harmless for immediate purposes—that (i) is a singular term:

(i) the referent of "Santorin".

There are good reasons for thinking this is wrong, that (i) is really a quantified noun phrase by virtue of being a Russellian definite description (see Ch. 4). On such an account, the relevant rule of inference will not be PSST but Whitehead and Russell's *14.15, a derived rule of inference for extensional contexts (see Chs. 4 and 7). The issue assumes some importance when we are asked to consider T-theories intended to produce theorems for sentences in the object-language containing modal opera-tors and when we discuss certain types of counterfactual claims about reference. There is a reading of (ii) that is false,

(ii) the referent of "Santorin" might not have been Santorini,

and this can be captured by reading the description as having large scope. To the extent that there is an additional true reading—some people want to dispute this—it is readily captured by reading the description as having smaller scope than the modal operator. Matters are further complicated by the fact that the description functioning as the subject noun phrase in (ii) contains a structural description as a part, giving it the same general form as (iii):

(iii) the recipient of the grant might not have been Santorini,

which is in several ways ambiguous.

(Ax. 3) $(\forall\alpha)(\forall\beta)(\ulcorner\alpha$ aime $\beta\urcorner$ is true $\equiv$ the referent of α loves the referent of β)

(Ax. 4) $(\forall\phi)(\forall\psi)$ $(\ulcorner\phi$ et $\psi\urcorner$ is true $\equiv \phi$ is true and ψ is true).[11]

(Here, "α" and "β" range over names and "ϕ" and "ψ" range over sentences.) Each axiom of a T-theory so constructed will have an impact on an infinite number of T-theorems, including those for sentences containing demonstrative and indexical elements, and this will have the effect of making it considerably harder for theories delivering non-interpretive T-theorems to produce only *true* T-theorems. In effect, then, the constraint of systematic compositionality narrows the class of T-theories towards convergence with the class of those that are interpretive. At least that is the idea.

But the question of potentially non-interpretive T-theories is still not behind us as we can see by examining the work done by reference axioms. The Greek island of Santorini has another name: 'Thira' (the Greek 'Thíra' is "more official" than 'Santoríni' and is the name typically (although not invariably) used in administrative or legal documents). The names 'Santorini' and 'Thira' are both used in English (i.e. by English speakers in sentences of English), and the names 'Santorin' and 'Thira' are both used in French (i.e. by French speakers in sentences of French). Now consider the T-theory obtained by replacing the reference axiom (Ax. 1) for "Santorin" by (Ax. 1*):

(Ax. 1*) the referent of "Santorin" = Thiera.

The resulting T-theory would deliver the following T-theorem in place of (7):

(10) "Santorin est volcanique" is true $\equiv$ Thira is volcanic.

(10) is just as true (and as lawlike) as (7); but is it interpretive? One's answer to this question is almost certainly going to be tied to one's views about what happens when "Santorin est volcanique"

---

[11] As it stands, (Ax. 3) does not actually respect syntactic structure. Syntactic theory tells us that "Pierre aime Claire" has more or less the following syntactic structure [$_S$ [$_{NP}$ Pierre] [$_{VP}$ aime [$_{NP}$ Claire]]]. For T-theories that respect syntactic structure, see Larson and Segal (1995). In order to produce axioms of the required form, Larson and Segal assign entities as semantic values of verbs and verb phrases, which involves an interesting departure from Davidson's austere line.

and other sentences are embedded in constructions that have triggered talk of *opacity* (the failure of PSST), for example sentences containing verbs of propositional attitude such as "croire" ("believe"). The nature of appropriate axioms for such verbs and the way in which T-theories should produce T-theorems for such sentences are matters of debate; but presumably when all is said and done, a T-theory containing (Ax. 1) for "Santorin" would deliver (11), whereas one containing (Ax. 1*) would deliver (12):

(11) "Pierre croit que Santorin est volcanique" is true ≡ Pierre believes that Santorini is volcanic

(12) "Pierre croit que Santorin est volcanique" is true ≡ Pierre believes that Thira is volcanic.

Following Frege, it is widely held that the right-hand sides of (11) and (12) are not synonymous, that there are circumstances in which they can differ in truth-value. Given the definite connections between (i) the English "Santorini" and French "Santorin", and (ii) the English "Thira" and French "Thira", it might plausibly be argued that (12) is not interpretive and that, in consequence, any T-theory producing it, although systematic and compositional, is not acceptable.[12]

(*e*) Axioms for predicates also leave room for non-interpretive T-theories. If the background logic is unconstrained, standard first-order logic with identity, then it is possible to produce T-theories that are non-interpretive by virtue of delivering T-theorems such as (13):

(13) "Santorin est volcanique" is true ≡ Santorini is volcanic and everything physical is physical.

---

[12] Similar issues arise in connection with sentence connectives such as "et" ("and") and "mais" ("but"). (Ax. i) is interpretive; but what about (Ax. i*)?

(Ax. i) $(\forall\sigma)(\forall\tau)$ ($\ulcorner\sigma$ mais $\tau\urcorner$ is true ≡ σ is true but τ is true)
(Ax. i*) $(\forall\sigma)(\forall\tau)$ ($\ulcorner\sigma$ mais $\tau\urcorner$ is true ≡ σ is true and τ is true).

For a card-carrying Fregean, there is an important difference between, on the one hand, "Santorin" and "Thira", and, on the other, "et" and "mais": the former differ from one another in *sense* whereas the latter have the same sense and differ from one another only in *colouring*. So even if sense can be invoked to decide between (Ax. 1) and (Ax. 1*) above—see McDowell (1977)—it will not help in distinguishing (Ax. i) from (Ax. i*) as these axioms express the same *thought* for Frege. For discussion, see Ch. 3 and Neale (1999c).

Some of these T-theories could be cut out by requiring the procedure by which T-theorems are derived to conform to the canons of some narrowly circumscribed proof procedure.[13] One would have to be careful, however, not to constrain the proof procedure so tightly as to deprive oneself of (i) resources needed to produce T-theorems that are still interpretive—for example, one would not want to leave any syntactic, logical, or set-theoretic junk on the right-hand side of T-theorems derived for French sentences containing quantified noun phrases ("chaque homme", "quelques hommes"), adverbs of quantification ("toujours", "jamais", etc.), indexicals and demonstratives ("je", "ici", "maintenant", "cet homme"), verbs of propositional attitude ("croire", "savoir"), or verbs that register quantification over events ("sortir", "se tomber"). But requiring a T-theory for French to produce its T-theorems in conformity to a canonical proof procedure will not eliminate *all* systematic and compositional theories that deliver (13). Replacing axiom (Ax. 2) above by (Ax. 2*) pre-loads the requisite trouble before the canonical proof procedure ever gets into action:

(Ax. 2*) ($\forall\alpha$) (⌜α est volcanique⌝ is true ≡ the referent of α is volcanic and everything physical is physical).

(*f*) At this point it is tempting to appeal to further considerations governing, or at least informing, the construction and testing of empirical theories: economy and simplicity.[14] It might be pointed out in connection with the case at hand that in comparing the T-theorems flowing from a T-theory θ_1 containing (Ax. 2) with those flowing from a T-theory θ_2 that differs only in containing (Ax. 2*) in place of (Ax. 2), the right-hand sides of certain T-theorems of θ_2 entail the right-hand sides of the corresponding T-theorems of θ_1 (and not vice versa), and that this is reason enough to cast θ_2 aside.

(*g*) If there remain further non-interpretive T-theories for French that have not been ruled out by any of the aforementioned constraints, it might be suggested that since a theory of meaning for French is meant to be (or be part of) an empirical theory about the

---

[13] See Davidson (1984: 61, 138).
[14] This idea is taken very seriously by Larson and Segal (1995) and Segal (1999), and for good reason: they aim to construct a T-theory that might form (at least the basis of) a theory of semantic competence.

utterances of members of our species, the theorist can dismiss any T-theory whose theorems do not possess some property P (to be elucidated) answering to general constraints governing the way we make sense of what other members of the species are doing.[15] To this it might be countered that once the appropriate conditions of dismissal are made sufficiently clear, they will be seen to invoke semantic concepts that render the larger enterprise hopelessly circular.

(*h*) Even if the class of interpretive T-theories for French is satisfactorily delimited, it is not obvious that an interpretive T-theory is *ipso facto* acceptable. For it might be argued that in addition to knowing what is stated by the T-theorems of an interpretive T-theory θ for French, in order to *understand* French one would need to know (or at least believe) something that is not deducible from θ's theorems, namely *that the theorems themselves are interpretive* (or at least that one would need to know (or believe) that the theorems satisfy a set of constraints that, as a matter of fact, render them interpretive (or at least nomic)).[16] The problem here is not that possessing this additional knowledge would require the possession of certain theoretical concepts not involved in knowing what is stated by θ's T-theorems—for this is unclear until more is said about what is involved in knowing what is stated by a T-theorem. Rather, the objection is that *no* T-theory will be acceptable because its T-theorems will never state enough information for understanding. To this it might be countered that the perceived need for such additional knowledge is symptomatic of reading too much into the notion of understanding. Knowledge of what θ's theorems state does, in fact, suffice for understanding French, but it does not, in addition, furnish anyone possessing that knowledge with direct grounds for knowing (or even thinking) that it does; and this is as it should be because that was never part of the original bargain.

Self-reflexive paradoxes are apt to drift into and out of focus at various junctures in thinking through these matters. Suffice to say the matter of whether a suitably constrained T-theory can serve as a theory of meaning has not been resolved to everyone's satisfaction.

---

[15] See Davidson (1984, ch. 9).
[16] See Davidson (1984, pp. xviii, 172–4); Foster (1976).

2.3 REFERENCE AND ONTOLOGY

We might think of the ontology of a sentence as those things that must exist for the sentence to be true; and we might think of the things in "our ontology" as the ontology of all the sentences we hold true. To specify what the ontology of a sentence is we need to invoke a semantic theory, and in this connection Davidson's approach to the construction of such a theory yields interesting ontological results.

There is a *double asymmetry* between sentences and singular terms within Davidson's theory. Thus far, no appeal to the notion of *reference* (or *predication*) has surfaced in the discussion of what an acceptable T-theory must do. A theory's deliverances with respect to *whole sentences* are all that matter: it is irrelevant how the internal workings of the theory treat the parts as long as things come out right for the wholes: "how a theory of truth maps non-sentential expressions on to objects is a matter of indifference . . . nothing can reveal how a speaker's words have been mapped onto objects" (1984, p. xix):

Since T-sentences say nothing whatever about reference, satisfaction, or expressions that are not sentences, the test of the correctness of the theory is independent of intuitions concerning these concepts. Once we have the theory, though, we can explain the truth of sentences on the basis of their structure and the semantic properties of the parts. The analogy with theories in science is complete: in order to organise and explain what we directly observe, we posit unobserved or indirectly observed objects and forces: the theory is tested by what is directly observed . . . what is open to observation is the use of sentences in context, and truth is the semantic concept we understand best. Reference and related notions like satisfaction are, by comparison, theoretical concepts (as are the notions of singular term, predicate, sentential connective, and the rest). There can be no question about the correctness of these theoretical concepts beyond the question whether they yield a satisfactory account of the use of sentences. . . . There is no reason to look for a prior, or independent, account of some referential relation. (1990: 300.)

In principle, then, it might be possible to construct an acceptable T-theory that does not utilize a notion of, say, reference at all. Only attempts to build a theory will reveal what appears to be needed.

According to Davidson, an acceptable T-theory will, in fact, utilize a *lean*, formal notion of reference, by virtue of containing axioms capable of handling quantification, and this fact is onto-logically significant. If we were dealing with an infinite extensional language *L* containing only (a finite number of) names, predicates, and sentence connectives, but no quantifiers, in fact it would not be necessary to invoke a concept like reference: a finite theory consist-ing of one axiom for each atomic sentence and one recursive axiom for each sentence connective would suffice because *L* would contain only finitely many *atomic* sentences. So it is not the exis-tence of singular terms per se that foists a referential notion upon us: it is *quantification* that does that, because it is quantification that forces us to abandon the construction of straightforward theo-ries whose axioms take the form

$$(14) \ \_ \, \_ \, \_ \ \text{is true} \equiv \ldots$$

in favour of T-theories that take a detour through *satisfaction*—"a generalised form of reference" (1990: 296)—a T-theory whose predicate and quantifier axioms take the form

$$(15) \ (\forall s)(s \text{ satisfies } \_ \, \_ \, \_ \equiv \ldots s \ldots),$$

where '*s*' ranges over (infinite) sequences of objects. The "logical form" of a sentence *S* belonging to a language *L* is, for Davidson, the structure imposed upon *S* in the course of providing an accept-able T-theory for *L* as a whole. Work on the syntax and semantics of natural language suggests we will not get very far in our attempts to construct acceptable T-theories for French, English, and so on unless we view the logical forms of certain sentences as encoding something very like the quantifier–variable structures familiar from formal languages such as the first-order predicate calculus. Following, for example, Field (1972), one formally useful way of pulling together names and variables (and other singular terms, if there are any) within a T-theory—a notational variant of many other ways, and perfectly consonant with Davidson's approach—is to use the notion of *reference-relative-to-a-sequence*, which we can abbreviate as *Ref*. On this account, the axiom for the name "Santorin" is given not by a simple reference axiom such as (Ax. 1) but by (Ax. 1′):

(Ax 1) the referent of "Santorin" = Santorini
(Ax 1′) $(\forall s)(Ref(\text{"Santorin"}, s) = \text{Santorini})$,

where '*s*' ranges over sequences. The purpose of this relativization will emerge shortly. (Ax. 1′) is just as much a "reference" axiom as (Ax. 1): it connects a piece of language with some entity or other, some piece of the world. (For ease of exposition, let us put aside names that allegedly fail to refer, if there are such expressions.) Reference, for Davidson, is no more than such a pairing—any pairing that works as far as grinding out T-theorems is concerned; there is no need, on Davidson's account, to provide an *analysis* of the reference relationship.

Axioms for verbs, adjectival expressions, and ordinary common nouns might treat such expressions as predicates as in the following:

(Ax. 2′) $(\forall s)(\forall \alpha)(s$ satisfies $\ulcorner \alpha$ est volcanique$\urcorner \equiv Ref(\alpha, s)$ is volcanic)

(Ax. 3′) $(\forall s)(\forall \alpha)(\forall \beta)(s$ satisfies $\ulcorner \alpha$ aime $\beta \urcorner \equiv Ref(\alpha, s)$ loves $Ref(\beta, s))$,

where "α" and "β" range over singular terms (for ease of exposition, let us put aside so-called intensional predicates like "faux").[17] Axioms for (truth-functional) sentence connectives will also be straightforward ("ϕ" and "ψ" range over sentences):

(Ax. 4′) $(\forall s)(\forall \phi)(\forall \psi)(s$ satisfies $\ulcorner \phi$ et $\psi \urcorner \ldots s$ satisfies ϕ and s satisfies ψ).

Axioms for individual variables can be read off the following axiom schema:

(Ax 5′) $(\forall s)(\forall k)(Ref(\ulcorner x_k \urcorner, s) = s_k)$,

where "k" ranges over the natural numbers and s_k is the kth element of s. The difference between a name and a variable, then, is that the *Ref* of a name is constant from sequence to sequence— see (Ax. 1′) above—whereas the *Ref* of a variable depends upon the sequence in question.[18] The utility of the axioms flowing from the axiom schema (Ax. 5′) lies in their interaction with axioms for

---

[17] There are notorious difficulties involved in providing a uniform predicational analysis of these categories. For present purposes, the differences between these categories can be ignored as they do not raise problems that bear directly on my main theme.

[18] The constant–variable distinction should not be confused with Kripke's (1980) rigid–nonrigid distinction: variables (with respect to sequences) are just as rigid as names.

quantifiers. If quantification in French turns out to be unrestricted and completely analysable in terms of the first-order quantifiers ∀ and ∃ (a more realistic proposal will be considered in due course) a T-theory for French can get by with an axiom based on (Ax. 6′) or its universal counterpart:

(Ax 6′) (∀s)(∀k)(∀φ)(s satisfies ⌜(∃x_k)φ⌝ ≡ there is at least one sequence differing from s at most in the kth place that satisfies φ).

A sentence is true if and only if it is satisfied by every sequence. Assuming an adequate background logic (e.g. extensional, first-order logic with identity), we could then prove T-theorems such as the following:

(16) 'Santorini est volcanique' is true ≡ Santorini is volcanic
(17) 'Pierre mange quelque chose' is true ≡ Pierre is eating something.[19]

If it turns out that an acceptable T-theory cannot be constructed without making use of a "generalised form of reference" such as satisfaction—or a notational variant tailored to singular terms such as *Ref* above—i.e. without axioms that connect pieces of language with other entities, let us say that such a notion is *theoretically ineliminable*.

According to Davidson, accepting that reference (in some form or other) is theoretically ineliminable does not mean accepting that *any particular set of reference axioms* is ineliminable. Indeed, it is Davidson's position that any acceptable set of T-theoretic axioms X can be transposed into another acceptable set Y that contains, as a subset, a set of reference axioms quite different from those contained in X. The predicate axioms would also differ, of course; but the axioms for the logical constants would remain fixed

---

[19] To be precise, we could prove such theorems if (i) we had a modicum of translational machinery for purging talk of sequences from the right-hand sides of T-theorems for quantified sentences and (ii) we treated '*Ref* ("Santorin", s)' either (a) as a Russellian definite description ('the referent of "Santorin" with respect to s') and hence as a first-order definable device of quantification, or (b) as a complex singular term formed from a singular term and a functional expression. If method (a) is selected, proofs will make use of Whitehead and Russell's *14.15, a derived rule of inference for extensional contexts, rather than straightforward applications of PSST (see Chs. 4 and 7). If method (b) is selected, a version of first-order logic with functors must be selected. There are, I believe, reasons for preferring method (a).

(indeed, they *must* remain fixed on Davidson's account in order to preserve first-order inferential relations).[20] The reason that reference and predication axioms can be transposed into others is because a particular axiomatization is tested only by its T-theorems, i.e. by its deliverances at the level of whole sentences. So the notion of reference employed by Davidson is philosophically lean in two senses: (i) no particular set of reference axioms is privileged; (ii) to say that 'Santorin' refers to Santorini is just to say that there is a successful axiomatization containing as one of its axioms (Ax. 1′)—or some notational variant that hooks up "Santorin" and Santorini.

Two points need to be made in this regard. First, as Davidson stresses repeatedly, the fact that an acceptable T-theory might make an "unnatural" assignment of objects to individual words does not affect the overall ontology to which the language is committed. (Of course, no *successful* assignment is really "unnatural" on Davidson's account.) Secondly, no appeal to modes of presentations, causal chains, informational packages, or intentionality is needed in order to characterize the theoretical notion of reference that Davidson employs. As Rorty (1986) observes, for Davidson "any 'theory of truth' which analyses a relation between bits of language and bits of non-language is already on the wrong track" (p. 333).

There is a crucial difference between the reference axioms and the predicate axioms in a successful T-theory. The former assign particular entities (individuals) as the semantic values (references or satisfiers) of expressions; the latter do no such thing (although they can still *have* satisfiers). This is important. On Davidson's account, since reference axioms are theoretically ineliminable, we must accept the entities that these axioms specify as satisfying our singular terms, even though we do not have to regard any particular satisfaction function as privileged. Predicate axioms invoke no new entities: the only semantically and ontologically significant notion they use is satisfaction, and satisfiers are just sequences of objects. By hypothesis, a successful axiomatization construes singular terms as *standing for* (or *satisfied by*) objects and construes sentences as

---

[20] It is debatable whether acceptable T-theories for languages containing Russellian descriptions together with words like 'necessarily' and 'possibly' allow of the sorts of straightforward reference permutations Davidson has in mind. This does not matter for present concerns.

satisfied by sequences of objects. Hence Davidson's "realism" about "the familiar objects whose antics make our sentences and opinions true or false" (1984: 198). (On the word 'realism', see below.)

Davidson reads an ontology of objects directly off an acceptable T-theory given the (standard and natural) way he views the axioms for singular terms and predicates: an adequate truth theory will require not just satisfaction axioms but satisfaction axioms that relate bits of language to *objects*. In his view, Tarski's work

make[s] it evident . . . that, for a language with anything like the expressive power of a natural language, the class of true sentences cannot be characterized without introducing a relation like satisfaction, which connects words (singular terms, predicates) with objects. (1990: 296)

. . . there is no way to give a [truth] theory without employing a concept like reference or satisfaction which relates expressions to objects in the world. (1990: 302)[21]

Events—which Davidson construes as unrepeatable particulars—will get into the picture along with objects because a successful axiomatization will have to deal with sentences which involve quantification over events, for example (18) and (19):

(18) There was a fire and there was a short-circuit
∃x(fire x • ∃y(short-circuit y))

(19) There was a fire because there was a short-circuit
∃x(fire x • ∃y(short-circuit y • y caused x)).

Sentences containing action verbs and adverbs ("John left quickly") and those containing bare infinitives ("John saw Mary

---

[21] There is room for substantial disagreement here. Colin McGinn, for example, has argued (in a seminar we taught together) that, without compromising the acceptability of a T-theory, the referential relations involved in term and predicate axioms can be inverted so that predicates have axioms that treat them as referring to *properties* while singular terms receive axioms structurally more akin to those commonly used for predicates. McGinn is certainly correct that the possibility of such an inversion, if systematic, would undermine Davidson's idea of unambiguously reading ontology off semantics. However, it is not clear to me that a systematic and acceptable inversion can be effected once two-place predicates, quantifiers, adverbs, and attitude verbs are introduced. Considerable ingenuity is going to be required to pull it off (if it can be pulled off), and the degree of ingenuity itself may provide a reason for Davidson to doubt the utility of such an axiomatization given other features of his philosophy, particularly his ideas about radical interpretation.

leave") also appear to require quantification over events.[22] In addition to claiming that we will need to pair bits of language with *objects* and *events* in order to construct an acceptable T-theory, Davidson suggests that if the need to posit a particular ontological category does not arise in the construction of such a theory, then the need cannot arise at all. (Of course, linguistic categories and set-theoretic entities like sequences are posited by the metalanguage.) The thought behind this suggestion appears to be (roughly) the following (although I have not actually found it stated quite this way anywhere in Davidson's work): An acceptable T-theory for *L* delivers a true theorem of the requisite form for *every* sentence of *L*; so there is nothing one can say in *L* that outstrips the ontology revealed by such a theory; so there is no sense to be made of ontological categories not forced upon us by the construction of a viable semantics.[23] (It might be objected that in doing semantics we can appeal only to entities that we think exist, so a semantic theory offers us no more by way of ontological insight than ordinary reflection upon our thought and talk. But this misses the fact that an adequate semantics is *systematic* in ways that ordinary reflection is not.)

One interesting question left open concerns competing T-theories with different ontologies. If θ_1 posits As, Bs, and Cs while θ_2 posits only As and Bs, then if both are acceptable T-theories for *L*, we have reason to posit only As and Bs. In this case our ontology is given by the intersection of the things posited by the competing theories. But what if θ_2 posited only Bs and Cs? Perhaps it is unlikely that we will find ourselves in such a situation (we are unlikely to find even *one* T-theory that covers all the data), but the question is still of philosophical interest if we take seriously the idea that ontology flows from semantics in the way Davidson suggests. Presumably Davidson will prefer a theory that posits objects and events over one that posits, for example, events and properties on the grounds that (i) identity conditions for objects and events are clearer than they are for properties, and (ii) our best

---

[22] See Davidson (1980) and Higginbotham (1983).

[23] Rovane (1984) argues that ontological commitments seem to be made *prior to* the construction of a theory of meaning—at least if such a theory is characterized in the way Davidson envisions—because articulating the conditions a theory must satisfy in order to qualify as a theory of meaning (see above) will itself involve such commitments.

accounts of nature and our most cogent statements of traditional philosophical problems concerning, for example, causation, time, change, human action, and the mind–body problem appear to presuppose the existence of objects and events. For present purposes, there is no need to pursue this matter.

2.4 CONTEXT AND OTHER COMPLICATIONS

Forms of semantic complexity we have hitherto ignored could, in principle, have a bearing on the ontology and final shape of an acceptable T-theory. Davidson sees a tidy ontology of objects and events flowing from such a theory: there are no facts, no situations, no states of affairs, no propositions, and no properties because (so far) we have seen no need to posit them. Davidson does not claim to have a *proof* that we need only objects and events; he is, in effect, throwing down the gauntlet: "Show me sentences that appear to require more than objects and events and I think I can show you that objects and events suffice." Various features of natural language might suggest Davidson needs more, and it is worth indicating some of the moves available to the Davidsonian semanticist in dealing with features of natural language that seem to engender complexity.

T-theoretic axioms for "I", "we", "you", "he", "she", "they", "this", "that", "these", "those", "yesterday", "today", "tomorrow", "here", "there", "local", "distant", "now", "then", "earlier", "later", "recent", "hitherto", "henceforth", "present", "current", "former", "long-standing", "contemporary", "previous", "prior", "next", "subsequent", and no doubt many other words must take into account contextual features of one sort or another. In view of this, the Davidsonian will naturally treat truth as a property not of sentences but of utterances or of sentences relativized to utterances or to contexts. The hope is that nothing of ontological consequence will arise because an utterance can be construed as an event or an event–object pair; and a context can be construed as some sort of n-tuple of objects or events. For example, if truth is taken as a property of utterances, then, simplifying somewhat, sample axioms might be rewritten as follows with metalanguage, semantic predicates taking on a parameter for an utterance event e, giving us, for example, (20) for "Santorini" and (21) for "I" (henceforth, I shall take the object-language to be English rather than French):

(20) $\forall s \forall e (Ref("Santorini", s, e) = Santorini)$
(21) $\forall s \forall e (Ref("I", s, e) = e_u)$,

where e_u is the utterer, the person producing the utterance (e.g. the speaker or writer).[24] It might be claimed that Davidson will need more than objects and events to implement this idea, but I am not aware of any good argument to this effect.

One matter that needs to be taken up at some point is the precise resources needed to derive T-theorems for indexical sentences. Another concerns the extent to which the T-theorems for such sentences are *interpretive* in the sense discussed earlier. Dealing with these matters will mean resuscitating questions about the delimitation of those T-theories that can do duty as theories of meaning, particularly if the idea of a canonical proof procedure is to play a role.

A sentence like (22) might be thought to present Davidson with an interesting challenge as it appears to involve quantification over colours, construed as *properties*:

(22) This is the same colour as that.

However, as Davidson (1999c: 88–9) has stressed, we need to distinguish two claims: (i) that the role of predicates in a theory of meaning consists in their standing for properties; (ii) that an interpretive T-theory will, at some point, require an ontology of properties. Davidson rejects (i), which he associates with Russell and others. But rejecting (i) need not involve rejecting (ii).[25] If there turns out to be no other way to account for the place of (22) within a language without positing properties, so be it, says Davidson, as long as properties are regarded as abstracta. In the meantime, he is perfectly justified in exploring whether (22) and related sentences

[24] For more sophisticated treatments of indexicals, see e.g. Burge (1974), Higginbotham (1988), Larson and Segal (1995), Taylor (1980), and Weinstein (1974).
[25] The importance of the general form of this distinction in Davidson's thinking about the relationship between meaning and ontology seems to have been spotted early on by Rovane (1984), who notes that when it comes to drawing ontology out of the theory of meaning, "The presumption is that the *large and constant* features of language that would emerge in any theory of meaning either correspond to, or reflect, or in some way gauge, certain large features of reality" (p. 417; my italics).

might bypass appeals to properties once their logical forms are properly revealed.

An acceptable T-theory for English must be able to handle sentences that contain modal expressions such as 'necessarily' and 'possibly'. Will this require an ontology of "possible worlds"? Or the use of non-extensional connectives that are sensitive to what sentences stand for, entities of finer grain than truth-values? If the axioms of a truth theory are modalized, a richer background logic (a suitable modal logic) can be used to derive T-theorems of the requisite form while treating modal adverbs as non-extensional sentence connectives. But Davidson himself has little time for such talk and, following Quine, he has argued that a slingshot argument can be used to demonstrate the impossibility of usefully non-extensional connectives. If, on the other hand, the axioms of a T-theory are left as is, it seems it will be necessary to allow the quantifiers to range over something like worlds. A question that then arises is whether, as some have suggested, the best way to make sense of worlds involves viewing them as very big facts, situations, or states of affairs, or as sets of propositions. There are, I believe, good reasons for thinking that all of the work can be done using models alone; if this is correct, there is considerably less of a threat to Davidson's project in modal talk than many have thought.[26]

It is well known that *natural* language quantification is more complex than its counterpart in standard first-order languages. However, work in generative linguistics and mathematical logic has revealed elegant methods for extending Tarski's insights so that T-theories can be provided for quantified fragments of natural languages while making precise the relationship between the superficial grammatical form of a sentence and its logical form. Many of the details need not concern us here. Suffice to say that noun phrases such as 'some man', 'no farmers', 'the king', 'most tall soldiers', etc. can be viewed as restricted quantifiers composed of quantificational determiners ('some', 'no', 'the', 'most', etc.) combined with simple or complex nouns ('man', 'tall man', etc.). Axioms such as the following (see Chapter 4) make things run very smoothly:

---

[26] This is something I explore in work in *Possibilities*.

(23) $(\forall s)(\forall k)(\forall \phi)(\forall \psi)$ (s satisfies $\ulcorner[some\ x_k\colon \phi]\ \psi\urcorner$ ≡ some sequence satisfying ϕ and differing from s at most in the kth place also satisfies ψ)

(24) $(\forall s)(\forall k)(\forall \phi)(\forall \psi)$ (s satisfies $\ulcorner[most\ x_k\colon \phi]\ \psi\urcorner$ ≡ most sequences satisfying ϕ and differing from s at most in the kth place also satisfy ψ).

It is not necessary to pack any additional set theory or overtly higher-order machinery into the right-hand sides of (23) and (24): they have the same form as axioms for the traditional unrestricted quantifiers *modulo* the relevant restriction concerning the satisfaction of ϕ.

A further complicating feature of natural language is the existence of anaphoric relations between expressions which cannot be handled in terms of either co-reference or standard variable-binding (e.g. those in "If a man owns a donkey he vaccinates it", "Several men who own donkeys feed them hay", or "Every pilot who shot at it hit the MiG that was chasing him"). I have argued at length elsewhere that the semantic facts are much simpler than is commonly supposed once a proper syntactic theory is in play and that the truth-conditions of sentences involving such links drop out systematically once it is recognized that some pronouns are referential while others are quantificational—as is the case with non-pronominal noun phrases—and that no new entities are quantified over.[27] If this is correct, just as there is nothing of semantical significance in anaphora, so there is nothing of ontological significance in the notion.

Finally, of course, propositional attitude ascriptions ("Pierre believes that Santorini is volcanic", "Marie doubts Cicero is Tully"). Notoriously Davidson (1984) has proposed a paratactic account that is meant to avoid talk of propositions by focusing again on acts of utterance. I feel no need to comment on the proposal here, except to say that it is widely held to be beset with difficulties (just like every other theory of propositional attitude ascriptions).[28]

---

[27] See Neale (1990, chs. 5 and 6; 1993*b*; forthcoming).
[28] See e.g. Burge (1986*a*) and Schiffer (1987).

2.5 FACTS AND CORRESPONDENCE

If we were to find we needed variables to range over, say, *facts* or *situations* in order to provide a theory of meaning, then on Davidson's account, facts or situations would also be part of our ontology. But Davidson suggests (i) that the need will not arise, and (ii) that entities like facts and situations (under their most common construals) are ruled out independently, as can be demonstrated by a slingshot argument.

(i) The sorts of sentence that might tempt one to posit facts include the following:

> (25) The fact that there was a short-circuit caused it to be the case that there was a fire
> (26) There was a fire because there was a short-circuit.

The thought here is that (25) and (26) express causal relations between two facts. But Davidson argues that these sentences do no more than express a relation between events, that (27) gives the logical form of both:

> (27) $\exists x$(fire x • $\exists y$(short-circuit y • y caused x)).[29]

(ii) Davidson (1984, 1990, 1996) has argued that we cannot have facts of any significance because of slingshot arguments: "facts or states of affairs have never been shown to play a useful role in semantics. . . . This is not surprising since there is a persuasive argument, usually traced to Frege (in one form) or Kurt Gödel (in another), to the effect that there can be at most one fact" (1996: 266).

One of the things I shall demonstrate later is that the various forms of slingshot argument do not actually *rule out* facts, although they do impose very definite constraints on what theories of facts must look like, constraints that many theories do not satisfy. As we shall see, Russell's Theory of Facts passes (assuming

---

[29] A more difficult case for Davidson might be the following:

(i) The fact that Mary left Bill's party did not upset him; but the fact that she left so suddenly did.

Davidson is surely correct that events, just like objects, can be described in a myriad of ways. But if Mary's leaving was Mary's sudden leaving, then how is it that (i) can be true if only an event upset Bill?

his Theory of Descriptions and a willingness to admit universals as components of facts); but many other theories fail.

Let us call any theory according to which true sentences stand for, or correspond to, facts—construed as non-linguistic entities—a "sentential-correspondence" theory. And let us call any sentential-correspondence theory that takes the *constituents* of true sentences to correspond to the *components* of facts—e.g. objects, properties, and relations—a "structural-correspondence" theory. Russell presents a theory of facts that involves structural correspondence. By contrast, Austin (1950, 1954) defends the intelligibility of a correspondence theory that does not presuppose structural correspondence. On Austin's account, there is, as he puts it, "no need whatsoever for the words used in making a true statement to 'mirror' in any way, however indirect, any feature whatsoever of the situation or event" (1950: 125). In English there are, in fact, words that stand for certain things in the world; but this is not, says Austin, a necessary feature of languages that can be used to make true statements. Austin's theory—which I shall examine later—is not, then, a structural-correspondence theory because the structure of a true statement does not reflect the structure of a fact to which it corresponds.

From his earliest work on truth and meaning in the 1960s to his most recent articles Davidson has consistently opposed the idea of sentential correspondence. In "True to the Facts" (1969), he did, however, call a Tarski-style T-theory a correspondence theory; but at the same time he argued against facts by providing a slingshot argument deemed to show that all facts, if there are any, collapse into a single Great Fact. This might seem odd: if there are no facts, to what do true sentences correspond? The tension is only verbal and is completely resolved in later work. In his preface to *Inquiries into Truth and Interpretation* Davidson points out that T-theories are correspondence theories only in the unassuming sense that their internal workings "require that a relation between entities and expressions be characterised ('satisfaction')" (1984, p. xv), and not in the sense that they presuppose any entities (facts) to which true sentences correspond. A T-theory was called a correspondence theory in 1969 because of the roles played by (sequences of) *objects* and *events*: we find correspondence lurking in the axioms, through reference and satisfaction, but not in the T-theorems (by recourse to which the theory is evaluated).

In his 1990 article "The Structure and Content of Truth" Davidson is blunt: it was a (verbal) mistake to call T-theories correspondence theories (p. 302), a source of regret (p. 304). All that was meant was that "there is no way to give such a theory without employing a concept like reference or satisfaction which relates expressions to objects in the world" (p. 302). Only in what Davidson now sees as a "contrived" sense is this correspondence:

Truth is defined on the basis of satisfaction: a sentence of the object language is true if and only if it is satisfied by every sequence of the objects over which the variables of the object language range. Take "corresponds to" as "satisfies" and you have defined truth as correspondence. The oddity of the idea is evident from the counterintuitive and contrived nature of the entities to which sentences "correspond" and from the fact that all true sentences would correspond to the same entities. (1990: 302 n. 36)[30]

Still more recently:

The sequences that satisfy sentences are nothing like the "facts" or "states of affairs" of the [sentential] correspondence theorists since if one of Tarski's sequences satisfies a closed sentence, thus making it true, then that same sequence also satisfies every other true sentence, and thus also makes it true, and if any sequence satisfies a closed sentence, every sequence does. (1996: 268)

The implication here is that if there is any remote sense to the idea that sequences function as "truth-makers", since every true sentence is satisfied by every sequence, sequences are less like facts than they are like the world (the Great Fact).

We must be careful, then, to distinguish the "unassuming" or "contrived" sense of 'correspondence' (associated with talk of satisfaction of formulae by sequences of objects) from the sense used in characterizing theories that appeal to entities (e.g. facts, situations, states of affairs, or propositions) to which *sentences* correspond. Following Davidson's lead, then, let us reserve the label 'correspondence theory' for sentential correspondence theories. The hallmark of a correspondence theory of truth is the idea that a sentence (or statement) is true if there is some particular fact (state of affairs, situation, or other non-linguistic entity) to which the sentence, if true, corresponds. (Some correspondence theories— such as Russell's—will also involve structural correspondence between constituents of sentences and components of facts; but this is not an essential feature of correspondence theories.)

One does not need to have Davidson's perspective on semantics in order to see little point in positing facts as truth-makers. Strawson (1950*a*), Quine (1960), and Geach (1972) see philosophers' appeals to facts as parasitic upon noun phrases of the form "the fact that φ", and in places they have heaped scorn on such entities. And along lines suggested by Frege in "The Thought" (1919), Brandom (1994) and Hornsby (1996) have argued that the only useful application of the words 'fact' and 'factual' is to thoughts (or claims) that are true.

Geach sees the postulation of facts as a relatively recent development and offers the following explanation:

Facts came to be counted among the entities in the philosopher's world only after the construction whereby "the fact", or its synonym in another language, is put in opposition with an indirect-statement clause had spread like the pox from one European language to another, largely by way of journalism. This happened at the turn of the last century; only then did philosophers come to postulate facts as individual entities, answering to the phrases so formed. Once stated, the philosophy of facts flourished mightily, especially in Cambridge. (1972: 21)[31]

In a discussion of *entia non grata* Quine (1960: 246–8) suggests that use of the noun 'fact' no more requires entities to which it applies than do the nouns "sake" and "mile". Moreover, says Quine, unreflective consideration of the way 'fact' is used seems to confer a spurious air of intelligibility on the distinction between analytic and synthetic: a sentence is analytic if and only if it is true and lacks factual content. Quine also offers arguments against facts being concrete objects and against explaining truth via the idea that facts are what make true sentences true. If true, the sentences "Fifth Avenue is six miles long" and "Fifth Avenue is a hundred feet wide" state distinct facts, "yet the only concrete or at least physi-

[31] Olson (1987) suggests this cannot be quite right because Mill, Bradley, and Peirce talk about facts before the atomistic Russell and Wittgenstein, before Moore and Ramsey, and before the expression-type "the fact that φ" took a firm hold. According to Olson, a deeper explanation for the emergence of facts must be sought, and he claims that Mill, Bradley, and Peirce took facts to be indispensable for making sense of *relations*; hence Russell's talk of relations when motivating facts. I suspect Olson is wrong about Bradley, but he is certainly correct to claim that Russell and Wittgenstein were moved by reflections on relations.

cal object involved is Fifth Avenue" (p. 247). And the two sentences are true "because of Fifth Avenue, because it is a hundred feet wide and six miles long . . . because of the way we use our words". The word 'fact', says Quine, in all of its uses can be paraphrased away or dealt with in some other way that avoids positing entities to which it applies.

In responding to Austin's (1950) paper "Truth", Strawson (1950*a*) says that although certain parts of a statement may refer or correspond to parts of the world,

> it is evident that there is nothing else in the world for the statement itself to be related to. . . . And it is evident that the demand that there should be such a relatum is logically absurd. . . . But the demand for something in the world *which makes the statement true* (Mr Austin's phrase), or *to which the statement corresponds when it is true*, is just this demand. (1950*a*: 194–5)

Davidson (1990: 303–4) cites this passage approvingly and endorses Strawson's claim that, "while we certainly say that a statement corresponds to (fits, is borne out by, agrees with) the facts", this is merely "a variant of saying it is true" (p. 304).[32] "There is nothing interesting or instructive to which true sentences might correspond" (p. 303). If Davidson's "nothing interesting or instructive" is read as "nothing potentially explanatory of truth", then Brandom (1994) and Hornsby (1996) concur when they endorse Frege's position that facts are just thoughts (or claims) that are true. (Brandom sees this position as supported by the fact that it is customary to say that facts are *about* objects rather than that they *contain* or *consist of* them (p. 622), an observation that should impress both Austin and Strawson.[33])

Davidson does more than simply nod in agreement with Strawson on this matter: he presents a logico-semantic collapsing argument aimed at showing that there is at most one fact to which true sentences correspond: "if we try to provide a serious semantics for reference to facts, we discover that they melt into one; there is no telling them apart" (2000: 66).

---

[32] Strawson's precise position on facts seems less clear than these remarks, taken alone, might suggest. He says that facts are not entities in the world and also that they are "pseudo-material". Some of the difficulties involved in piecing together Strawson's overall position and what it entails about facts are discussed fruitfully by Searle (1998).

[33] The same observation is made by Aune (1985).

2.6 THE GREAT FACT

Davidson's explicit argument against facts is a version of an argument first used by Church (1943*b*, 1956) against Carnap's idea that sentences stand for propositions.[34] Davidson's specific claim is this: "starting from the assumptions that a true sentence cannot be made to correspond to something different by the substitution of co-referring singular terms, or by the substitution of logically equivalent sentences, it is easy to show that, if true sentences correspond to anything, they all correspond to the same thing" (1990: 303).[35] This simply summarizes a claim Davidson made in 'True to the Facts' (1969), and for the details he (rightly) refers his readers back to that work. By way of softening up the terrain, in 'True to the Facts' he asks us to consider when statements of the following form hold:

(28) the statement that *p* corresponds to the fact that *q*.

He replies as follows:

Certainly when "*p*" and "*q*" are replaced by the same sentence: after that the difficulties set in. The statement that Naples is farther north than Red Bluff corresponds to the fact that Naples is farther north than Red Bluff, but also it would seem, to the fact that Red Bluff is farther south than Naples (perhaps these are the same fact). Also to the fact that Red Bluff is farther south than the largest Italian city within thirty miles of Ischia.

---

[34] Church sees the argument as originating with Frege. The extent to which anything approximating this argument can be found in Frege's work is discussed in Ch. 3.

[35] Davidson sees C. I. Lewis (1923) as led to the same conclusion by a different route: Lewis, he says, "challenged the correspondence theorist to *locate* the fact or part of reality, or of the world, to which a true sentence corresponded" and in the absence of a plausible answer concluded that "if sentences correspond to anything at all, it must be the universe as a whole" and consequently that "all true sentences correspond to the same thing" (1990: 303). Manning (1998) sees mention of Lewis as two-edged: the whole world will be the *denotation* of a true sentence, but in addition to its denotation (which is just its extension) an expression is also assigned a *signification* in Lewis's system (1994), and the signification of a sentence is a state of affairs. In his amusing response to Baylis (1968), Lewis (1968) downplays his use of the word 'fact' in his 1923 article, noting that it is "one of the trickiest words in any language", and pronounces "the final and authoritative Lewis theory of fact. A fact is an actual state of affairs. But 'fact' is a crypto-relative term, like 'landscape'. A landscape is a terrain, but a terrain as seeable by an eye. And a fact is a state of affairs, but a state of affairs as knowable by a mind and stateable by a sentence" (1968: 660).

When we reflect that Naples is the city that satisfies the following description: it is the largest city within thirty miles of Ischia, and such that London is in England, then we begin to suspect that if a statement corresponds to one fact, it corresponds to all. (1984: 41–2)

Davidson's next step involves two principles "implicit" in the above train of thought: "if a statement corresponds to the fact described by an expression of the form 'the fact that p', then it corresponds to the fact described by 'the fact that q' provided either (1) the sentences that replace 'p' and 'q' are logically equivalent, or (2) 'p' differs from 'q' only in that a singular term has been replaced by a coextensive singular term" (1984: 42). Davidson appears to regard these two assumptions as embodying traditional and intuitive wisdoms about facts that many friends of facts might be willing to accept. As Taylor (1980) aptly puts it, the assumptions seem to embody the idea that "sentences so closely connected as to be guaranteed by logic alone to share a truth-value cannot differ in truth-relevant entities" (p. 30) and hence must describe, correspond to, or stand for the same fact. (Cursory glances at Russell's (1918) Theory of Facts and of Gödel's (1944) discussion reveal that both men thought an adequate theory of facts should entail the second assumption; see Chapters 4 and 5.) Let us call these Assumptions 1 and 2, respectively.

Before examining whether friends of facts might antecedently want to deny either of these assumptions—there are, I believe, antecedently good reasons for *some* fact theorists to deny Assumption 2—let us follow Davidson's train of thought.

Once the two assumptions are granted, says Davidson, the conclusion that there is just one fact is not far behind:

The confirming argument is this. Let "p" abbreviate some true sentence. Then surely the statement that p corresponds to the fact that p. But we may substitute for the second "p" the logically equivalent "(the x such that x is identical with Diogenes and p) is identical with (the x such that x is identical with Diogenes)". Applying the principle that we may substitute coextensive singular terms, we can substitute "q" for "p" in the last quoted sentence, provided "q" is true. Finally, reversing the first step we conclude that the statement that p corresponds to the fact that q, where "p" and "q" are any true sentences. (1984: 42)

The moral we are to draw from this is that definite descriptions of the form 'the fact that so-and-so', if they describe at all, describe the same thing: The Great Fact. No point remains in distinguishing among various names of the Great Fact when written after "corresponds to"; we may as well settle for the single phrase "corresponds to the Great Fact". This unalterable predicate carries with it a redundant whiff of ontology, but beyond this there is apparently no telling it apart from "is true" (1984: 42)

It would seem, then, that Assumptions 1 and 2 lead to a collapse of all facts into one. And this, Davidson later adds,

trivialise[s] the concept of correspondence completely; there is no interest in the relation of correspondence if there is only one thing to which to correspond, since, as in any such case, the relation may as well be collapsed into a simple property: thus, "*s* corresponds to the universe", like "*s* corresponds to (or names) the True", or "*s* corresponds to the facts" can less misleadingly be read "*s* is true". (1990: 303)

This tricky argument needs to be decompressed if it is to be examined in a fruitful manner. I shall provide a detailed appraisal of arguments of this form later. For the moment, a few important observations will suffice. Let '*d*' abbreviate 'Diogenes' and let $\iota x(x{=}d \bullet \phi)$ do duty for the definite description 'the *x* such that *x* is identical with Diogenes and ϕ'. Davidson's claim is that, given Assumptions 1 and 2, if ϕ and ψ are both true, then the following sentences all correspond to the same fact:

> (I) ϕ
> (II) $\iota x(x{=}d) = \iota x(x{=}d \bullet \phi)$
> (III) $\iota x(x{=}d) = \iota x(x{=}d \bullet \psi)$
> (IV) ψ.

Proof: Suppose sentences (I)–(IV) correspond to facts f_I–f_{IV} respectively. Since (I) and (II) are logically equivalent, by Assumption 1 we know that $f_I = f_{II}$; since (III) and (IV) are logically equivalent, by the same assumption we know that $f_{III} = f_{IV}$; and on the assumption that $\iota x(x{=}d \bullet \phi)$ and $\iota x(x{=}d \bullet \psi)$ are "co-referring singular terms" (taking ϕ and ψ to be true), by Assumption 2 we know that $f_{II} = f_{III}$; hence $f_I = f_{II} = f_{III} = f_{IV}$.

If Davidson's argument is based on Assumptions 1 and 2 *as I have stated them*, then it would appear to depend crucially for its success upon the viability of a semantics for definite descriptions satisfying the following properties:

(*a*) it must render sentences (I) and (II) above logically equivalent (similarly sentences (III) and (IV));

(*b*) it must treat definite descriptions as singular terms (and not, for example, as quantificational noun phrases as they are in Russell's Theory of Descriptions (Chapter 4));

(*c*) when ϕ and ψ are both true, it must declare the definite descriptions $\imath x(x{=}d \bullet \phi)$ and $\imath x(x{=}d \bullet \psi)$ co-referential; more accurately, given Davidson's view of reference as whatever it takes to get acceptable T-theorems, it must declare the following *sentence* true:

(29) $\imath x(x{=}d \bullet \phi) = \imath x(x{=}d \bullet \psi)$.

In his published writings Davidson does not tell us how he intends to treat definite descriptions, so he leaves us guessing about key aspects of the argument *as I have stated it*. In fact, there is a considerable amount of work to be done before the argument can be stated in such a way that it delivers an exact conclusion. The relevant work will be carried out in Chapters 4–9. Right now all I want to do is set out Davidson's contribution to the debate about facts and indicate precisely where the main batch of work needs to be done. First, several side issues.

(i) The main issues are unaffected by whether the slingshot is reformulated using class abstracts (e.g. $\{x: x{=}d\}$ and $\{x: x{=}d \bullet \phi\}$) rather that *iota*-expressions ($\imath x(x{=}d$) and $\imath x(x{=}d \bullet \phi)$). For the same questions need to be asked about the semantics of $\{x: x{=}d \bullet \phi\}$ that are being asked about the semantics of $\imath x(x{=}d \bullet \phi)$. (For elaboration, see Chapter 8.)

(ii) It is sometimes said that Davidson blunders when he attempts to use a slingshot argument against facts because, if successful, such an argument would be equally damaging to events, demonstrating that there is at most one Great Event. This claim betrays a serious misunderstanding. Davidson's slingshot is aimed at theories that propose to treat *sentences* as standing for things; in particular, it is aimed at theories that propose to treat true sentences as standing for things. Certainly the argument has whatever formal structure and consequences it has whatever one *calls* the things that true sentences stand for. A semanticist might be inclined to take true sentences (or true sentences containing just certain main verbs) to stand for events; for example, such a semanticist might take (30) to stand for the event of Socrates' drinking hemlock:

(30) Socrates drank hemlock.

The slingshot would, in principle, have a bearing on such a theory. But it is vital to see that *Davidson* does not take (30) or any other sentence to stand for an event (or anything else). True, on Davidson's account the logical form of (30) is given by the existential quantification (31) because he construes an ordinary action verb such as 'drink' as containing an argument place for an event variable (see above):

(31) $\exists x\ drink(Socrates, hemlock, x)$.

But (31) no more stands for an event than (32) stands for an object, and no more than (33) stands for a number:

(32) Socrates likes something
$\exists x(loves(Socrates, x))$

(33) Nine exceeds something
$\exists x(exceeds(9, x))$.

The claim that slingshot arguments can be turned on theories of events is correct *only where events are treated as things for which sentences stand*, which is not something Davidson claims. For present purposes, such theories might as well be lumped with theories that treat sentences as standing for states of affairs or (when true) facts.

(iii) Davidson does not discuss the notion of logical equivalence *per se*; so it is reasonable to suppose (especially given his affinity to Tarski and his attraction to the first-order predicate calculus) that he is assuming the standard Tarskian conception of this notion: two sentences are logically equivalent just in case they have the same truth-value in every model (equivalently: the same truth-value under all systematic reinterpretations of their non-logical vocabulary; equivalently (given soundness and completeness) each is derivable from the other). (Other options are considered in Chapter 10.)

(iv) It is sometimes claimed that Davidson's slingshot can be dismissed on the grounds that since ϕ is a closed sentence—ϕ needs a truth-value if it is to be logically equivalent to $\iota x(x=d) = \iota x(x=d \bullet \phi)$—the description $\iota x(x=d \bullet \phi)$ is illicit, ill-formed, or uninterpretable by virtue of containing a closed sentence in its matrix. Ultimately, this objection has no force. It is a mistake to suppose that every atomic formula within the matrix of a description must

contain at least one occurrence of x that ιx can bind; certainly
where ϕ is a closed sentence it would often be odd to use anything
like a natural language analogue of $\iota x(x=d \bullet \phi)$ in ordinary or theoretical talk; but there is no more formal difficulty involved in
making sense of such a description (or plain $\iota x \phi$) than there is in
making sense of $\exists x(x=d \bullet \phi)$ (or plain $\exists x \phi$). Interestingly, Gödel's
(1944) version of the slingshot does not make use of a closed
sentence within the matrix: it uses the description $\iota x(x=d \bullet Fx)$
rather than $\iota x(x=d \bullet \phi)$. As we shall see in Chapter 9, this turns out
to give it a decisive *semantic* edge.

(v) Officially, it ought to be Davidson's position that the question of whether definite descriptions are referential or quantificational is of little substance outside the context of particular,
acceptable T-theories. As already noted, in the first instance a T-
theory is tested in connection with whole sentences not their parts,
i.e. in terms of its T-theorems not its axioms. So there should be
nothing to choose between two acceptable T-theories even if the
axioms of one treat descriptions referentially while those of the
other treat them quantificationally.[36]

(vi) On a related note, it might be suggested that if descriptions
are treated referentially, then *Davidson's* use of a slingshot argument does not sit well with his austere conception of reference. For
Davidson, the status of any reference axioms for singular terms
within a T-theory is exhausted by their role within the theory, and
the T-theory itself is evaluated in connection with whole sentences
not their parts. Officially, then, there is nothing to choose between
acceptable T-theories containing different sets of reference axioms.
So what does it mean to say that $\iota x(x=d \bullet \phi)$ and $\iota x(x=d \bullet \psi)$ are
co-referential when ϕ and ψ are true? Does it mean they are co-
referential when ϕ and ψ are true in *every* acceptable T-theory? If
so, what reason is there to think this is so?

To these questions Davidson might reply as follows. The assumption of co-reference in moving from (II) to (III) in the slingshot

---

[36] In fact, matters are rather complex, as one can see by attempting to construct
a T-theory whose axioms treat descriptions referentially but whose T-theorems are
meant to correspond to those flowing from a T-theory whose axioms treat descriptions in accordance with, say, Russell's quantificational treatment. A number of
thorny issues emerge concerning (*a*) the distinction between semantics and analysis,
(*b*) the precise syntax of T-theorems, and (*c*) the question of the exact syntactic and
conceptual resources a T-theory needs if it is to produce T-theorems of a form that
make it possible to see the theory as a candidate theory of meaning.

(I) ϕ
(II) $\iota x(x{=}d) = \iota x(x{=}d \bullet \phi)$
(III) $\iota x(x{=}d) = \iota x(x{=}d \bullet \psi)$
(IV) ψ

amounts to an assumption about *sentences*, namely that (34) is a *logical consequence* of (35):

(34) $\iota x(x{=}d \bullet \phi) = \iota x(x{=}d \bullet \psi)$
(35) $(\phi \bullet \psi)$.

Again, Davidson's affinity to Tarski and his attraction to the first-order predicate calculus suggest an endorsement of the standard Tarskian definition of *logical consequence*, which is definitionally tied to the standard Tarskian definitions of *logical truth* and *logical equivalence* (which Davidson appeals to when he says that (I) and (II) are logically equivalent and that (III) and (IV) are logically equivalent). A sentence q is a logical consequence of a sentence p just in case there is no model in which p is true and q is false (equivalently: there is no systematic reinterpretation of the non-logical vocabulary under which p is true and q is false; equivalently (given soundness and completeness): q is derivable from p). (Other options will be discussed in Chapter 10.)

The upshot of all this is that Davidson's appeal to a notion of co-reference in stating his slingshot does not directly undermine his views about reference. It does, however, serve as a stark reminder of (i) Davidson's reliance on well-understood logical notions and on a pre-selected set of logical constants whose T-theoretic axioms are fixed in advance, and (ii) an assumption built into the slingshot: = is a logical constant. Without this assumption, there would be no getting from (I) to (II) or from (III) to (IV); and if Davidson's own view of reference is assumed, there would be no way of getting from (II) to (III).

Henceforth, I want to evaluate all slingshot arguments on their own terms, avoiding the independent issue of whether there are features of the philosophical system of the *originator* of any particular slingshot that might lead one to question his use of the argument in the first place. The central question raised by Davidson's slingshot, *as stated above*, is this: how are its descriptions to be treated? If they are treated as singular terms, the slingshot needs supplementing with a theory of descriptions according to which

(*a*) φ and ιx(x=a) = ιx(x=a • φ) are logically equivalent, and
(*b*) ιx(x=a • φ) and ιx(x=a • ψ) are co-referential whenever φ and ψ
are both true. As I shall demonstrate later, it is no trivial matter to
come up with a theory of descriptions that is antecedently plausible and which also has both of these features. If, on the other hand,
Russell's Theory of Descriptions is assumed—descriptions are not
singular terms but complex quantificational devices—then the relevant logical equivalences come for free.[37] On Russell's account,
G(ιxFx) is simply shorthand for

(36) $\exists x(\forall y(Fy \equiv y=x) \bullet Gx)$.

Thus (II) of Davidson's slingshot is shorthand for (II′), which is
indeed logically equivalent to φ:

(II) ιx(x=a) = ιx(x=a • φ)
(II′) $\exists x(\forall y((y=a \bullet \phi) \equiv y=x) \bullet \exists u(\forall z(z=a \equiv z=u) \bullet u=x))$.

But of course, on this theory, descriptions are *not* singular terms, so
the crucial claim that ιx(x=a • φ) and ιx(x=a • ψ) are "co-referring
singular terms" cannot be used to justify the claim that (II) and (III)
stand for the same fact. Of course, there may be some *other*, closely
related reason for thinking (II) and (III) stand for the same fact, but
this would need to be explained within the context of an account of
the relationship between predicates (and logical vocabulary) and the
facts stated by sentences containing them. It will become clear that
this is far from nit-picking. As Gödel (1944) so astutely points out,
Russell's Theory of Descriptions appears to play an important
supporting role in connection with Russell's Theory of Facts. Facts,
for Russell, are structured entities, and he is happy to accept that two
sentences stand for the same fact if one of them differs from the other
only in the replacement of co-referring singular terms. For example,
on Russell's account (36) and (37) stand for the same fact (assuming
'Cicero' and 'Tully' are names and not disguised descriptions):

---

[37] I shall assume until stated otherwise that we are dealing with classical logic.
Various forms of so-called *free logic* have been constructed in order to permit singular terms that fail to refer. From a model-theoretic perspective, a free logic might be
characterized as one in which an interpretation is not required to assign an object
to every name. Such logics thereby reject the classical inference principle of existential generalization. There is, however, considerable disagreement among those who
attracted to free logic over the status of sentences containing empty names. For
discussion of free logic in connection with slingshot arguments, see Ch. 9.

(37) Cicero snored
(38) Tully snored.

But Russell rejects the idea that two sentences stand for the same fact if one differs from the other in the replacement of a singular term *t* by a description that happens to be *true of* the thing *t refers to*, or if one differs from the other in the replacement of descriptions true of the same thing. For example, on Russell's account (38) and (39) do *not* stand for the same fact:

(39) The author of *De fato* snored
(40) The orator who denounced Catiline snored.

And neither (39) nor (40) stands for the unique fact that (37) and (38) stand for (Chapter 4).

The moral, then, is that if a slingshot argument is to succeed in ridding the landscape of facts (or at least ridding it of traditional ways of construing facts and making them philosophically useful), it will need to be supplemented with a precise theory of descriptions.

2.7 SCHEME AND CONTENT

Davidson (1984, 1989) argues that no good sense can be made of (*a*) conceptual relativism—the idea that different people, communities, cultures, or periods view, conceptualize, or make the world (or their worlds) in different ways—or (*b*) a distinction between 'scheme' and 'content', i.e. a distinction between conceptual scheme (representational system) and empirical content ("something neutral and common that lies outside all schemes" (1984: 190).

The main argument against relativism is intertwined in subtle ways with one of two arguments deployed against scheme–content dualism, a dualism which relativism is meant to presuppose. For concreteness, Davidson associates conceptual schemes with sets of intertranslatable languages (some find this problematic, but for my purposes here it is not). The first argument against scheme–content dualism proceeds by way of undermining the notion of a scheme; the second by way of undermining the (relevant) notion of content. The former involves an appeal to the conditions something must satisfy in order to qualify as a conceptual scheme (conditions that some have found too stringent). I shall not discuss it here. Rather, I want to examine the anti-content argument and explain why its success depends upon the rejection of facts. I can then explain the relevance of this for talk of "anti-representationalism".

Davidson detects two contenders for the role of "content" in writings advocating forms of relativism: (1) *reality* (*the world, the universe, nature*) and (2) *uninterpreted experience*. And since we find talk of conceptual schemes (languages, systems of representation) either (*a*) *organizing* (*systematizing, dividing up*) or (*b*) *fitting* (*describing, matching, corresponding to*) reality or experience, there are four distinct ways of characterizing the relationship between scheme and content: schemes organize reality, organize experience, fit reality, or fit experience.

None of the four possibilities is meant to be viable. For present concerns, it is the argument against *schemes fitting reality* that is important as it connects directly with talk of an ontology of facts. But a few brief remarks about schemes organizing will help forestall potential confusion.

A good ordinary language point gets the ball rolling. No clear meaning can be attached to the notion of organizing a single object (the world, nature, etc.) unless the object in question is understood to contain (or consist in) other objects. As Davidson observes, someone who sets out to organize a closet or a desk arranges the things in or on it. A man who is told to organize not the shoes and shirts in a closet, but the closet itself, would be bewildered (1984: 192).

He continues: "A language may contain simple predicates whose extensions are matched by no simple predicates, or even by any predicates at all, in some other language. What enables us to make this point in particular cases is an ontology common to the two languages, with concepts that individuate the same objects" (1984: 192). Davidson is not here making the mistake of claiming that if we are to render intelligible the idea that there is "something neutral and common that lies outside all schemes" organised by two purportedly distinct schemes, then the schemes must have the same *concepts*; rather, he is making the point that they must have the same *ontology*. The closet analogy is useful again. If we are to make sense of the idea of different ways of organizing the same closet, we must make sense of the idea of different ways of organizing the things that are in it. And this we can do only by thinking of the entities in the closet as fixed across ways of organizing them, whether we separate things into shirts, trousers, and shoes, or into black things, white things, and things that are neither black nor white, or into woollens, cottons, and leathers.

Notice that this line of thought does not *directly* undermine the scheme-organizing-reality form of scheme–content dualism: rather, it undermines the idea that this particular form of scheme-content dualism can be used to make sense of radically different conceptual schemes. Within the context provided by Davidson's objectives, however, this is not a severe limitation. For if the intelligibility of the idea that there are radically different conceptual schemes presupposes a scheme–content distinction, and if there are just four ways of making the distinction viable—the four ways that Davidson mentions—then even if he manages to demonstrate only that each of the four ways *either* fails to be intelligible or else entails that alternative schemes are not radically different, then he will have shown that the idea of radically different schemes is unintelligible. And surely this will be enough for Davidson to have shown, in addition, that the scheme–content distinction itself is unintelligible: he will have shown that there is at most one conceptual scheme; and we cannot make sense of the idea of *one* conceptual scheme unless we can make sense of more than one; and this we cannot do if we have shown that there is *at most* one; so there are none. That is the idea.

I want no quarrel with Davidson on the matter of schemes organizing. I see him as presenting a more serious challenge: to show how the idea of schemes *fitting* experience or reality is intelligible and at the same time allows for the possibility of distinct schemes. According to Davidson,

When we turn from talk of organization to talk of fitting, we turn our attention from the referential apparatus of language—predicates, quantifiers, variables, and singular terms—to whole sentences. It is sentences that predict (or are used to predict), sentences that cope or deal with things, that can be compared or confronted with the evidence. It is sentences also that face the tribunal of experience, though of course they must face it together. (1984: 193).

A sentence or a theory (i.e. a set of sentences) "successfully faces the tribunal of experience . . . provided that it is borne out by the evidence", by which Davidson means "the totality of possible

sensory evidence past, present, and future" (ibid.). And for a set of
sentences to fit the totality of possible evidence is for each of the
sentences in the set to be true. If the sentences involve reference to,
or quantification over, say, material objects and events, numbers,
sets, or whatever, then what those sentences say about these entities is true provided the set of sentences as a whole "fits the sensory
evidence" (ibid.). Davidson then adds that "One can see how, from
this point of view, such entities might be called posits. It is reasonable to call something a posit if it can be contrasted with something
that is not. Here the something that is not is sensory experience—
at least that is the idea" (ibid.). The allusion to the theory of meaning is clear. A set of sentences involves reference to, or
quantification over, material objects, events, or whatever only if an
acceptable T-theory for the language as a whole must appeal to
such entities in delivering T-theorems for the sentences in the set.
And the entities in question are part of our ontology: they are the
posits of our 'scheme' and can be contrasted with (sensory) experience, i.e. 'uninterpreted content'.

But now Davidson makes what I take to be an important move,
a move against schemes fitting either experience or reality. There is
no alternative to quoting the relevant passage in close to its
entirety:

The trouble is that the notion of fitting the totality of experience, like the
notion of fitting the facts, or of being true to the facts, adds nothing intelligible to the simple concept of being true. To speak of sensory experience
rather than the evidence, or just the facts, expresses a view about the
source or nature of evidence, but *it does not add a new entity* [my italics]
to the universe against which to test conceptual schemes. ... all the
evidence there is is just what it takes to make our sentences or theories
true. Nothing, however, no *thing*, makes sentences or theories true: not
experience, not surface irritations, not the world, can make a sentence
true. *That* experience takes a certain course, that our skin is warmed or
punctured, that the universe is finite, these facts, if we like to talk that way,
make sentences and theories true. But this point is put better without
mention of facts. The sentence "my skin is warm" [as uttered by me, here,
now] is true if and only if my skin is warm [here and now]. Here there is
no reference to a fact, a world, an experience, or piece of evidence.
Footnote: See Essay 3 [i.e. "True to the Facts"] (pp. 193–4).

Here there is allusion both to the theory of meaning and to a
collapsing argument against the viability of *facts*. The theory of

meaning doesn't need them, and the collapsing argument (slingshot) is meant to show that we can't have them anyway.

On Davidson's conception of a scheme—which I shall not contest here—if the *schemes-fitting-reality* story is to succeed, there must be something extralinguistic for true sentences or beliefs to fit, match up to, or correspond to. He sees just two plausible candidates: the world itself or individual facts.[38] But neither will work, he claims, because each trades on the idea that the entity in question "makes the sentence true". Why, exactly, does Davidson think that no legitimate appeal can be made to the idea of an extralinguistic entity that "makes the sentence true"? He thinks individual true sentences are not made true by individual facts because he has confidence in his collapsing argument, which is meant to show that there is at most one fact; this is surely part of what is suggested by his back-reference to 'True to the Facts' (first published in 1969) in the footnote quoted above. So if this attack on the scheme–content distinction is to succeed, an argument against facts is required in order to thwart the schemes-fitting-reality option.

---

[38] The idea that the objects true beliefs and sentences are *about* will suffice is not canvassed. On Davidson's view, "The question what objects a particular sentence is about, like the questions what object a term refers to, or what objects a predicate is true of, has no answer" (1984, p. xix); "nothing can reveal how a speaker's words have been mapped onto objects" (ibid.).

If the (true) belief that Brutus stabbed Caesar is about Brutus and Caesar, isn't the (true) English sentence that expresses that belief, namely

(i) Brutus stabbed Caesar

also about them? And if so, do Brutus and Caesar themselves constitute enough for the sentence and belief to match up to? Russell (1918) thought not (see Ch. 4). The sentence

(ii) Brutus knew Caesar

is also true. If the things a sentence (or belief) matches up to are restricted to the objects it is about, then (i) and (ii) match up to the same things. It is here that Russell invokes *relations* and ends up with *facts*, composed of objects and relations, as the things that true sentences stand for. Composition is not a matter of simply lumping together particulars and universals, witness the truth of (ii) and falsity of (iii):

(iii) Caesar stabbed Brutus.

"The failure of correspondence theories of truth based on the notion of fact", says Davidson, "traces back to a common source: the desire to include in the entity to which a true sentence corresponds not only the objects the sentence is 'about' (another idea full of trouble) but also whatever it is the sentence says about them" (1984: 49). "Theory of truth based on satisfaction is instructive partly because it is less ambitious about what it packs into the entities to which sentences correspond: in such a theory these entities are no more than arbitrary pairings of the objects over which the variables of the language range with those variables" (ibid. 49).

Now what of the alternative position, that individual true sentences are made true not by facts but by *the world*? Why does Davidson say explicitly, in the passage quoted above, that not even *the world* will do? In the course of rejecting the idea of schemes *organizing* the world, he points out that such a story presupposes distinct entities in the world to be organized. Distinct entities are called for by the meaning and use of the word "organize" (you cannot organize a closet without organizing the things in it). But they do not appear to be called for by the meaning and use of the word "fit". And, interestingly, in later works Davidson seems to suggest that the world—or at least how it is arranged—is, in fact, one of two things that does make a (true) sentence true, as in the following passage:

What Convention T, and the trite sentences it declares true, like " 'Grass is green' spoken by an English speaker, is true if and only if grass is green" reveal is that the truth of an utterance depends on just two things: what the words as spoken mean, and how the world is arranged. There is no further relativism to a conceptual scheme, a way of viewing things, a perspective. Two interpreters, as unlike in culture, language, and point of view as you please, can disagree over whether an utterance is true, but only if they differ on how things are in the world they share, or what the utterance means. (1990: 304)

If the sentence 'Smith is in London' is true, it is true because of "how the world is arranged": one of the entities in the world, Smith, is in London. Indeed, this much is given by a T-theory (and no appeal to an alternative set of axioms will alter this fact). So the world makes the sentence true in at least this sense: if the world had been arranged differently—i.e. if the *things* in the world had been arranged differently (for a world to be arranged, the things in it must be arranged)—if Smith were, say, in Paris, the sentence 'Smith is in London' would not be true. To deny this would be to drain all content from the concept of objective truth (see below).

There might seem to be no barrier, then, to making the scheme–content distinction viable by thinking of schemes fitting reality (the world), for it is still open to pursue the idea that a true sentence fits, or is made true by, the world without endorsing the (possibly hopeless) idea that it fits, or is made true by, a particular fact. Davidson (1999e, 2000) recognizes how harmless this way of talking really is: "can't we say that true sentences represent, or better correspond to, or are made true by the world, as Neale suggests? As long as this way of talking isn't thought to explain anything about the concept of truth, it is harmless and may even make those happy who want to be sure that the truth of empirical sentences depends on something more than words and speakers" (1999*e*: 668). There is nothing to console the sentence–fact correspondence theorist here. It is no more illuminating to be told that a sentence is true if and only if it corresponds to the world than it is to be told that a sentence is true if and only if it is true, states a truth, says the world is as the world is, or fits the facts. For the last of these phrases, perfectly ordinary as it is—unlike the philosopher's invention 'corresponds to a fact'—seems to be an idiomatic form of 'is true'. Indeed it is sometimes hard to resist the points that all talk of "facts" is idiomatic and that the logical forms of sentences do not involve quantification over facts ("it is a fact that *p*" = "it is true that *p*"; "that's a fact" = "that's true"; "the fact that *p* caused it to be the case that *q*" = a sentence involving quantification over events).[39]

Davidson goes on to suggest that ultimately there is nothing here to console the conceptual relativist either:

> Meanwhile there is the question raised by Neale: why isn't the fact that the world can be said to make our sentences true or false enough to justify the scheme–content distinction and conceptual relativism? Why, he asks, did I say in "The Very Idea of a Conceptual Scheme" that "Nothing . . . no *thing*, makes our sentences and theories true: not experience, not surface irritations, not the world, can make a sentence true"? That was a mistake. I was right about experience and surface irritations, but I gave no argument against saying the world makes some sentences true. After all, this is exactly as harmless as saying that a sentence is true because it corresponds to the One Great Fact, and just as empty. . . . Maybe we can't locate a part of the world that makes an individual sentence true, but the world itself makes the true sentences true . . . those three little words ("not the world") were seriously misleading. (1999*e*: 668–9)

A separate argument is needed, Davidson recognizes, to show that if the world is what makes true sentences true, then the resulting conceptual relativism is of only "a mild sort that I have always

---

[39] See Strawson (1950*a*) and Davidson (1984). Related to this point is Brandom's (1994) observation that the word 'fact' has clear application only to thoughts (or claims), facts being those thoughts (or claims) that are true.

accepted" (p. 668), an argument that focuses on the fact that the notion of a scheme falls apart if the basic conceptual resources of two divergent schemes differ in any non-trivial way. I have no need to dicuss that argument here as my work on the scheme-content distinction is done. My main conclusion is this: in order to demolish the scheme–content distinction, Davidson needs (i) an argument against facts, and (ii) an argument showing that interestingly divergent schemes are not forthcoming on the view that true sentences are made true not by facts but by the world.

2.8 REALISM AND OBJECTIVITY

A number of philosophers claim to see in Davidson's recent work a denial of "realism" or an inconsistency or unclarity in his positions on the external world, objectivity, and truth. Claiming that someone is (or is not) in the extension of 'realist' is a risky business because the word has been applied so widely in philosophy, often in ways that are quite at odds with one another. Once certain anachronisms and terminological issues are ironed out, however, Davidson's position seems rather robust. First, he is explicit that rejecting the scheme–content distinction "does not mean that we must give up the idea of an objective world independent of our knowledge of it" (1984, p. xviii) or give up "an objective public world which is not of our own making" (1986: 310):

In giving up the dependence on the concept of an uninterpreted reality, something outside all schemes and science, we do not relinquish the idea of objective truth—quite the contrary. Given the dogma of a dualism of scheme and reality, we get conceptual relativity, and truth relative to a scheme. Without the dogma, this kind of relativity goes by the board. Of course the truth of sentences remains relative to a language, but that is as objective as can be. In giving up the dualism of scheme and world, we do not give up the world, but re-establish unmediated touch with the familiar objects whose antics make our sentences and opinions true or false. (1984: 198)

Secondly, there is Davidson's original response to epistemological scepticism and its relation to the idea that an ontology flows naturally from an acceptable T-theory:

What stands in the way of global skepticism of the senses is, in my view, the fact that we must, in the plainest and methodologically most basic cases, take the objects of a belief to be the causes of that belief. And what we, as interpreters, must take them to be is what they in fact are. Communication begins where causes converge: your utterance means what mine does if belief in its truth is systematically caused by the same events and objects. (1986: 317–18).

. . . the general outlines of our view of the world are correct; we individually and communally may go plenty wrong, but only on condition that in most large respects we are right. It follows that when we study what our language—any language—requires in the way of overall ontology, we are not just making a tour of our own picture of things: what we take there to be is pretty much what there is. (1984, pp. xviii–xix)

Davidson seems to be responding to the sceptic as follows. Creatures to whom it makes sense to ascribe beliefs at all must be substantially right in what they believe. More precisely, the act of ascribing erroneous beliefs to an agent makes sense only in so far as the person making such an ascription is willing to see the agent in question as possessing a much more substantial set of *true* beliefs—a set of beliefs can be more *substantial* than another in other than a numerical way.[40] And in the most basic cases—but certainly not in all cases—ascribing true beliefs to an agent makes sense only in so far as we are willing to see the objects of beliefs as their causes.[41]

The passages just quoted sit well with Davidson's general ontological outlook: ontologies of objects and events flow straightforwardly from acceptable T-theories (unlike ontologies of, say, facts and properties). Giving up the scheme–content distinction does not mean abandoning the view that objects and events are (or were)

---

[40] Following Lepore (1986), I am reluctant to couch what Davidson really has in mind in terms of the sheer *number* of beliefs.

[41] According to Rorty (1986, 1991), rejecting the scheme–content distinction provides a much shorter way with the sceptic, without representations and facts, the sceptical problematic cannot even be stated; "Once we give up *tertia*, we give up (or trivialise) the notions of representation and correspondence, and thereby give up the possibility of epistemological scepticism" (1991: 139). On this view, the debate between "sceptics" and "anti-sceptics" evaporates with representations and facts. There is an alarming simplicity to this train of thought; whatever its merits, it presupposes the rejection of the scheme–content distinction, which in turn presupposes there are no facts. By contrast, Davidson's original argument against scepticism can be deployed even by those who have eked out for themselves theories of facts in the narrow gully which, as we shall see, provides limited cover from Gödel's slingshot.

"out there" or "happening" in an objective world (largely) not of our own making. That Davidson is not averse to talk of an objective world is reinforced in two recent passages:

> I believe in the ordinary notion of truth: there really are people, mountains, camels, and stars out there, just as we think there are, and those objects and events frequently have the characteristics we think we perceive them to have. Our concepts are ours, but that doesn't mean they don't truly, as well as usefully, describe an objective reality. (1999a: 19)

> I certainly don't reject realism, at least not until I know what it is I am rejecting. I decided not to call myself a realist because I found that for a large number of philosophers being a realist meant accepting a correspondence theory of truth which held that one could *explain* the concept of truth as correspondence with the facts. I have always been clear that I was not an antirealist about any theoretical entities over which a theory I held true quantified. Quantification (in Quine's ontic sense) is the key to the significant connections between language and belief and the world, since there is no way to give an account of the truth of sentences in a language with general quantification except by relating parts of sentences to entities. Tarski's device of satisfaction expresses such a relation: it is, of course, a fancy form of reference. (1999d: 123)

This is not the place for a full-scale examination of the way the word 'realism' has been used in philosophy; but once we distinguish several distinct uses, Davidson's positions on particular issues that might be stated using the word "realism" can be located with some precision and seen to cohere rather well with what he says elsewhere about T-theories, reference, correspondence, facts, representation, and the scheme–content distinction.[42]

(i) In older (particularly medieval) literature, a realist is sometimes said to be someone who claims that, outside the mind and in addition to particulars, there exist universals (or properties, or qualities, or attributes, or Platonic Forms, or at any rate things that particulars can share, partake of, instantiate, exemplify, or participate in). The opponent of realism in this sense is usually said to be a nominalist. Such a realism is likely to be held in conjunction with

---

[42] I am concerned here only with the word "realism" as it might be used to label certain doctrines in metaphysics. Some metaphysical doctrines are also irrelevant (e.g. modal realism) as well as certain semantic doctrines: Davidson might be said to be a non-realist about reference if this means only that he sees no particular set of reference axioms as more faithful to the truth than any other set forming part of an acceptable T-theory.

the semantic view that predicates typically stand for universals (or whatever), although certain nouns (e.g. "wisdom", "courage") might stand for them too (or things very like them). Davidson certainly does not hold the semantic view: the semantic role of a predicate, on his account, is exhausted by its contribution to the T-theorems flowing from an acceptable T-theory for the language to which the predicate belongs. And since Davidson holds that an acceptable T-theory can probably be assembled without positing entities other than particular objects and events, he is not endorsing realism in this narrow sense.

(ii) A realist in the sense just adumbrated might be said to be a realist in another, broader sense. Someone who believes that there exist Xs, where "X" is a label for a basic ontological category, is sometimes said to be a realist about Xs.[43] Thus a realist in the sense of (i) above would be a realist about universals (or whatever). But it is perfectly possible to deny realism about universals while affirming realism about some other ontological category, for example objects or events. Davidson is a realist (in this sense) about objects and events (construed as particulars), but he is not a realist about universals or facts.[44] (Is there an important connection between realism about universals and realism about facts? Russell seemed to think so: universals were components of facts on his account, and this was no arbitrary decision. For discussion, see Chapter 4.)

(iii) Perhaps the most common use of the term "realism" today is in application to various elaborations of the following meagre claim: at least some portion of reality ("what there is") exists independently of our minds (or anything else's mind).[45] (The opponent of realism in this sense might be called an idealist.) This very non-committal "realism" can be elaborated in a dizzying array of non-equivalent

[43] This is to be distinguished from realism about X where "X" picks out a region of discourse, e.g. ethics, aesthetics, or psychology (to avoid potential confusion I shall use "realism with respect to X" for this): the realist with respect to X claims that statements in X are apt for truth or falsity. Someone who denies this is often called a non-factualist with respect to X.

[44] Orthogonally, it is possible to ask whether someone is a realist about *mental* entities, e.g. mental events. Davidson's (1980) position is that any mental event that enters into causal relations with material events can be redescribed in a material vocabulary.

[45] The qualification is meant to allow the "realist" to deny that mental or social facts (among other things) are mind-independent.

ways, which may overlap in some places and conflict in others. Some
elaborations invoke the concepts of truth or correspondence and, as
such, may seem to presage a change of subject matter; indeed it is
in this connection that some of the contemporary battles over the
word 'realism' have been (and perhaps still are being) fought. My
aim here is not to pass judgement on competing uses or to come
down on any particular side. I seek only to understand the evolution of Davidson's own position with respect to various elaborations of the meagre thesis and its connection to his avowed
"realism" (in sense (ii) above) about the entities flowing from an
acceptable T-theory and his consequent "non-realism" (in sense (ii)
above) about facts and rejection of the scheme–content distinction.
Some of the attempted elaborations I shall outline give rise to
commitments involving truth, correspondence, facts, and uniquely
privileged descriptions. As the last of the passages just quoted
reveals, it is precisely the threat of such commitments that makes
Davidson reluctant, at times, to call himself a realist.[46]

A first, weak, elaboration might be the following: (*a*) Material
objects exist (and material events occur) objectively, i.e. they exist
(and occur) independently of our thoughts, languages, or perspectives; they are "out there" to be discovered (in principle) rather
than constituted or brought about by our thoughts, languages, or
perspectives. As a way of trying to say a little more, some philosophers have added epistemic or linguistic colouring: (*b*) The objects
(and events) we perceive, think about, and talk about—or at least
a good number of them—are among the objective existents (and
occurrents); and so are many objects (and events) whose existence
(or occurrence) we infer in one way or another, and many objects
(and events) we never perceive, think about, or talk about. Certain
philosophers have sensed a need to invoke the notion of *truth* in
order to fill out the idea, a move others have seen as instantly self-
defeating: (*c*) Many beliefs and statements about objective existents
and occurrents are objectively *true* or *false*, i.e. true or false independently of our thoughts, languages, or perspectives. An appeal to
"correspondence" sometimes follows close behind: (*d*) Beliefs and

---

[46] I should mention that I find *all* of the following elaborations problematic
where they are not vague; certainly a great deal of work would be required to spell
them out in ways that would make any of them simultaneously precise and interesting.

statements that are objectively true correspond to an objective reality (and those that are false do not). The idea of correspondence is sometimes fleshed out by appeal to individual facts: (*e*) In order for a belief or statement to correspond to an objective reality, there must be an objective fact to which it corresponds (where an objective fact is another objective existent). Talk of an objective reality, facts, and truth has encouraged some philosophers to fill out the meagre thesis with talk of a uniquely privileged description of reality: (*f*) In order for a true statement to correspond to an objective reality (or to a fact within it) the statement must form part of a unique description of that reality (or of the objective facts which comprise it), a description of "Reality As It Is In Itself".

Davidson accepts elaborations (*a*) and (*b*); but what of the others? He rejects (*f*) outright: "no sensible defender of the objectivity of attributions of truth to particular utterances or beliefs is stuck with this idea" (2000: 66). (If Rorty thinks otherwise, he is mistaken.) And he certainly rejects (*e*), which entails "realism" about facts in the sense of 'realism' given in (ii) above. With (*d*) matters are more complicated, but the work has already been done. If 'correspondence' is understood as expressing a relation between sentences and facts, then Davidson rejects (*d*) because it amounts to (*e*). But if, on the other hand, 'correspondence' is understood as invoking only a relation between singular terms and particular objects and events, then Davidson accepts (*d*).

This leaves us with (*c*), which goes beyond (*b*) in bringing in truth: "Many beliefs and statements about objective existents and occurrents are objectively true or false, i.e. true or false independently of our thoughts, languages, or perspectives." Seen one way, this might seem an obviously false, paradoxical, or self-defeating elaboration; but seen another, it might seem just an overly cognitive or linguistic way of restating (*b*). A recent paper by Davidson (2000) brings together what is needed to see where he stands. The key notion is *objectivity*—at least once this is detached from any problematic notion of sentential correspondence. There is no good reason, says Davidson, to depart from the "traditional" view that truth is objective (pp. 67 and 72) where "Truth is objective if the truth of a belief or sentence is independent of whether it is justified by all our evidence, believed by our neighbors, or good to steer by" (p. 67). At the same time he explicitly rejects the idea that objective truth requires truth to be an object (p. 65): truth, he maintains, is "a concept . . . intelligibly attributed to things like sentences, utterances, beliefs, and propositions, entities which have a propositional content" (p. 65). Furthermore—and this is the key—truth "depends upon how the world is" (p. 73):

It is possible to have a belief only if one knows that beliefs may be true or false. I can believe it is now raining, but this is because I know that whether or not it is raining does not depend on whether I believe it, or everyone believes it, or it is useful to believe it; *it is up to nature*, not me or my society or the entire history of the human race. (p. 72; my italics)

Whether my belief that it is raining is true is "up to" nature, the world, reality; and there is no harm in stating this as follows: my belief that it is raining is, if true, *made true* by the world. There is neither harm nor explanatory value in saying that a true belief, sentence, or statement is made true by the world as long as this is not taken to mean that individual facts in the world are truth-makers. Davidson is embracing a notion of objective truth without the trappings of what he once called the "realist" conception of truth, with its seeming commitment to facts.[47] In short: Davidson accepts elaboration (*c*) as long as it can be further and fruitfully elaborated without commitment to facts.[48]

It is now easy to say everything that needs to be said about Rorty in connection with Davidson's "realism". Davidson is an "anti-representationalist", says Rorty, because he rejects the "reciprocal relations" of "making true" and "representing"; and the anti-representationalist eschews discussion of "realism" by denying that the notion of "representation" or that of "fact of the matter" has any useful role in philosophy (1991: 2). When the smoke has cleared, all Rorty's Davidson is doing is rejecting "realism" in the sense of elaboration (*e*)—scarcely news. That Rorty himself has

---

[47] As he once put it, "The realist view of truth, if it has any content, must be based on the idea of correspondence, correspondence as applied to sentences or beliefs or utterances—entities that are propositional in character, and such correspondence cannot be made intelligible" (1990: 304). It cannot be made intelligible because it would require individual facts to which true sentences or beliefs or utterances correspond.

[48] Davidson (2000) also insists that without a grasp of the concept of objective truth, language and thought are impossible: no sentence can be understood and no belief entertained by someone lacking the concept of objective truth (p. 72). For discussion of this paper, especially of the idea that Davidson's notion of objectivity amounts to the thesis that we can never tell which of our beliefs are true, see Bilgrami (2000).

only elaboration (*e*) in mind seems to be supported by his claim that Davidson is an anti-representationalist because he is committed to the thesis that "there is no point to debates between realism and antirealism, for such debates presuppose the empty and misleading idea of beliefs 'being made true' " (1986: 128). By undermining the scheme–content distinction, he says, Davidson has made it impossible to get the realist–anti-realist debate off the ground:

If one gives up thinking that there are representations, then one will have little interest in the relation between mind and the world or language and the world. So one will lack interest in either the old disputes between realists and idealists or the contemporary quarrels within analytic philosophy about "realism" and "antirealism". For the latter quarrels presuppose that bits of the world "make sentences true", and that these sentences in turn represent those bits. Without these presuppositions, we would not be interested in trying to distinguish between those true sentences which correspond to "facts of the matter" and those which do not (the distinction around which the realist-vs.-antirealist controversies revolve). (1992: 372).

If Rorty had meant to be claiming that Davidson denies elaborations (*a*) or (*b*), or "realism" about objects and events in the sense of (ii) above, then he would have been wrong. Charity dictates that we see Rorty as trying to say something true but uncontroversial about Davidson and "realism": Davidson rejects elaboration (*e*).

2.9 REPRESENTATION

According to Davidson, if we are able to demonstrate that there are no facts, the consequences for "correspondence" and "representation" are clear:

The correct objection to correspondence theories [of truth] is . . . that such theories fail to provide entities to which truth vehicles (whether we take these to be statements, sentences, or utterances) can be said to correspond. If this is right, and I am convinced it is, we ought also to question the popular assumption that sentences, or their spoken tokens, or sentence-like entities or configurations in our brains, can properly be called "representations," since there is nothing for them to represent. If we give up facts as entities that make sentences true, we ought to give up representations at the same time, for the legitimacy of each depends on the legitimacy of the other. (1990: 304)

If there are no individual facts, then we cannot say with any felicity that a true sentence (or belief) corresponds to, or represents a fact. When Davidson says that neither "sentences, [n]or their spoken tokens, [n]or sentence-like entities [n]or configurations in our brains can properly be called "representations", since there is nothing for them to represent", he is proposing an injunction against certain statements of the forms (R) and (C):

(R) *X* represents *Y*
(C) *X* corresponds to *Y*,

where "represents" and "corresponds to" are transitive verbs and "*X*" and "*Y*" are replaced by noun phrases. First, instances of (R) and (C) are not true if the noun phrase replacing "*X*" describes a sentence (statement or utterance)—one minor concession, noted earlier: if "*X*" is replaced by a description of a true sentence *S* and "*Y*" is replaced by "the world" (or, in a Fregean vein, "the True"), the resulting sentence will be true but no more informative than the statement that *S* is true.[49] Secondly, instances of (R) and (C) are not true if the noun phrase replacing "*Y*" is meant to describe (or refer to) a *fact* (*situation, state of affairs, circumstance*). So no sentence, statement, utterance, gesture, mental state, computer state, sculpture, painting, or photograph can be said to represent a fact.

It is important to see that Davidson is not claiming that there *cannot be* useful representatives of *objects* or *events*. Without any charge of inconsistency, Davidson can accept the truth of many instances of (R) where the noun phrase replacing "*X*" describes or refers to (e.g.) a painting or a sculpture and the noun phrase replacing "*Y*" describes or refers to (e.g.) a person, a place, or an event (e.g. a battle). He can say that a map of London represents London, that various marks on the map represent its streets, parks, churches, and so on. Similarly for remarks one might make about wind-tunnel or computer-generated models of objects (e.g. aircraft and automobiles) or events (e.g. hurricanes and earthquakes). So anyone seeking an explicit argument against the existence of representations of objects and events had better look elsewhere; no such argument can be extracted from the rejection of facts or the rejection of the

---

[49] Of course certain philosophically irrelevant instances are acceptable. We might adopt a convention according to which sentences of French are used to represent the temperature or chess moves.

scheme–content distinction. I mention this because it appears Rorty wants to draw more from these rejections, for example when he says that "anti-representationalism"—to which he sees Davidson as subscribing—is "the claim that *no* linguistic items represent *any* non-linguistic items" (1991: 2). If we are meant to take this at face value—the italics are Rorty's—then Rorty is drawing a conclusion that Davidson is not from the rejection of facts and scheme–content dualism.

Schematically, Rorty is ascribing to Davidson the view that there are no true sentences of form (R) where the noun phrase replacing "*X*" describes or refers to a linguistic item and the noun phrase replacing "*Y*" describes or refers to a non-linguistic item. But Davidson's position is that there are no true sentences of this form where the noun phrase replacing "*X*" describes or refers to *anything whatsoever* and the noun phrase replacing "*Y*" describes or refers to a *fact* (*situation, state of affairs, circumstance*); and this entails only that no linguistic items represent *facts* (etc.), not that no linguistic items represent *any* non-linguistic items. Davidson holds there are no true instances of (R) where the noun phrase replacing "*Y*" is of the form "the fact that so-and-so" (or some similar form designed to describe a fact) because he believes he can show (by way of a slingshot) that there are no facts. It's as simple as this: nothing can be said to represent a fact since there are no facts to be represented. There is no reason to see a stronger injunction flowing from Davidson's reasoning.

It is possible that Rorty wants to draw the stronger conclusion about linguistic representations because the only viable linguistic contenders for being described by noun phrases replacing "*X*" are sentences and singular terms (including variables under assignments), and the only viable non-linguistic contenders for being described by noun phrases replacing "*Y*" are objects, events, and facts. If sentences and singular terms cannot represent facts (because there aren't any), then the only way for linguistic entities to represent non-linguistic entities is for sentences or singular terms to represent objects or events.

Davidson's slingshot is meant to show that any two true sentences will represent the same entity (by whatever name); so there is no merit to the idea that sentences are representations. We are left, then, with the task of making sense of singular terms representing (i.e. referring to) objects or events. But the thesis that no singular term can represent an object or event certainly does not follow from the rejection of facts or scheme–content dualism. However, there is another thread of Davidson's work that Rorty might pick up here: no particular set of reference (i.e. satisfaction) axioms for singular terms is privileged on Davidson's account since no complete set of truth-theoretic axioms (of which a set of reference axioms will form a proper subset) is privileged; so the reference relation cannot be considered usefully representational in any sense that will satisfy a "realist" about reference or representation. Perhaps it is this feature that encourages Rorty to say that no linguistic item represents any non-linguistic item for Davidson. But the theoretical ineliminability of reference (i.e. satisfaction) within such a theory threatens to take the sting out of this. For while it is true that no particular set of working reference axioms is privileged, and while it is true that no philosophical account of the reference relation is invoked beyond the idea of a theory-internal pairing of singular terms and objects (and events)—Davidson does not have to see reference as determined by, for example, description, baptism, or causal or informational chains—reference is theoretically ineliminable (he says) in the sense that any adequate axiomatization for a natural language will treat names and variables (relative to sequences, and via axioms of satisfaction) as "standing for" particular objects and events. The theory of meaning reveals an ontology of objects and events. We should not, I think, infer from Davidson's faith in the existence of alternative axiomatizations (containing different singular-term axioms) that he means to be claiming that there is no useful sense in which a singular term can be said to stand for or represent an object or event: relative to a particular axiomatization (and assignment) that is precisely what such an expression is doing.

3

Frege: Truth and Composition

'Facts, facts, facts' cries the scientist if he wants to emphasize
the necessity for a firm foundation for science. What is a fact?
A fact is a thought that is true.

(G. Frege)

3.1 REFERENCE AND COMPOSITION

Frege (1892) distinguishes between the *reference* (*Bedeutung*) and
the *sense* (*Sinn*) of an expression, where the latter is a "mode of
presentation" of the former. The referent of a declarative sentence,
for Frege, is its truth-value—Truth or Falsity—and its sense is a
thought (*Gedanke*). So the thought expressed by a sentence *S* is a
mode of presentation of *S*'s truth-value.

Church, Gödel, and Davidson have claimed to see in Frege's
work at least the glimmer of an argument purporting to show that
there is no viable alternative to the view that if sentences refer, then
there is a unique entity to which every true sentence refers, and a
unique and distinct entity to which every false sentence refers.
Russell (1918) and others have baulked at the idea that all true
sentences stand for the same thing. According to Russell, a true
sentence stands for a *fact*, and there are many distinct facts (his
position will be discussed in the next chapter). In a similar vein,
many philosophers view sentences, whether true or false, as standing for *propositions* or *states of affairs*, and there are meant to be
many more than two propositions or states of affairs.

It is unclear whether Frege provides anything that should be
viewed as a deductive argument for the thesis that the reference of
a sentence is a truth-value; but he does juggle a number of inter-
connected logical and epistemological points in ways that make the
thesis attractive, or at least palatable. The formal arguments that

Church and Gödel produce cannot be found in Frege's work; but it is not difficult to see Frege's influence in these arguments, largely through the *Principle of Composition*, which is meant to express the idea that the reference of an expression φ is determined by φ's syntax and the references of φ's parts (*mutatis mutandis* for sense).

Singular terms and sentences—Frege often views the latter as complex examples of the former—are the building blocks of his system. The syntax of an expression belonging to any other major category is a function of those of singular terms and sentences. Suppose, for the moment, that we have just singular terms, one-place sentence connectives (e.g. "it-is-not-the-case-that"), two-place sentence connectives (e.g. "and" and "but"), and intransitive verbs (e.g. "smile"). The notation of categorial grammar serves well here, where S is the category *sentence* and N the category *singular term*. A one-place sentence connective is of the syntactic category S/S (a device that combines with a sentence to form another sentence); a two-place connective is of the category S/(S,S) (a device that combines with a pair of sentences to form a sentence); an intransitive verb is of the category S/N (a device that combines with a singular term to form a sentence).

Given (i) that singular terms refer to objects and sentences refer to truth-values (whether truth-values are themselves objects is of no importance to the concerns of this book), (ii) the Principle of Composition, and (iii) a syntax, we can characterize the references of expressions belonging to other syntactic categories.[1] Sentence connectives refer to truth-functions: a one-place connective such as ~ refers to a function $V \rightarrow V$ from truth-values to truth-values, i.e. a function from sentence referents to sentence referents; a two-place sentence connective such as "and" or "but" refers to a function $\langle V, V \rangle \rightarrow V$ from *pairs* of truth-values to truth-values, i.e. a function from pairs of sentence referents to sentence referents; an intransitive verb (effectively a one-place predicate) refers to a function $O \rightarrow V$ from objects to truth-values, i.e. a function from singular term referents to sentence referents.

---

[1] In order to avoid issues that are irrelevant to the immediate expository concerns of this chapter, where singular terms are concerned let us restrict attention to proper names that do, in fact, refer; and where sentences are concerned let us restrict attention to declarative sentences that are true or false. Some will see these restrictions as vacuous, others as draconian; for immediate purposes it does not matter in the least.

3.2 INNOCENCE ABANDONED

Matters get slightly more interesting when transitive verbs (e.g. "like") are added. It is common in logic and philosophy to treat transitive verbs as two-place predicates. On such an account, a transitive verb belongs to the category S/(N,N) and refers to a function ⟨O,O⟩ → V from ordered pairs of objects to truth-values. But contemporary linguistic theory will have none of this: a transitive verb and its direct object combine to form a sentence constituent (a verb phrase), i.e. an expression of the category S/N (just like an intransitive verb). On such an account, the Fregean should say that a transitive verb is of the category (S/N)/N and refers to a function O → (O → V) from objects to functions from objects to truth-values.

Excitement begins once sentential verbs (e.g. "believe" and "say") are thrown into the mix: Frege's Principle of Composition *seems* to be threatened. A sentential verb appears to be of the category (S/N)/S—an expression that combines with a sentence to form a verb phrase—and should therefore refer to a function V → (O → V) from truth-values to functions from objects to truth-values. But this seems wrong. "Phosphorus" and "Hesperus" refer to the same object, so (1) and (2) have the same truth-value:

(1) Phosphorus is the brightest object in the sky before sunrise
(2) Hesperus is the brightest object in the sky before sunrise.

But (3) and (4), according to Frege, need not have the same truth-value:

(3) Philip believes that Phosphorus is the brightest object in the sky before sunrise
(4) Philip believes that Hesperus is the brightest object in the sky before sunrise.

This looks problematic for Frege's system because (3) appears to differ from (4) only in the replacement of parts with the same reference (namely sentences (1) and (2), which have the same truth-value).

But the way Frege proceeds, the Principle of Composition remains intact. There is an important disanalogy between transitive verbs and sentential verbs. The verb "like" takes as its complement the sort of expression that refers to an object; this comports with the intuitive idea that things liked are objects.[2] The verb "believe" takes a sentence as its complement (on Frege's account), and a sentence is the sort of expression that refers to a truth-value. This would seem to lead to the thoroughly *counter-intuitive* idea that things believed are truth-values. Frege wanted to capture the idea that things believed are *thoughts*, i.e. the sorts of thing that are the *senses* rather than the references of sentences. And so he reaches the position that a sentence subordinate to a verb like "believe" has as its reference, in such a linguistic environment, its customary sense (i.e. the sense it would have if it were unembedded). And since (1) and (2) do not have the same sense—they contain parts that differ in sense, namely "Phosphorus" and "Hesperus"—substituting one for the other as the complement of "believe" need not preserve reference (truth-value) of the whole, i.e. (3) and (4) can differ in truth-value.[3] In short, the Principle of Composition remains intact, but a *second*, antecedently plausible, principle has now been rejected. It might be thought reasonable to assume that the reference of an unambiguous expression does not depend on the surrounding linguistic environment. This assumption is often called the *Principle of Semantic Innocence* after a famous remark of Davidson's:

Since Frege, philosophers have become hardened to the idea that content sentences in talk about propositional attitudes may strangely refer to such entities as intensions, propositions, sentences, utterances, and inscriptions. . . . If we could recover our pre-Fregean semantic innocence, I think it would seem to us plainly incredible that the words "the earth moves," uttered after the words "Galileo said that," mean anything different, or refer to anything else, than is their wont when they come in other environments. No doubt their role in *oratio obliqua* is in some sense special; but that is another

---

[2] For simplicity, I am ignoring the fact that quantified as well as referential noun phrases may function as direct objects. On a Fregean account, whereas a referential noun phrase is of the category N, a quantificational noun phrase (e.g. "every man") is of the category S/(S/N): in either case the result of combining a noun phrase with a one-place predicate is a sentence. A quantificational noun phrase on this account refers to a function $(O \rightarrow V) \rightarrow V$ from functions from objects to truth-values to truth-values.

[3] The matter of what a sentence refers to when it is doubly (triply, . . .) embedded as in "Phaedo believes Socrates believes Plato is wealthy" has attracted some attention. Some have argued that it still refers to its customary sense, i.e. a mode of presentation of its customary reference; others have maintained that it must refer to a mode of presentation of a mode of presentation of its customary reference. In fact, neither party is right: once the possibility of multiple embeddings is introduced, Frege's theory becomes inconsistent, but there is no need to go into this matter here.

story. Language is the instrument it is because the same expression, with semantic features (meaning) unchanged, can serve countless purposes. (1984: 108)

Frege has abandoned Semantic Innocence and thereby saved the Principle of Composition. In this he was followed by Church, for example; but to some the price has seemed exorbitant, and many able philosophers have attempted to construct semantic theories that respect both Semantic Innocence and the Principle of Composition.[4]

A third principle that has loomed large in recent semantic investigations is the *Principle of Direct Reference*. In connection with a singular term α, this principle holds that the referent of α is the only thing associated with α that is relevant to determining the proposition expressed by an utterance of a sentence containing α, and so the only thing associated with α that is relevant to determining the truth-value of an utterance of a sentence containing α. From the fact that Frege accepts the Principle of Composition in connection with sense as well as reference, it follows that he rejects the Principle of Direct Reference: the *sense* of the unembedded sentence "Phosphorus is the brightest object in the sky before sunrise" serves as its *reference* when embedded in, for example, "Philip believes that Phosphorus is the brightest object in the sky before sunrise", and this sense depends upon the customary sense of "Phosphorus". So Frege and Church propose theories that are

(5) +Composition
    −Semantic Innocence
    −Direct Reference.

---

[4] The distinction between semantic theories that are Semantically Innocent and those that are not is somewhat analogous to the distinction in syntax between grammars that are context-free and those that are not. A context-free phrase structure grammar countenances only rules that are context-free, i.e. rules of the form

(i) $\alpha \rightarrow \beta_1 \ldots \beta_n$,

which may be contrasted with context-sensitive rules of the form

(ii) $X\alpha Y \rightarrow X \beta_1 \ldots \beta_n Y$.

The point of analogy is that rules of the form of (ii) specify that if α occurs in the context $X\alpha Y$ it can expand to $\beta_1 \ldots \beta_n$. Some syntacticians and semanticists prefer context-free grammars and innocent semantic theories because of the simplicity and uniformity they appear to provide; others seem not to be moved by such considerations. Nothing in this book involves taking a stand on this issue.

Non-Fregeans have discussed the extent to which it is possible, and desirable, to construct semantic theories that respect two or three of the principles; for example, many of a Russellian leaning have suggested treating the reference of a sentence as a structured proposition (rather than a truth-value) as the obvious first step towards the construction of such a theory.

3.3 THE REFERENCE OF A SENTENCE

Let us turn to the matter of *why* sentences should refer to truth-values on Frege's account. Since reference is subject to the Principle of Composition, the reference of a sentence, says Frege, "must remain unchanged when a part of the sentence is replaced by an expression with the same reference. ... What feature except the truth-value can be found that belongs to ... sentences quite generally and remains unchanged by substitutions of the kind just mentioned?" (1892: 64–5). This passage seems to admit of two interpretations. On one, Frege appears to be suggesting that if the reference of a sentence can be altered only by replacing one of its parts X by an expression that does not have the same reference as X, then all true sentences have the same reference, and similarly all false ones. On the other interpretation, he appears to be suggesting that, given the same condition, the reference of a sentence must be a truth-value because the truth-value of a sentence is the only *semantically relevant entity* associated with a sentence that survives all substitutions of co-referential expressions. Some scholars feel the latter reading is supported by the fact that in the next paragraph Frege gives us the following conditional: "If now the truth-value of a sentence is its reference, then on the one hand all true sentences have the same reference and so, on the other hand, do all false sentences" (1892: 65).

Let us assume, with Frege, that sentences *do* refer and see if we might find ourselves pointed in the direction of the idea that truth-values serve as their references by other features of Frege's theory. On Frege's account, two singular terms, e.g. "Phosphorus" and "Hesperus", might agree in reference yet differ in sense, a fact that he exploits in addressing puzzles involving identity and substitution. On the assumption that the Principle of Composition applies to both reference and sense, two sentences agreeing in reference

could still differ in sense. However, on the Fregean assumption that
sense determines reference (that reference is a function of sense),
two sentences cannot agree in sense yet differ in reference.

But what does it take for two sentences to agree in sense, to
express the same thought? In a letter to Edmund Husserl written on
30 October and 1 November 1906 Frege says that "In logic one
must decide to regard equipollent propositions as differing only
according to form. After the assertoric force with which they have
been uttered is subtracted, equipollent propositions have something in common in their content, and this is what I call the thought
they express. This alone is of concern to logic. The rest I call the
colouring and the illumination of the thought" (1906a: 67). This
naturally leads one to ask for a precise characterization of equipollence, for the criterion of identity for thoughts that Frege has in
mind. A clear statement of Frege's view on this matter comes in
another letter to Husserl, written on 9 December 1906 in response
to two letters (now lost) that Husserl had written in response to the
letter quoted from above.⁵ Frege appears to suggest the following
criterion for identifying thoughts: for any two sentences A and B,
if (i) "A • ~B" and "~A • B" can *both* be shown to be contradictions using only "purely logical laws" (and without relying on
knowledge of the truth-value of either sentence), and (ii) neither A
nor B contains a logically "self-evident" sentence as a part, then A
and B have the same sense.⁶ *Modulo* his prohibition on "self-

---

⁵ According to Heinrich Scholz, the first of these two letters deals with equipollence and colouring.

⁶ "It seems to me that an objective criterion is necessary for recognising a
thought again as the same, for without it logical analysis is impossible. Now it seems
to me that the only possible means for deciding whether a proposition A expresses
the same thought as proposition B is the following, and here I assume that neither
of the two propositions contains a logically self-evident component part in its sense.
If *both* the assumption that the content of A is false and that of B true *and* the
assumption that the content of A is true and that of B false lead to a logical contra-
diction, and if this can be established without knowing whether the content of A or
B is true or false, and without requiring other than purely logical laws for this
purpose, then nothing can belong to the content of A as far as it is capable of being
judged true or false, which does not also belong to the content of B. . . . Thus what
is capable of being judged true or false in the contents of A and B is identical, and
this alone is of concern to logic, and this is what I call the thought expressed by both
A and B. . . . Is there another means of judging what part of the content of a proposition is subject to logic, or when two propositions express the same thought? I do
not think so." (Frege 1906b: 70–1)

In "A Brief Survey of my Logical Doctrines", also written in 1906 (Frege 1906c:

evident" subsentences, Frege seems to be fairly close to making the suggestion that sentences which are "logically equivalent" have the same sense (and hence the same reference). So given the Principle of Composition, we find ourselves heading in the direction of the idea that in non-oblique contexts (*a*) *co-referring singular terms* may be substituted for one another without altering the reference of the whole and (*b*) *logically equivalent sentences* may be substituted for one another without altering the reference of the whole. If this were established, it would not, of course, demonstrate that there are only two possible references for a sentence; rather it would call out for an argument from the premiss that the substitution of neither co-referring singular terms nor logically equivalent sentences can affect the reference of a sentence, to the conclusion that there are just two possible references for a sentence. It is just this sort of argument that Church (1943*a*) and Gödel (1944) present (although there is no evidence to suggest that either was influenced by the discussion in Frege's letter to Husserl). From the soundness of such arguments it would still not follow that the possible references of a sentence are Truth and Falsity: *any* two distinct things would do, for example the numbers 1 and 0. However, truth-values would have an obvious appeal, if only for the reason that an adequate Principle of Composition would very likely dictate that a sentence lacks a reference if one of its parts lacks a reference, and taking truth-values to be the references of sentences would square nicely with the antecedently plausible suggestion that a sentence lacks a *truth-value* if one of its parts lacks a reference. (Frege scouts other considerations, but they do not bear on any of the points I wish to make here.)

197–202), Frege is less precise on the logic of equipollence, offering a closely related psychological or epistemological characterization. Two sentences *A* and *B* are said to be equipollent when "anyone who recognises the content of *A* as true must thereby also recognise the content of *B* as true and, conversely, that anyone who accepts the content of *B* must straightway accept that of *A*" (p. 197). At the very least, this characterization still invites the thought that mutual entailment is at the heart of the notion. (There is an obvious problem with all of this: if logically equivalent sentences have the same sense, then such sentences ought to be intersubstitutable *salva veritate* in contexts of propositional attitude. But this is simply not the case according to Frege (1892).)

4

Russell: Facts and Descriptions

It is generally agreed that, if Frege had to ascribe reference to sentences at all, then truth-values were by far the best thing he could have selected as their referents: at least, he did not go down the dreary path which leads to presenting facts, propositions, states of affairs or similar entities as the referents of sentences.

(M. Dummett)

4.1 FACTS AND THEIR PARTS

It is common in philosophy, logic, and linguistics to see sentences as structured entities and to see the semantic powers of certain favoured constituents—so-called "singular terms"—as deriving from the fact that they stand for (refer to, designate) things. The name "Socrates", for example, might be said to stand for Socrates. It is much less usual, indeed it seems strained or artificial, to say that verbs, adverbs, connectives, articles, or prepositions stand for things in any similar way. Yet many philosophers, logicians, and linguists are happy to treat such expressions as standing for things within their semantic theories; for example, as standing for properties, relations, sets, or functions. And, more importantly for present concerns, whole sentences are commonly seen as standing for things; for example: truth-values, propositions, states of affairs, situations, or (when true) facts. Frege, as we have seen, had the idea that a declarative sentence stands for either Truth or Falsity. Russell (1918) wanted none of this and argued that a true sentence stands for a *fact*; so did Wittgenstein (1921). In this they were joined by a number of other philosophers at Cambridge, including, for a while at least, G. E. Moore and F. P. Ramsey. Around the same time C. I. Lewis (1923) was also arguing for facts.

Russell and Wittgenstein argued that the world contains (or is composed of) facts, construed as "logical complexes"; and they made use of the idea that true sentences are simply those that *correspond to* facts.[1] They also argued that no adequate description of reality and the way it connects to language could be provided without positing facts. For immediate purposes, I want to focus on Russell's theory and on Gödel's (1944) claim that the tenability of the theory relies heavily on the viability of Russell's Theory of Descriptions. (Wittgenstein's theory of facts and the applicability of Gödel's point will be addressed later.)

Russell draws our attention to the first of a series of "truisms . . . so obvious that it is almost laughable to mention them" (1918: 182): "the world contains *facts*, which are what they are whatever we may choose to think about them, and . . . there are also *beliefs*, which have reference to facts, and by reference to facts are either true or false" (p. 182). On Russell's account, a fact is "the sort of thing expressed by a whole sentence, not by a single name" (pp. 182–3): "we express a fact, for example, when we say that a certain thing has a certain property, or that it has a certain relation to another thing" (p. 183). Russell's reason for positing facts and his view of their ontological status are summarized thus: "the outer world—the world, so to speak, which knowledge is aiming at knowing—is not completely described by a lot of 'particulars' . . . you must also take account of these things I call facts, which are the sorts of things that you express by a sentence, and . . . these, just as much as particular chairs and tables, are part of the real world" (p. 183). The claim here is simply that no complete descrip-

---

[1] Frege explicitly rejects this sort of position:

"It might be supposed . . . that truth consists in correspondence of a picture with what it depicts. Correspondence is a relation. This is contradicted, however, by the use of the word "true", which is not a relation-word and contains no reference to anything else to which something must correspond. . . . A correspondence . . . can only be perfect if the corresponding things coincide and are, therefore, not distinct things at all . . . if the first did correspond perfectly with the second, they would coincide. But this is not at all what is wanted when truth is defined as the correspondence of an idea with something real. For it is absolutely essential that the reality be distinct from the idea. But then there can be no complete correspondence, no complete truth. So nothing at all would be true; for what is only half true is untrue." (1919: 18–19).

After rejecting the correspondence theory of truth Frege answers the question "What is a fact?" with "A fact is a thought that is true" (p. 21). For a fruitful discussion of these passages, see Hornsby (1996).

tion of reality and the way it connects to language can be provided if one posits only particulars (or even, it would seem, particulars and their attributes); facts are needed too. I'll come to Russell's argument in a moment. But first, what *are* facts, and how are they to be individuated on his account? The following statements give Russell's basic picture: (i) facts, "just as much as particular chairs and tables, are part of the real world" (ibid.); (ii) a fact is "the sort of thing expressed by a whole sentence, not by a single name . . . We express a fact, for example, when we say that a certain thing has a certain property, or that it has a certain relation to another thing" (pp. 182–3); (iii) facts are "complexes" of *objects* (particulars) and *properties* (universals); (iv) the (major) "constituents" of a true sentence correspond to the "components" of the fact to which the sentence corresponds; (v) facts are individuated by their components and the way they are related to one another.[2] The argument for facts goes more or less as follows. Consider sentence (1):

(1) Brutus knew Caesar.

Since it is true, (1) says something correct about the world. But this cannot be explained unless the world provides some *thing*, or some *things*, to which (1) corresponds. Does the world provide enough by way of containing (or at least having contained) Brutus and Caesar, objects to which the singular terms in (1) correspond? No. The following sentence is true and concerns the same two individuals:

(2) Brutus stabbed Caesar.

Requiring the world to provide *relations* corresponding to the transitive verbs in (1) and (2) seems to get us part of what is required. But if the world provides only objects and relations, what is it about the world that makes (2) true and (3) false?

(3) Caesar stabbed Brutus.

The three parts of (2) and (3) correspond to the same three parts of the world. We need a *fourth* part of the world, it seems, a complex

---

[2] Brandom (1994: 622) makes the ordinary language observation that it is customary to say that facts are *about* objects rather than that they contain or consist of them. He sees this as evidence for the Fregean view that facts are just thoughts (or claims) that are true. See also Hornsby (1996).

entity composed of Brutus, Caesar, and the relation expressed by "stabbed", a *structured* entity in which Brutus and Caesar stand in different relations to the relation expressed by the verb. And this fourth entity—call it a fact—is that part of the world to which the sentence as a whole corresponds.

Thus emerged a modern "correspondence" theory of truth: a sentence (or belief) is true just in case there is some *fact* to which it corresponds, where a fact is a non-linguistic entity in an objective external world.³ In recent years the sort of rationale Russell provided for facts has been converted into something forming the core of a linguistic and modal statement of the correspondence theory. Every true sentence, it is said, must have a *truth-maker*, something in the world that grounds or explains its truth, for there is no other way of making sense of the idea that the world must be a certain way in order for the sentence in question to be true. *T* is a truth-maker for sentence *S* if, and only if, it is necessary that if *T* exists then *S* is true. Objects and properties seem not to suffice as truth-makers. Brutus and Caesar and the relation expressed by "stabbed" do not make sentence (2) true—they could all exist without the sentence being true, just as they all exist without (3) being true. Enter facts: the fact that Brutus killed Caesar does the trick—or so it is claimed.

4.2 REPRESENTING RUSSELLIAN FACTS

Philosophical problems cannot be solved by inventing a notation; but sometimes the injection of a perspicuous notation can sharpen a discussion, help frame key points, or eradicate potential ambiguity. With a view to highlighting the fact that Russells facts have objects and properties as components, I want to borrow a notation for facts used by van Fraassen (1969).⁴ Take a true atomic sentence

---

³ I say 'modern' because as Olson (1987: 16) stresses, it is usual to view Aristotle and others as holding correspondence theories of truth without postulating facts. "The failure of correspondence theories of truth based on the notion of fact", says Davidson, "traces back to a common source: the desire to include in the entity to which a true sentence corresponds not only the objects the sentence is 'about' (another idea full of trouble) but also whatever it is the sentence says about them" (1984: 49). For discussion of Davidson's approach, see Ch. 2.

⁴ Van Fraassen aims to show that facts can provide a semantic explication of "tautological entailment" in the sense of Anderson and Belnap (1962). Nothing of

Fa ("*a* is *F*"); van Fraassen uses $\langle a, F \rangle$ for the complex *that-Fa*, and says that the fact

(4) $\{\langle a, F \rangle\}$

makes "*a* is *F*" true. $\{\langle a, F \rangle\}$ has as its components the property for which the predicate *F* stands and the object for which the term *a* stands.[5]

On a Russellian account, then, the (true) sentence (5) stands for the fact represented by (6):

(5) Caesar is mortal
(6) $\{\langle \text{CAESAR, MORTAL} \rangle\}$.

This fact has as its components (i) Caesar (the person himself, represented here by "CAESAR"), corresponding to "Caesar", the singular term occupying the subject position of (5), and (ii) the property of being mortal (given here by "MORTAL"), corresponding to the predicate expression "is mortal". (5) might be said to "depict" (6); and the structure of (6) might be said to "mirror" the structure of (5). (While essential to the philosophical projects that Russell set himself, the last feature is inessential to most of the points I shall be making.)

How might we represent (7)?

(7) Brutus stabbed Caesar.

Given the way Russell motivates facts, we want to indicate that

consequence turns on using van Fraassen's notation (or his sketch of "conjunctive" facts). I do not mean to be committing myself to any of van Fraassen's theses (or their denials), or even to a theory of facts at all. Similar quasi-set-theoretic notations are used by a number of philosophers to represent situations (e.g. Barwise and Perry 1983), states of affairs (e.g. Taylor 1976, 1985), events (e.g. Kim 1993), and propositions (e.g. Kaplan 1978, 1989a). There is nothing wrong with such notation per se, but it is a mistake to read too much philosophy into it.

[5] If we are Russellians, we can think of "$\{\langle a, F \rangle\}$" as a definite description of a fact—"the fact that *a* is *F*"—though not a name of that fact. Why does van Fraassen put braces around "$\langle a, F \rangle$"? Consider a true non-atomic sentence, such as the conjunction (*Fa* • *Gb*) or the disjunction (*Fa* ∨ *Gb*). Russell hoped to avoid postulating "conjunctive" or "disjunctive" facts (more generally, "molecular" facts) to which such sentences correspond. Nothing of vital importance to immediate concerns turns on any decision taken about such entities; but for thoroughness, continuity, and simplicity I propose to follow van Fraassen (and others who feel that fact-theorists will probably need molecular facts, if only in a weak sense) and say that $\{\langle a, F \rangle\}$ makes (*Fa* ∨ *Gb*) true, as does $\{\langle b, G \rangle\}$, and that the "conjunctive" fact $\{\langle a, F \rangle, \langle b, G \rangle\}$ makes (*Fa* • *Gb*) true.

Brutus and Caesar stand in different relationships to the relation expressed by "stabbed". As van Fraassen (1969) and Kaplan (1978) note, we can get what we want here if our notation is allowed to group items in a way that mirrors the grouping imposed on sentences by their syntactic structures. Assuming (8) adequately captures the principal syntactic divisions in (7), we can represent the fact that (7) stands for as (9), which mirrors the division between the subject noun phrase (NP) and the verb phrase (VP) in (7):

(8) [$_S$ [$_{NP}$ Brutus [$_{VP}$ stabbed [$_{NP}$ Caesar]]]]
(9) {⟨ BRUTUS ⟨CAESAR, STABBED⟩⟩}.

An important question that must be faced by any theory that purports to get at truth by way of facts concerns quantified sentences. To what facts do the following sentences correspond?

(10) Every human is mortal
(11) Some humans are mortal.

According to Russell, they correspond to *general* rather than *particular* facts. In order to sidestep questions that are not relevant to immediate concerns, we can adopt a neo-Russellian account of general facts rather than follow the details of Russell's own account. Again, in representing the fact we mirror the syntactic structure of the sentence that is meant to stand for it. Assuming (12) adequately captures the principal syntactic divisions in (10), we can represent the general fact to which (10) corresponds as (13), which mirrors the division between the subject noun phrase (NP) and the verb phrase (VP) in (10):

(12) [$_S$ [$_{NP}$ [every human] [$_{VP}$ is mortal]]]
(13) {⟨⟨EVERY, HUMAN⟩, MORTAL⟩}.

And we might think of this fact as having as its components (i) the logical complex composed of (*a*) the property of being human, and (*b*) the EVERY-relation (a relation that holds between pairs of properties ⟨P,Q⟩—here represented by "⟨⟨—, P⟩, Q⟩"—if and only if there is nothing that has P that does not also have Q), and (ii) the property of being mortal. (The fact corresponding to (10) differs from the one corresponding to (11) only in that its first component is a logical complex that has as a component not the EVERY-relation but the SOME-relation—a relation that holds between pairs of properties $\langle P, Q \rangle$ if and only if there is something that has P that also has Q.)

Of course, talk of properties and relations as components of facts will not be to everyones taste, especially when it is stressed that, on Russellian accounts, properties are not to be construed extensionally, i.e. co-extensional predicates need not stand for the same property.

4.3 THE THEORY OF DESCRIPTIONS

The idea that certain words are syncategorematic, defined in linguistic context rather than in isolation, is an old one, much favoured by those afflicted with ontological angst. Nominalistic strands of medieval philosophy exploited this idea; so did a later nominalist, Jeremy Bentham, who called it "definition by paraphrasis" and deployed it in connection with seemingly categorematic expressions that he felt referred to "fictions", among which he included qualities, relations, classes, and indeed all of the entities of mathematics. Bentham's strategy was to provide a systematic method for converting any sentence containing a dubious term X into a certain type of sentence that is X-free, thereby revealing X to be syncategorematic, despite grammatical appearances. And his point was to avoid embarrassing ontological commitments while still getting some basic grammatical work out of terms of dubious denotation.

These days the method of paraphrasis is commonly called the method of *contextual definition*, and it impinged upon recent philosophy largely through the work of Frege and then Russell, most famously through the latter's Theory of Descriptions. We are apt to take this for granted today, but occasionally someone like Quine reminds us of what has happened:

Contextual definition precipitated a revolution in semantics: less sudden perhaps than the Copernican revolution in astronomy, but like it in being a shift of center. The primary vehicle of meaning is seen no longer as the word, but as the sentence. Terms, like grammatical particles, mean by contributing to the meaning of the sentences that contain them. The heliocentrism propounded by Copernicus was not obvious and neither is this ... the meanings of words are abstractions from the truth conditions of sentences that contain them.

It was the recognition of this semantic primacy of sentences that gave us contextual definition, and vice versa. I attributed this to Bentham. Generations later we find Frege celebrating the primacy of sentences, and Russell giving contextual definition its fullest exploitation in technical logic. (1981: 69)

On Quine's account, ordinary singular terms—put variables aside for a moment—are ultimately redundant: any sentence containing an ordinary singular term can be replaced without loss—and in a manner suggested by Russell's Theory of Descriptions—by a sentence that is term-free. On such an account, ordinary singular terms, e.g. names, are no more than "frills" (1970: 25) or convenient "conventions of abbreviation" (1941a: 41); contextual definition is our "reward", as Quine sees it, "for recognising that the unit of communication is the sentence not the word" (1981: 75).

This is a rich idea and goes well beyond anything Frege or Russell envisaged. It has led some philosophers to ask whether Quine is trying to have his terms and eat them. For at the same time as he has championed the elimination of singular terms by paraphrasis, he has attempted to draw powerful philosophical conclusions from arguments involving the *substitution* of purportedly co-referential singular terms within the scope of purportedly non-truth-functional sentence connectives. In particular, he has presented a slingshot argument designed to show that any sentence connective satisfying minimal logical conditions must be truth-functional, an argument that appears to make crucial use of the idea that complex definite descriptions (or class abstracts) are singular terms. In order properly to evaluate this type of argument, it is necessary to examine in detail precisely what is involved in Russell's contextual definition of such expressions and a worry Gödel (1944) expresses about Russell's "elimination" of descriptions.

According to Russell, a true sentence of the form "the F is G" stands for a *general* fact because definite descriptions are quantificational expressions, not singular terms. In view of what is to come, and in order to forestall potential confusion, this point and its ramifications need to be spelled out.

From a syntactic perspective, the definite article "the" is a *determiner* on a par with "every", "some", "a", and "no", a device that combines with a nominal expression to form a noun phrase. Russell argued that "the" is also *semantically* like these determiners in so far as it introduces quantification. On his account, phrases of the form "the *F*" are not singular terms at all; they are quantificational noun phrases ("denoting phrases") like those of the forms "every *F*", "some *F*", "an *F*", and "no *F*". According to his Theory of Descriptions, (an utterance of) a sentence of the form "the *F* is *G*" is true if and only if the corresponding sentence of the form "every *F* is *G* and there is exactly one *F*" is true. So whereas the logical form of a sentence of the form "α is *G*" can be given by a formula of the form "*G*α", the logical form of a simple sentence of the form "the *F* is *G*" is given by a quantificational formula (14), which can be reduced to the logically equivalent formula (15):

(14) $\forall x(Fx \supset Gx) \bullet \exists x \forall y(Fy \equiv y{=}x)$
(15) $\exists x(\forall y(Fy \equiv y{=}x) \bullet Gx)$.

It is not uncommon to find philosophers appealing to Russell's Theory of Descriptions when attempting to shed light on the logical forms of certain statements, perhaps the premises or the conclusions of certain philosophical arguments. One philosopher might accuse another of committing a "substitution fallacy" by treating a particularly significant expression as a singular term when really it is a description; or one might accuse another of committing a "scope fallacy" involving the interpretation of a description with respect to, say, a modal, temporal, or causal operator.

Curiously, it is less common for such philosophers to construe Russell's theory as a component of a systematic semantics for natural language. Now I would have thought that it is only *because* the Theory of Descriptions can be construed as a component of a systematic semantical theory that philosophers are entitled to appeal to it in the ways they do. Consequently, I would maintain that there is an onus on anyone who wishes to appeal to the theory in explicating the logical forms of statements of English to be explicit about its place within a systematic semantics for English.

In *Descriptions* (1990) and in a paper published a few years later I attempted to articulate all of this in detail, to defend the truth-conditional correctness of the theory from the most pressing syntactic, semantic, and pragmatic objections, and to explain the philosophical significance of the theory in various semantic domains.[6] For the early purposes of this chapter, then, I propose to

[6] See Neale (1993*a*.

proceed on the assumption that Russell's theory is right.[7] And later in the book I will scrutinize the most promising competing theories, for it will become crucial, at various junctures, to specify the semantics of descriptions being assumed and to compare the net result should some plausible alternative theory be assumed in its stead.

In view of the use of formulae involving devices of description and abstraction in collapsing arguments of the sorts that will concern us in later chapters, we need to settle in advance a number of formal and philosophical issues about abbreviation, definition, elimination, and notation, issues about which there is still lingering confusion in the literature, some of it the result of misunderstandings of Russell's theory inherited from the work of Gödel (1944), Carnap (1947), Quine (1940, 1953c, 1961), and Russell (1905) himself. Surprisingly, even among those who, like Quine, profess allegiance to the truth-conditional deliverances of Russell's theory, there is sometimes resistance to (i) the idea that (14) comprises one way of revealing the *logical form* of "the F is G", (ii) the idea that descriptions may take various "scopes", and (iii) the idea that descriptions are "incomplete symbols". Such resistance seems to be based on either a failure to separate essential from inessential features of Russell's presentation of his theory, or else a failure to grasp the nature of the connection between logical form and semantics. Misunderstandings by detractors of Russell's theory tend to be based on the same failures, as we shall see.

4.4 ABBREVIATION

Consider a language L containing several one-place predicates, an unending supply of variables $x_1 \ldots x_n$, left and right parentheses as devices of punctuation, and the following logical vocabulary: $\forall, \vee, \sim, =$. Assume a rudimentary Tarskian truth-definition for L (where s ranges over infinite sequences of objects in the domain, k ranges over the natural numbers, s_k is the object in the kth position in s, and ϕ and ψ range over formulae of L):

---

[7] In an appendix, I deal with some alleged problems of implementation. In a new edition of *Descriptions*, I deal with some alleged counter-examples. See also my "This, That, and the Other" (forthcoming).

(i) $\forall s \forall k$ (with respect to s, the referent of $x_k = s_k$)

(ii) $\forall s \forall k \forall \phi (\forall x_k \phi$ is satisfied by s if and only if ϕ is satisfied by every sequence differing from s at most in the kth position)

(iii) $\forall s \forall \phi$ ($\sim\phi$ is satisfied by s if an only if ϕ is not satisfied by s)

(iv) $\forall s \forall \phi \forall \psi ((\phi \lor \psi)$ is satisfied by s iff ϕ is satisfied by s or ψ is satisfied by s).

(I avoid corner quotes. Where absolutely necessary—which is hardly ever—I use ordinary double quotes. Mostly I do not bother putting quotation marks around symbols as it is obvious I am talking *about* them rather than using them. No confusion should arise.) Now suppose we were to find ourselves using a great number of formulae involving negation and disjunction (because we wanted to express conjunction) and wanted to save ink. Within a broad range of options we can distinguish (i) introducing some metalinguistic shorthand and (ii) adding new symbols to L.

An attractive way of introducing metalinguistic shorthand would be to use "quasi-formulae" to represent genuine formulae of L. For example, we could use $(\phi \bullet \psi)$ as a convenient shorthand for $\sim(\sim\phi \lor \sim\psi)$ without actually adding $\bullet$ to L.

One way of adding to L itself would be to introduce a two-place connective $\bullet$ by way of an appropriate syntactical rule and a new semantical axiom involving the connectives $\lor$ and $\sim$:

(v) $\forall s \forall \phi \forall \psi ((\phi \bullet \psi)$ is satisfied by s if and only if $\sim(\sim\phi \lor \sim\psi)$ is satisfied by s).

Alternatively, we might prefer to add $\bullet$ to L more directly, i.e. by way of an appropriate syntactical rule and a new semantical axiom that does not involve any other expressions of L:

(vi) $\forall s \forall \phi \forall \psi ((\phi \bullet \psi)$ is satisfied by s if and only if ϕ is satisfied by s and ψ is satisfied by s).

Similarly, any of methods (i), (ii*a*) or (ii*b*) could be used in connection with other symbols we might consider, for example $\supset$, $\equiv$, $\neq$, and $\exists$.

Consider now a language L', just like L but containing the following logical vocabulary: $\forall, \exists, \sim, \bullet, \lor, \supset, \equiv, =, \neq$. There is nothing that can be said in L' that cannot be said in L; but there are many things that can be said with fewer symbols in L' and in ways that are more readily understandable.

Within a middle range there is a trade-off between economy of symbols and ease of interpretation. Economy of symbols is not the only criterion we invoke in designing formal languages with which we work. If we are doing the metatheory of first-order logic, we are naturally drawn to the economy afforded by a language with fewer symbols; when we come to *use* (rather than discuss) first-order logical formulae, we are naturally drawn to the economy of length and simplicity afforded by a language with a greater number of symbols. (Imagine how difficult it would be to train ourselves readily to understand sentences whose logical vocabulary contains just $\exists$, =, and | (Scheffer's two-place stroke, expressing incompatibility). Whitehead and Russell were sufficiently impressed by | to say, in the introduction to the second edition of *Principia*, that the whole work should be understood as rewritten with just that one sentence connective. (At the same time Russell was confident that negation is more primitive *psychologically* than stroke.)

Finally, consider a language L'', just like L' but containing three individual constants a, b, c understood as primitive singular terms (names if you like). Suppose we were to find ourselves wanting to talk about things in the domain not named a, b, or c, or about things satisfying certain descriptive conditions and not known by us to be named by a, b, or c. We could render the statement that the unique thing satisfying the predicate F also satisfies the predicate G (i.e. the statement that the F is G) as follows:[8]

(16) $\exists x(\forall y(Fy \equiv y=x) \bullet Gx)$.

(In place of x_1, x_2, etc., occasionally I will use x, y, etc.) Again, there are things we could do to save ink and present ourselves with more readily interpretable formulae. We could introduce some shorthand. In particular, we could follow Russell, who viewed (16) as rendering the logical form of an English sentence "the F is G". Adapting Peano's *iota*-notation, Russell represents a definite description "the F" by an expression of the form ιxFx, read as "the unique x such that Fx". The *iota*-operator *looks like* a variable-binding operator for creating a term $\iota x\phi$ from a formula ϕ. But there is an important feature of Russell's theory that makes this characterization a little misleading. True, a simple one-place predicate symbol G may be prefixed to a description $\iota x\phi$ to form some-

[8] See Russell (1905) and Whitehead and Russell (1925, *14).

thing of the form $G\iota x\phi$. But this is not a formula of Russell's formal language; it is a quasi-formula, an abbreviation, a piece of short-hand for a genuine formula of the form of (17) (where $\phi(y)$ is the result of replacing all free occurrences of x in ϕ by y):

(17) $\exists x(\forall y(\phi(y) \equiv y=x) \bullet Gx)$.

For Russell, a phrase of the form $\iota x\phi$ is *not* a genuine singular term; it is an *abbreviatory device* that permits (provably legitimate) short cuts in the course of proofs, and the use of quasi-formulae that are usually easier to grasp than the genuine formulae for which they go proxy. The important point for present concerns is that *the iota operator has not been added to L" itself*. A quasi-formula of the form $G\iota x\phi$ is just shorthand for a genuine formula of the form of (17).[9]

At this point, then, the following contextual definition of defi-nite descriptions might be considered, where $\Sigma(\iota x\phi)$ is a sentence containing $\iota x\phi$, $\Sigma(x)$ is the result of replacing an occurrence of $\iota x\phi$ in $\Sigma(\iota x\phi)$ by x, and $\phi(y)$ is the result of replacing free occurrences of x in ϕ by y:

(18) $\Sigma(\iota x\phi) =_{df} \exists x(\forall y(\phi(y) \equiv y=x) \bullet \Sigma(x))$.

But this will not suffice once more complex examples are examined. Whitehead and Russell bring this out with the quasi-formula (19):

(19) $G\iota x\phi \supset \psi$.

Depending upon how definition (18) is applied, (19) could be viewed as shorthand for either (20) or (21), which are not equiva-lent in respect of truth-conditions:

(20) $(\exists x(\forall y(\phi(y) \equiv y=x) \bullet Gx) \supset \psi)$
(21) $\exists x(\forall y(\phi(y) \equiv y=x) \bullet (Gx \supset \psi))$.

So unlike any genuine formula of $L"$ (or the language of *Principia*), a quasi-formula of the form of (19) is, at the moment, ambiguous. Consequently, some sort of modification of or supplement to the system of abbreviation is required if it is to be of service.

---

[9] Strictly speaking, even (17) is shorthand for Russell because $\bullet$, $\equiv$, and = are to be analysed away at some point for certain of Russell's purposes, perhaps using | if we are to take seriously comments in the introduction to the second edition of *Principia*. I have never seen (17) rendered in true primitive notation, i.e. in a format that makes use of just $\exists$ and |, and I have no desire to.

The point is worth stressing in connection with another sort of example that is of more immediate interest. Depending upon how (18) is applied, the quasi-formula ~$G\iota x\phi$ could be viewed as shorthand for either (22) or (23), which are not equivalent in respect of truth-conditions:

(22) ~$\exists x(\forall y(\phi(y) \equiv y{=}x) \bullet Gx)$
(23) $\exists x(\forall y(\phi(y) \equiv y{=}x) \bullet {\sim}Gx)$.

(The former, unlike the latter, can be true if nothing uniquely satisfies ϕ.) Whitehead and Russell adopt a rather cumbersome supplementation of their shorthand in order to eradicate ambiguity in their quasi-formulae: they place a copy of the description inside square brackets at the front of the formula that constitutes the scope of the relevant existential quantifier. Thus (22) and (23) are abbreviated as (22′) and (23′) respectively:

(22′) ~$[\iota x\phi]G\iota x\phi$
(23′) $[\iota x\phi]{\sim}G\iota x\phi$.

Since they are concerned mostly with formulae in which descriptions have minimal scope, Whitehead and Russell allow themselves to omit the square-bracketed copy of the description whenever the scope of the description is understood to be minimal. Thus (22′), but not (23′), can be simplified to ~$G\iota x\phi$, now understood as unambiguous—after all, this is just an abbreviatory notation that has no effect on the primitive language.

Using these scope conventions, the Theory of Descriptions can be summarized in two succinct propositions. The central proposition is the following contextual definition:

$^*14.01$ $[\iota x\phi]\Sigma(\iota x\phi) =_{df} \exists x(\forall y(\phi(y) \equiv y{=}x) \bullet \Sigma(x))$.[10]

The second proposition is relevant only to statements that seem to involve talk of existence. For Russell, a genuine singular term cannot fail to refer, so no predicate letter in the language of *Principia* stands for "exists". But a statement of the form "the *F* exists" is meaningful and Russell introduces an abbreviatory symbol E! that may be combined with a description $\iota x\phi$ to create a

---

[10] Throughout, I shall use $\iota x\phi$ where Russell uses $(\iota x)(\phi x)$. This policy will be applied in all contexts, even when I quote from *Principia*.

second type of quasi-formula E!ιxφ, which is also to be understood in terms of a contextual definition:

$$^*14.02 \quad E!ιxφ =_{df} \exists x \forall y (φ(y) \equiv y=x).$$

The Theory of Descriptions claims that any well-formed formula containing a definite description (regardless of the complexity of $\Sigma(ιxφ)$ in $^*14.01$) can be replaced by an equivalent formula that is description-free.[11] It is clear that using Russell's abbreviatory convention does not add to the expressive power of L''.

Once certain derived rules of inference have been proved for truth-functional contexts, most importantly,

$$^*14.15 \quad (ιxφ=α) \supset \{\Sigma(ιxφ) \equiv \Sigma(α)\}$$
$$^*14.16 \quad (ιxφ=ιxψ) \supset \{\Sigma(ιxφ) \equiv \Sigma(ιxψ)\},$$

it is useful for certain purposes of proof to be able to regard the definite descriptions $s(x)$, $\sqrt{x}$, $\log x$, $\sin x$, $x + y$, and so on *as if* they were singular terms.[12]

Another useful theorem for truth-functional contexts in *Principia Mathematica* is $^*14.18$:

---

[11] In unpublished work Saul Kripke has produced examples of what he calls "hydras" which cast doubt on the systematicity of unpacking using solely $^*14.01$ and $^*14.02$. That there might be interesting issues in this area is hinted by Mates (1973), who informs me that he became convinced by problem cases concocted by Tarski in seminars at Berkeley.

[12] The *iota*-notation is rarely used in *Principia* after ^{*14}, "being chiefly required to lead up to another notation" (Whitehead and Russell 1925: 67), namely the inverted comma *of*-notation: $R'z$ is used as shorthand for "the object that bears R to z" and is introduced by a further contextual definition:

(i) $R'z =_{df} ιxRxz$.

Russell calls both (i) and $^*14.01$ "contextual definitions", and he also says that $ιxφ$ and $R'z$ are both "defined in use". Notice that in $^*14.01$ we get whole formulae on both the right and left of $=_{df}$, whereas in (i) we do not. On Russell's account, then, technically it is not in the nature of a contextual definition that it involve whole formulae (Quine's shift from terms to sentences is not mandatory). Of course, (i) can easily be recast in terms of formulae—just attach a one-place predicate to either side—but this would buy Russell nothing. According to (i), (ii) is analysed as (iii), which, according to $^*14.01$, is, in turn, analysed as (iv):

(ii) $G(R'z)$
(iii) $G(ιxRxz)$
(iv) $\exists x(\forall y(Ryz \dots y=x) \bullet Gx)$.

$^*14.01$ differs from (i) in that it involves a *logical reparsing*. It is only in the context of a whole formula that the analysis of $ιxφ$ can be stated. Of course, *ultimately* this is true of $R'z$ too.

*14.18 $E! \iota x\phi \supset \{\forall x\Sigma(x) \supset \Sigma(\iota x\phi)\}$.

This says that if there exists exactly one thing satisfying ϕ, then that thing "has any property which belongs to everything" (Whitehead and Russell 1925: 174). The description $\iota x\phi$ "has (speaking formally) all the logical properties of symbols which directly represent objects ... the fact that it is an incomplete symbol becomes irrelevant to the truth-values of logical propositions in which it occurs" (p. 180).

The fact that Whitehead and Russell prove some interesting theorems about contextually defined definite descriptions occurring in truth-functional contexts should not obscure the quantificational character of the Theory of Descriptions, which comes through clearly not only in *14.01 and *14.02 themselves but also in Russell's talk of *general* propositions and *general* facts. By the time of *Principia*, having more or less given up on the notion of propositions as non-linguistic entities of theoretical utility, Russell takes a true sentence to stand for a fact. But in order to avoid unnecessary distractions that emerge in connection with false sentences, it will be convenient, for a moment, to go back a few years to when Russell was first presenting the Theory of Descriptions, to a period when he took propositions more seriously as non-linguistic entities.

For Russell, a singular term α may be combined with a one-place predicate phrase "$-$ is G" to express a proposition that simply could not be entertained or expressed if the entity referred to by α did not exist. Russell often puts this by saying that the referent of α is a *constituent* of such a proposition, a so-called *singular* proposition whose existence is contingent upon the existence of the referent of α.

A sentence of the form "the F is G" does *not* express a singular proposition; it expresses a *general* (or *quantificational*) proposition, a proposition that is not *about* a specific entity (described by "the F"), and whose existence is not contingent upon the existence of the entity which in fact satisfies the predicate F (if anything does).[13] If one does not see that on Russell's account "the F is G"

---

[13] For Russell, all of this is intimately tied up with his epistemology and psychology. Just as one can grasp the proposition expressed by an utterance of a sentence of the form "every F is G" or "no F is G" without knowing who or what satisfies the matrix Fx, indeed independently of whether or not anything does satisfy it, so

expresses a *general* proposition, that "the *F*" *never* refers, one simply does not understand the theory.

To say that the proposition expressed by a sentence *S* is singular is really just to say that the grammatical subject of *S* *stands for* an object and *contributes* that object to the proposition expressed by an utterance of *S* (or, if you prefer, contributes that object to the truth-conditions of an utterance of *S*). To say that a sentence *S* expresses a *general* proposition is just to say that the grammatical subject of *S* is not the sort of expression that stands for an object or contributes an object to the proposition expressed by (or the truth-conditions of) an utterance of *S*. This is the heart of Russell's position that English phrases of the form "the *F*", as well as those of the form "every *F*", "some *F*", and so on—i.e. all "denoting phrases"—are *incomplete* symbols: they are incomplete because they do not "stand for" or "directly represent" objects in the way proper names and predicates do.[14] Which is not to say, of course, that one could not construct theories according to which "the *F*", "every *F*", and so on stand for entities—higher-order functions, for example, as in numerous theories that use generalized quantifiers—theories which also deliver the same Russellian truth-conditions.

The literature on Russell's Theory of Descriptions contains various complaints about its formal properties, complaints that seem to do serious injustice to the theory and its place in a semantic theory for natural language. Some recurrent claims of this nature are the following. (i) If ϕ is a formula containing a singular term that refers to *A* and if ϕ itself is uniquely satisfied by *A*, then the definite description $\iota x \phi$ is not really Russellian: it is a singular term that refers to *A*. (ii) Russell's theory artificially deprives languages of definite descriptions. (iii) It gives rise to problems of scope. (iv)

one can perfectly well grasp the proposition expressed by an utterance of a sentence of the form "the *F* is *G*" without knowing who or what satisfies *Fx* and independently of whether or not anything does satisfy it. As it is sometimes put, one can perfectly well grasp the proposition expressed without knowing who or what is "denoted" by "the *F*", indeed independently of whether or not anything actually is "denoted" by it. To this extent, it makes no sense to say that the existence of the proposition depends upon the identity of the "denotation" of "the *F*"; so the proposition expressed is not singular.

[14] There is a tendency in some of the literature on Russell to construe the notion of an incomplete symbol as driven by largely notational considerations, and to see Russell's theory as requiring the use of a privileged formula in rendering the logical form of "the *F* is *G*". See e.g. Evans (1977, 1982) and esp. B. Linsky (1992*b*, forthcoming). For discussion, see the appendix.

Russell's notion of the scope of a description has no formal analogue in natural language; furthermore, any theory of logical form that contains the resources necessary to represent descriptions as taking various scopes will have an ad hoc character. (v) Russell's theory cannot constitute a serious contribution to the semantics of natural language because the logical forms it delivers bear so little relation to surface syntax or to what we know now about syntactical structure in the light of advances in theoretical linguistics. (vi) Attempts to provide theories that deliver improved logical forms conflict with Russell's theory, which uses a privileged sentence of a fixed primitive notation to capture the logical form of any particular sentence containing "the *F*". (vii) Attempts to render sentences containing descriptions in terms of formal sentences that make use of restricted quantifiers must involve fundamental departures from Russell's theory because descriptions have "no meaning in isolation", being "incomplete symbols" that "disappear on analysis". (viii) The existence of complex definite descriptions that contain as proper parts quantified noun phrases upon which subsequent ("donkey") pronouns are anaphoric—as in, for example, "the farmer who bought a donkey vaccinated it"—demonstrates conclusively that descriptions in natural language cannot be treated as logical or semantical units.

As we shall see, there is little substance in these charges, which seem to stem from misunderstandings of the inherently quantificational character of Russell's theory, the distinction between the theory itself and the notation used in its formal implementation, and the concepts of scope, incompleteness, analysis, contextual definition, and variable-binding.

4.5 SCOPE

A proper understanding of the concept of *scope* is vital for comprehending the rest of this book. In this section I want to talk about scope only in connection with definite descriptions. In Chapter 6 I shall set out a fully general account applicable to any expression whatsoever that occurs as part of another.

A truth-function, according to Whitehead and Russell, is "a function whose truth or falsehood depends only upon the truth or falsity of its arguments. This covers all the cases with which we are ever concerned" (1925: 184). The restriction of the theorems of *Principia Mathematica* to formulae containing descriptions in truth-functional contexts comes out clearly in *14.3 below, which is meant to state that when φ is uniquely satisfied, the scope of ιxφ does not matter to the truth-value of any truth-functional sentence in which it occurs:

*14.3 $\forall f\,[\{\forall p \forall q\,((p \equiv q) \supset f(p) \equiv f(q)) \bullet E!\iota x\phi)\}$
$\supset \{f([\iota x\phi]G\iota x\phi) \equiv [\iota x\phi]\,f(G\iota x\phi)\}]$.

The variable *f* is meant to range over functions of propositions (I have added the quantifier ∀*f*, which is not present in *Principia*, but retained the authors' desire to keep the theorem short by ignoring issues of use and mention that will not lead to confusion).[15] Whitehead and Russell conclude their discussion of this topic with the observation that "the proposition in which ιxφ has larger scope always implies the corresponding one in which it has the smaller scope, but the converse implication holds only if either (*a*) we have E!ιxφ or (*b*) the proposition in which ιxφ has the smaller scope implies E!ιxφ" (p. 186).

The restriction of scope permutation to truth-functional contexts expressed (or meant to be expressed) by *14.3 is something Quine (1953c, 1961) overlooked in his responses to Smullyan's (1948) postulation of truth-conditional ambiguity in sentences containing descriptions and modal operators. Mirroring Russell's postulation of an ambiguity of scope in sentences containing descriptions and psychological verbs—an ambiguity Russell milked to tackle puzzles about substitutivity—Smullyan sought to characterize in terms of scope what he saw as an example of the same type of ambiguity in modal contexts. Using *Px* for "*x* numbers the planets in our solar system", the surface sentences (24) and (25) can be given their respective (*a*) and (*b*) readings below:

---

[15] Whitehead and Russell do not appeal to *14.3 in subsequent proofs because of its use of propositions as values of variables, "an apparatus not required elsewhere" (p. 185). They proceed by individual cases, as they arise. Notice that *14.3 does not entail that the scope of a *relativized* description—i.e. a description containing a free variable such as ιxWxy (representing, say, "the woman sitting opposite him" as it occurs in "every man talked to the woman sitting opposite him")—is irrelevant in truth-functional contexts. In order for E!ιxφ to be true, ιxφ cannot contain a free variable.

(24) George wondered whether the number of planets in our
solar system > 7
   (a) George wondered whether $\exists x(\forall y(Py \equiv y{=}x) \bullet (x > 7))$
   (b) $\exists x(\forall y(Py \equiv y{=}x) \bullet$ George wondered whether $(x > 7))$
(25) necessarily the number of planets in our solar system > 7
   (a) necessarily $\exists x(\forall y(Py \equiv y{=}x) \bullet (x > 7))$
   (b) $\exists x(\forall y(Py \equiv y{=}x) \bullet$ necessarily $(x > 7))$.

Notoriously, Quine has expressed the view that the interpretations of (24b) and (25b) pose great philosophical difficulties. For
present purposes, it will suffice to make a minor point on behalf of
Smullyan (1947, 1948), who mistakenly thought he had defused
Quine's worries.[16] As Quine later recognized, he erred in *From a
Logical Point of View* in 1953 and again in a revised 1961 edition
when he accused Smullyan of "propounding, in modal contexts, an
alteration of Russell's familiar logic of descriptions" by "allow[ing]
difference of scope to affect truth value even in cases where the
description concerned succeeds in naming [*sic*]" (1961: 154). By the
time of the 1980 reprinting of the book the charge against Smullyan
on page 154 has been excised. In a new foreword Quine points out
that the page in question originally "contained mistaken criticisms of
Church and Smullyan" (p. vii).[17] The relevant part of the page now
reads as follows: "Then, taking a leaf from Russell [1905], he
[Smullyan] explains the failure of substitutivity [in modal contexts]
by differences in the structure of the contexts, in respect of what
Russell called the scopes of the descriptions. *Footnote*: Unless a
description fails to name [*sic*], its scope is indifferent to extensional
contexts. But it can still matter to intensional ones" (1980: 154).
   I mention this because it highlights a lingering misunderstanding in
discussions of Smullyan's position on the failure of substitutivity in
modal contexts: Smullyan does *not* claim that substitutivity is
restored by appealing to the scopes of descriptions; his position is

---

[16] This claim is defended by Neale (2000a) in the face of the (bad) arguments and
scholarship of Neale (1990) on this matter. A more thorough defence will appear in
Possibilities.
[17] While in residence at the Villa Serbelloni in Bellagio in 1975 Quine donated to
the library some of his books, including a copy of the 1961 edition of *From a
Logical Point of View*. In the margin of page 154, next to the footnote in which he
chastises Smullyan, Quine inscribed "Kripke has convinced me that Russell shared
Smullyan's position. See *Principia* pp. 184f. esp. *14.3: the explicit condition of
extensionality".

that, on Russell's account, (i) descriptions are not singular terms and so do not appear in primitive notation, and (ii) the false reading of (25), namely (25*b*), cannot be derived from "necessarily 9 > 7" and "9 = the number of planets". The putative existence and truth (cf. Smullyan) or unintelligibility (cf. Quine) of (25*a*) is irrelevant to *this* point—which is *not* to say that Smullyan's observation defuses Quine's objections to quantified modal logic (it does not).[18]

Quine's initial interpretative error about applications of Russell's Theory of Descriptions in modal contexts has been repeated by others, and in some cases this has led to further error.[19] The fact that the error is so widespread naturally leads one to speculate why, especially as Russell is explicit as early as 1905 in "On Denoting", that altering the scope of a description—even one whose matrix is uniquely satisfied—*can* alter truth-value in non-extensional constructions: that is how he deals with the puzzle involving "George IV wondered whether Scott was the author of *Waverley*". (The point is made again in *Principia*.) I suspect the answer lies in the contrast between, on the one hand, the discussion of descriptions in the introduction to *Principia* and in the informal remarks at the end of *14 and, on the other, the formal presentation of the theory and the relevant theorems. For example, in the introduction, Whitehead and Russell say that "when E!$\iota x\phi$, we may enlarge or diminish the scope of $\iota x\phi$ as much as we please without

---

[18] The situation with respect to propositional attitudes and logical modality appears to be mirrored elsewhere, as noted by Chisholm (1965), Føllesdal (1965), Sharvy (1969), Kaplan (1986), and others. If, as a result of some astronomical cataclysm, Mercury gets sucked into the sun in the year 3001, the number of planets will be reduced from 9 to 8—assuming no consequences for the other planets—but 9 would not be so reduced. And if "in 3001" functions semantically as some sort of one-place connective—there may be better treatments of course—and if (i*a*) and (i*b*) are intelligible, then in the year 3002 an utterance of (i) will be true when read as (i*a*), false when read as (i*b*), where > is shorthand for "exceeded":

(i) In 3001 the number of planets in our solar system > 8
   (*a*) In 3001 $\exists x(\forall y(Py \equiv y=x) \cdot (x > 8))$
   (*b*) $\exists x(\forall y(Py \equiv y=x) \cdot$ in 3001 $(x > 8))$.

Difficult questions about $\exists$ and tense need to be answered before this sort of observation can be developed properly.

[19] See e.g. Carnap (1947), Føllesdal (1966), Hintikka (1968), Hintikka and Kulas (1985), Hintikka and Sandu (1991), Kalish *et al* (1980), Lambert (1991), B. Linsky (1992*b*, forthcoming), L. Linsky (1966), Scott (1967), Thomason (1969), Wallace (1969), Wedberg (1984), and Wilson (1959*b*).

altering the truth-value of any proposition in which it occurs" (1925: 70); and at the end of *14 they say, "when E!ιxφ, the scope of ιxφ does not matter to the truth-value of any proposition in which ιxφ occurs. This proposition cannot be proved generally, but it can be proved in each particular case" (p. 184). But then they go on to add that "The proposition can be proved generally when ιxφ occurs in the form χιxφ and χιxφ occurs in what we may call a 'truth function', i.e. a function whose truth or falsehood depends only upon the truth or falsehood of its argument or arguments" (p. 184). This, of course, is what theorem *14.3 says.

In this terrain, errors readily compound. Consider what Hintikka (1968) has to say:

> when the Russellian theory [of descriptions] is put to work in modal and other complicated contexts, much of its success depends on a clever choice of scope conventions and on similar adjustments. With a clever choice of these, a suitable modification of the theory gives us a certain amount of mileage (cf. e.g. Smullyan [1948], Montague and Kalish [1959], Linsky [1966]), but the deeper reasons for the choice remain unaccounted for, and cry out for further analysis. (p. 5)

Thus far, Hintikka is amplifying Quine's original error. But from here he goes straight on to say,

> Donnellan [1966*a*, *b*] has even argued that definite descriptions are used in two essentially different ways in ordinary language. No matter whether these can be caught by juggling the scope conventions, the reasons for doing so will remain in the dark. . . . Thus it also seems to me that the theoretical significance (or lack thereof) of the ingenious use of the theory of descriptions to simplify one's "canonical notation" by Quine [1960, ch. 5] and others is too incompletely understood to be evaluated here. (p. 5)

This passage betrays confusion. It has seemed attractive to some philosophers to explicate the *de re* readings of sentences containing descriptions and non-extensional devices in terms of something like Donnellan's (1966*a*) "referential" (rather than "attributive" ≅ Russellian) interpretation of the relevant description. For example, Rundle (1965) makes this suggestion for descriptions in modal contexts; and Hintikka (1968), Stalnaker (1972), and others suggest that a referential interpretation can be used in characterizing the *de re* readings of descriptions in non-extensional contexts more generally. But this is will not do. Cartwright (1968) and Kripke (1971, 1977) have pointed out that attempts to provide accounts of either the large scope–small scope distinction or the *de re–de dicto* distinction in terms of a referential–attributive distinction are misguided. A speaker may make a *de re* use of (25), or the variant (26), without using the definite description "the number of planets" referentially:

(26) The number of planets, whatever it is, is necessarily odd.

The following passage from Kripke makes the point very clearly:

Suppose I have no idea how many planets there are, but (for some reason) astronomical theory dictates that that number must be odd. If I say, "The number of planets (whatever it may be) is odd," my description is used attributively. If I am an essentialist, I will also say, "The number of planets (whatever it may be) is necessarily odd," on the grounds that all odd numbers are necessarily odd; and my use is just as attributive as the first case. (1977: 9)[20]

The point, quite simply, is that the proposition expressed by an utterance of (26) is not singular, even if the description is understood *de re*. The Russellian account is quite consistent with this fact. The proposition expressed is general; the *de re* reading is obtained by giving the description large scope over the modal operator as in (25*b*) above. (The *de dicto–de re* distinction cannot, however, replace Russell's notion of scope. A description may be assigned a scope intermediate to the scopes of two operators in a sentence and the reading of the sentence will not be *de re* nor will it be fully *de dicto*. Thus Russell's notion of scope may be used to capture so-called *de dicto–de re* ambiguities, but the *de dicto–de re* distinction cannot always be used to capture ambiguities of scope.) As Kripke goes on to point out, we find exactly the same situation with definite descriptions in attitude contexts. Suppose Smith has a singular wonder concerning the man who lives upstairs: he wonders whether the man is Greek. I may correctly report this state of affairs by saying

(27) Smith wonders whether the man who lives upstairs is Greek

with the definite description "the man who lives upstairs" understood *de re*. But this does not mean that I have used the description referentially. I may have no relevant object-dependent thought about the man who lives upstairs and no intention of communicating such a thought. Russell captures this *de re* reading by giving the definite description maximal scope:

(27′) $\exists x(\forall y(My \equiv y=x)$ • Smith wonders whether x is Greek).

It is also stressed by Kripke that no binary semantical distinction can *replace* Russell's notion of scope. A sentence like (28) is *three* ways ambiguous according as the description is given maximal, intermediate, or minimal scope:

    (28) Smith hopes that Jones believes that the man upstairs is Greek
        (*a*) $\exists x(\forall y(My \equiv y=x)$ • (Smith hopes that (Jones believes that x is Greek)))
        (*b*) Smith hopes that $\exists x(\forall y(My \equiv y=x)$ • (Jones believes that x is Greek))
        (c) Smith hopes that (Jones believes that $\exists x(\forall y(My \equiv y=x)$ • x is Greek)).

The reading given by (28*b*) is neither *de re* nor fully *de dicto*.[21]

These facts demonstrate quite conclusively that descriptions understood *de re* cannot, in general, be identified with descriptions understood referentially, and that a semantical ambiguity between Russellian and referential interpretations of descriptions cannot *replace* either the *de re–de dicto* distinction or the large scope–small scope distinction as it shows up in non-extensional contexts. So even if one could provide good arguments for the existence of referential interpretations of the definite and indefinite descriptions in some of the examples we have been considering, *the large-scope readings would still be needed*.[22]

---

[21] Again, the situation is mirrored with indefinite descriptions. As Kripke (1977) observes, the following example is three ways ambiguous according as "a high American official" is given large, intermediate, or small scope:

    (i) Hoover charged that the Berrigans plotted to kidnap a high American official.

Similar examples can be constructed using iterated modalities.

[22] With the publication of Kripke's (1977) therapeutic remarks on scope, the tendency to confuse referential and large scope readings has largely faded. Hornstein (1984) proposes accounts of both definite and indefinite descriptions that are undermined by the behaviour of such expressions in non-extensional contexts. Hornstein's theory predicts (falsely) that only *large* scope readings are available for the definite descriptions in sentences such as the following:

If it were not for the particular aims of *Principia*, Whitehead and Russell could have pushed their abbreviatory conventions to their logical resting place. The square-bracketed occurrence of a description that is used to indicate scope is effectively marking the scope of an existential quantifier, and to that extent it is actually functioning rather like a quantifier itself. So why not replace the *original occurrence* of the description in the formula to which the square-bracketed occurrence is attached by a *variable* bound by the square-bracketed occurrence? After all, this is just an abbreviatory notation. On this simplification, (29) reduces to (29'), and (30) reduces to (30'), effectively yielding the notation of restricted quantification (see below):

(29) $\sim[\iota x\phi]G\iota x\phi$
(29') $\sim[\iota x\phi]Gx$
(30) $[\iota x\phi]\sim G\iota x\phi$
(30') $[\iota x\phi]\sim Gx.$

If this notational suggestion had been adopted, *14.01 and *14.02 would have looked like this:

*14.01′ $[\iota x\phi]Gx =_{df} \exists x(\forall y(\phi(y) \equiv y{=}x) \bullet Gx)$
*14.02′ $[\iota x\phi]E!x =_{df} \exists x\forall y(\phi(y) \equiv y{=}x).$

This would be real progress, but it is not what Whitehead and Russell do, for reasons to which I have already alluded.

If we were so disposed, we could add the *iota*-operator directly to L'' by way of other symbols of L''. There would be some work involved if *iota*-compounds were to continue to occupy singular term positions yet not be subject to reference axioms.[23] It would be much easier to use the more transparently quantificational notation

(i)   Ralph believes that the man who lives upstairs is a spy
(ii) John claims to have proved that the largest prime number lies somewhere between 10^{27} and 10^{31}
(iii) The first man in space might have been American
(iv) The number of planets is necessarily odd.

[23] In fact, there is even work to be done if *iota*-compounds are to occupy singular term positions and be subject to reference axioms, as in those non-Russellian theories that treat descriptions as singular terms. The work is caused by the fact that descriptions contain formulae (sometimes quantified formulae) but at the same time occupy term positions in formulae; this makes it impossible to define first the class of terms, and then the class of formulae, as one does standardly; the classes must be defined together. This fact is often overlooked by those proposing referential theories of descriptions (or of class and functional abstracts for that matter).

above according to which expressions of the form $\iota x\phi$ are one-place variable-binding operators:

(vii) $\forall s \forall k \forall j \forall \phi \forall \psi$ $\{[\iota x_k \phi]\psi$ is satisfied by s if and only if $\exists x_k(\forall x_j\, (\phi(y) \equiv x_j = x_k) \bullet \psi)$ is satisfied by $s\}$.

Alternatively, we could add the *iota*-operator to L'' by way of the same syntactic rule and a semantic axiom that does not involve any other primitive symbols of L'':

(viii) $\forall s \forall k \forall \phi \forall \psi$ $\{[\iota x_k \phi]\psi$ is satisfied by s if and only if ϕ is satisfied by exactly one sequence differing from s at most in the kth position and ψ is satisfied by every such sequence$\}$.

The right-hand side of (viii) simply encodes Russell's truth-conditions. It is a very short step from here to understanding how the Theory of Descriptions fits into a systematic account of quantification in natural language, quantified noun phrases analysable in terms of restricted quantifiers.

4.6 QUANTIFICATION AND NOTATION

For most of the philosophical and formal tasks of the present work, Whitehead and Russell's *iota*-notation is perfectly adequate; and for some of these tasks it is actually much better than the notation of restricted quantification I used in *Descriptions* because it can be used in ways that permit one to be agnostic, in certain settings, on the matter of whether descriptions might be treated as singular terms rather than as quantificational noun phrases. However, I want to say a few things about restricted quantifiers here in order to deal with a worry Gödel had about Russell's Theory of Descriptions and several more recent worries that have bubbled away in corners of the philosophical literature.

Russell's own formal implementation of the Theory of Descriptions suggests a significant gap between surface syntax and logical form. But upon reflection it is clear the gap has little to do with descriptions per se. In order to characterize the logical forms of quantified sentences "every *F* is *G*" or "some *F* is *G*" in standard first-order logic we have to use formulae containing sentence connectives, no counterparts of which occur in the surface forms of the sentences. And when we turn to a sentence like "just two *F*s are

G", we have to use many more expressions that do not have counterparts in surface syntax, as well as repetitions of a number that
do:

(31) $\exists x \exists y((x{\neq}y \bullet Fx \bullet Fy \bullet Gx \bullet Gy) \bullet \forall z((Fz \bullet Gz)$
$\supset (z{=}x \lor z{=}y)))$.

The case involving descriptions is a symptom of—and also helps us
to see the severity of—a larger problem involving the use of standard first-order notation to characterize the logical forms of
sentences of natural language. Similarly, if Russell's theory predicts
that ambiguities of scope arise where there actually *is* ambiguity in
natural language, this is a virtue rather than a vice; and if there is
any "problem", it concerns only the fact that the use of Russell's
abbreviatory conventions may, on occasion, require the insertion of
scope indicators in order to make it clear which of two (or more)
unambiguous formulae in primitive notation is being abbreviated
by a particular pseudo-formula. It is nonsense to claim that
Russell's Theory of Descriptions suffers from complications
concerning scope.

For the purposes of providing a systematic semantics for natural
language we can capture Russell's insights about the logic and
semantics of descriptions—that descriptions are not singular terms,
that sentences containing definite descriptions have quantificational truth-conditions—without using his notation (or even the
notation of standard first-order logic). Indeed, a more perspicuous
notation is not hard to construct and is already widely used.
Suppose we were to modify our simple quantificational language
L'' by throwing out the two unrestricted quantifiers $\forall$ and $\exists$ (and
associated rules of syntax and semantics) and bringing in two
quantificational determiners *every* and *some*, devices which are
used to create *restricted* quantifiers. A determiner Δ_k combines
with a formula ϕ to form a restricted quantifier of the form (32),
exemplified by (33) and (34):

(32) $[\Delta_k: \phi]$
(33) $[every_1: man\ x_1]$
(34) $[some_1: man\ x_1]$.

And a restricted quantifier of this form combines with a formula ψ
to form a formula of the form of (35), exemplified by (36) and (37):

(35) $[\Delta_k: \phi]\psi$
(36) $[every_1: man\ x_1]$ *snores* x_1
(37) $[some_1: man\ x_1]$ *snores* x_1.

Adding axioms such as the following will suffice for defining truth:

(i) $\forall s \forall k \forall \phi \forall \psi ([every_k: \phi]\psi$ is satisfied by s if and only if ψ is satisfied by every sequence satisfying ϕ and differing from s at most in the kth position)

(ii) $\forall s \forall k \forall \phi \forall \psi ([some_k: \phi]\psi$ is satisfied by s if and only if ψ is satisfied by some sequence satisfying ϕ and differing from s at most in the kth position).

In this system we could represent *no man snores* as (38) or (39) (henceforth I shall often, but not always, make use of the convention I adopted in earlier work (1993*b*) of dropping the obvious variable inside the quantifier and attaching its subscript directly to the predicate[24]):

(38) $\sim[some_1: man_1]$ *snores* x_1
(39) $[every_1: man_1]\sim$*snores* x_1.

But of course we could make for a more direct mapping between sentences of English and our new formalism by adding to the latter a new quantificational determiner *no* and an appropriate axiom. Sentence (40) would be subject to the axiom iii:

(40) $[no_1: man_1]$ *snores* x_1
(iii) $\forall s \forall k \forall \phi \forall \psi ([no_k: \phi]\psi$ is satisfied by s if and only if ψ is satisfied by no sequence satisfying ϕ and differing from s at most in the kth position).

This might be particularly useful if we are interested in constructing a systematic semantic theory for English that respects facts about syntactic structure uncovered by theoretical linguistics.

Now what about definite descriptions? The particular formalism and notation of *Principia* are not essential to the Theory of Descriptions itself, except in so far as one has orthogonal philo-

---

[24] As Graff (2001) notes, getting rid of the clutter (and this is all it is) allows us to get a little closer to English not just in a superficial sense but ultimately in allowing us to see determiners as attaching to predicates in a logical sense. Of course, this presupposes tailoring axioms of satisfaction for predicates accordingly. We could also drop the colon without harm.

sophical aims, as Russell did. Indeed, the theory was presented in
"On Denoting" without this particular formalism and notation;
but in *Principia* the theory was presented much more clearly *with*
it. It would be a mistake to equate the theory with that particular
formal implementation itself, despite the fact that the consequences
of the theory, in that notation, are exhausted by the consequences
of *14.01 and *14.02. If we want, we can use the formal language
containing restricted quantifiers, i.e. we can use (41) to represent
"the king snores":

(41) [*some*$_1$: *king*$_1$] [*every*$_2$: *king*$_2$] (x_1=x_2 • x_1 *snores*).

To do this would *not* be to present a serious *alternative* to the
Theory of Descriptions; it would be to choose a language other
than that of *Principia* in which to state it.

In fact there is no need for anything as indirect as (41). In
English, the word "the" is a one-place determiner along with
"every", "some", "no", and so on; so we could add to our new
formalism yet another quantificational determiner *the* and an
appropriate axiom. Sentence (42) would be subject to the axiom
(iv), which captures Russells insights perfectly:

(42) [*the*$_1$: *king*$_1$] snores x_1

(iv) $\forall s \forall k \forall \phi \forall \psi$([*the*$_k$: ϕ]ψ is satisfied by s if and only if ψ is
satisfied by the sequence satisfying ϕ and differing from s at
most in the kth position).

I have used the English determiner "the" in the metalanguage so as
to make (iv) congruent with the axioms for the other determiners,
(i)–(iii) above. The right-hand side of (iv) is to be understood as
equivalent to "ϕ is satisfied by exactly one sequence differing from
s at most in the kth position and ψ is satisfied by every such
sequence".[25] The viability of a formal language containing

[25] For discussion, see Neale (1993*a*). The axiom can be simplified; however, questions about the syntax, semantics, and systematicity of the axioms (and the metalanguage in which they are stated), as well as questions about the distinction
between semantics and analysis, have a considerable bearing on the proper form of
any truth-definition that is to play a serious role in a semantical theory for natural
language and on the characterization of that role itself.
Variants of axiom (iv) are readily produced for plural and dual descriptions,
which are first-order-definable just like singular descriptions. "The *F*s are *G*" is true
if and only there are at least two *F*s and every *F* is *G*. "Both *F*s are *G*" is true if and
only if there are exactly two *F*s and every *F* is *G*. To produce the variant for "the"

restricted quantifiers shows that the language of *Principia* is not an essential ingredient of a theory of quantification and logical form; in particular, it is not an essential ingredient of the Theory of Descriptions construed as a component of a systematic semantics for natural language.

The restricted quantifier implementation of the theory I have outlined has much to commend it. For one thing, it draws out the syntactical and semantical similarities between "every", "some", "a", "the", and so on; for another, it makes the scope of a description utterly transparent in the formal notation. For example, Russell's (43) and (44) will be rendered as (43') and (44') respectively:

(43) $\sim[\iota x_1 F x_1] G \iota x_1 F x_1$
(44) $[\iota x_1 F x_1] \sim G \iota x_1 F x_1$
(43') $\sim[the_1: F x_1] G x_1$
(44') $[the_1: F x_1] \sim G x_1.$

To use a restricted quantifier notation in connection with descriptions is to make a move that Russell failed to make when he did not simplify his abbreviatory notation in the way I mentioned earlier, according to which (43) reduces to (43'') and (44) to (44''):

(43'') $\sim[\iota x_1 F x_1] G x_1$
(44'') $[\iota x_1 F x_1] \sim G x_1.$

Russell's failure to make this elementary simplification has already been explained.

Many English sentences containing two or more quantified noun phrases admit of distinct readings, i.e. readings with distinct truth-conditions; and in many cases the readings can be captured in terms of relative scope; thus "every man likes some woman" can be read as either (45') or (45''):

(45') $[every_1: man_1][some_2: woman_2] \, x_1 \text{ likes } x_2$
(45'') $[some_2: woman_2][every_1: man_1] \, x_1 \text{ likes } x_2.$

Permuting quantifiers does not always result in a difference in truth-conditions. For example, the truth-conditions of "every man

as it combines with a plural noun complex replace "the sequence" by "the sequences"; to produce one for "both" replace $[the_k: \phi]$ by $[both_k: \phi]$ and replace "the sequence" by "both sequences".

likes every woman" are unaffected by relative scope (reflecting the
fact that $\forall x_1 \forall x_2 R x_1 x_2$ and $\forall x_2 \forall x_1 R x_1 x_2$ are equivalent):

(46') [$every_1$: man_1][$every_2$: $woman_2$] x_1 likes x_2
(46") [$every_2$: $woman_2$][$every_1$: man_1] x_1 likes x_2.

Nonetheless, (46') and (46") are distinct formulae (just as
$\forall x_1 \forall x_2 R x_1 x_2$ and $\forall x_2 \forall x_1 R x_1 x_2$ are), and to the extent that quantifiers in natural language need to be assigned scope for interpreta-
tion, we can say that "every man likes every woman" is structurally
ambiguous without being truth-conditionally ambiguous.
Sameness of quantificational determiner is neither necessary nor
sufficient for a scope ambiguity to engender a truth-conditional
ambiguity. "Most men like most women" is truth-conditionally
ambiguous; "every man likes the queen" is not (as noted by
Whitehead and Russell). Although the original motivation in logic
for positing ambiguities of scope involved ambiguity of truth-
conditions, clearly the right strategy for thinking about these
matters *now* within the context of a general theory of quantifier
scope is to treat structural ambiguity seriously whether or not it is
of truth-conditional import.

Analogues of (43') and (44')—for purely local convenience I
have reinserted variables in the matrices—can be used to represent
the notorious ambiguities that arise in natural language when non-
extensional connectives and verbs of propositional attitude occur
with definite descriptions.

(43') ~[the_1: Fx_1]Gx_1
(44') [the_1: Fx_1]~Gx_1.

For example, it should be possible to characterize the so-called *de
dicto* and *de re* readings of (47) and (48) posited by Russell (1905)
and Smullyan (1948) using the respective (a) and (b) sentences
below: [26]

(47) George wonders whether Scott is the author of *Waverley*
  (a) George wonders whether [the_1: x_1 authored *Waverley*]
  Scott = x_1

---

[26] Adding an appropriate axiom even for □ is not straightforward; difficult
choices have to be made which have repercussions for the rest of the axiomatization
and the philosophical status of the axioms themselves. For discussion, see Davies
(1981).

(b) [the_1: x_1 authored *Waverley*] George wonders whether Scott = x_1

(48) necessarily, nine is the number of planets
(a) □ [the_1: x_1 numbers the planets] 9 = x_1
(b) [the_1: x_1 numbers the planets] □ 9 = x_1.

The claim that (47) and (48) are ambiguous in this way has gained the status of something of an orthodoxy and has gone largely unchallenged for decades, as has the claim that the ambiguities multiply in the obvious way when (47) and (48) are further embedded, as in, say "Mary doubts that George wonders whether Scott is the author of *Waverley*".[27] In interesting recent work, Delia Graff (2001) has challenged the orthodoxy, claiming that a sentence in which a description combines with the copula to form a verb phrase is *always* equivalent to the reading the Russellian obtains by giving the description small scope. Among other things, this entails the rejection of both (47b) and (48b) as genuine readings of (47) and (48), which might strike some as a disastrous result.

Graff's proposal appears to have been designed, at least in part, with the aim of treating instances of the negated form "*a* is not the *F*" as unambiguous, the description always understood as taking small scope.[28] The issues here are not always in the sharpest of relief, but ultimately they do not seem to support this stringent proposal. Consider the following:

(49) Cicero is Tully
(50) Cicero is the winner
(51) The winner is Cicero.

It is commonly—but not universally—held that the copula in (49) expresses identity, the whole sentence understood as the relational

---

[27] I say largely because Quine (1947, 1953e, 1961, 1980) has attempted to show that (48b) is unintelligible, at least when □ is read as expressing logical or analytic necessity.

[28] It is often said that the indefinite counterpart, "*a* is not an *F*", is unambiguous, that if "an *F*" is a quantified noun phrase then it is one that insists on small scope when it combines with the copula in this way. One way of accounting for this would be to take the seemingly unreflective practice in logic and philosophy of treating indefinite descriptions in this position as ordinary predicates as basically correct. Graff's article is (roughly) an attempt to extend such a predicational analysis of indefinites to definites.

(49′) Cicero = Tully.[29]

This raises a question as to its syntax. (49′) is usually assumed to have a symmetrical structure; but linguistic theory is more likely to favour an asymmetric structure in which "is Tully" is a constituent verb phrase:

(49″) $[_S [_{NP}$ Cicero] $[_{VP}$ is $[_{NP}$ Tully]]].

There is nothing in this structure, of course, that prohibits its being *interpreted* as true if and only if (49′) is true.

It has been common practice for some time to see the copula as behaving in the same way in (50) and (51), to see these sentences as differing from (49) only in the presence of quantification induced by the descriptions.[30] On such an account, (50) and (51) will be read as (50′) and (51′) respectively:

(50′) $[the_I: winner \, x_I]$ Cicero $= x_I$
(51′) $[the_I: winner \, x_I] \, x_I =$ Cicero.

If one were to give up the idea that the copula expresses identity in (50) and (51), certainly one would be strongly inclined to give it up for (49) too, and vice versa. Graff provides an interesting argument for giving it up in (50) based on an alleged asymmetry between (52) and (53) (the negation of (50)), which, on a rote Russellian account, should be ambiguous according as the description or the negation takes larger scope:

(52) Cicero did not meet the winner
    (a) $\sim[the_I: winner \, x_I]$ Cicero met x_I
    (b) $[the_I: winner \, x_I] \sim$Cicero met x_I
(53) Cicero is not the winner
    (a) $\sim[the_I: winner \, x_I]$ Cicero $= x_I$
    (b) $[the_I: winner \, x_I] \sim$Cicero $= x_I$.

---

[29] See e.g. Russell (1905), Smullyan (1947, 1948), and especially Kripke's (1971) discussions of (49), "Saul Kripke is Saul Kripke", "Hesperus is Phosphorus", and other examples.
[30] Again, see Russell (1905), Smullyan (1948), and Kripke (1971). I followed suit in *Descriptions* (1990). In particular, I treated sentences of the forms "*a* is the *F*" and "the *F* is *a*" occurring in psychological and modal statements such as (47) and (48) in this traditional way. Given my long—and glaringly misguided—discussion of (48) and similar modal sentences, it is odd that Graff claims I do not discuss descriptions combining with the copula.

Graff feels that although (52) is ambiguous in this way, (53) has to be read as (53*a*); the feeling that (53*b*) is a genuine reading is the product of illusion, she suggests, and should be explained in terms of conversational implicature.[31] Graff proposes to obtain what she regards as the right result by treating "is the *F*", as it occurs in structures like (50) and (53) as a complex predicate (*Yx: Fx*) contextually defined as follows:

(54) $\Sigma[(Yx: Fx)\alpha] =_{df} \Sigma[F\alpha \bullet \forall x(Fx \supset x = \alpha)]$.

Assuming existential generalization, obviously Graff's analysis of (50) is equivalent to the Russellian (50′) for it says that Cicero wins (Cicero is a winner) and every winner is Cicero. It is in connection with (53) that the analyses diverge, the Russellian analysis serving up (53*a*) and (53*b*) to Graff's solitary reading, equivalent to (53*a*).

Similarly, where the Russellian quantificational analysis delivers (47*a*) and (47*b*) as readings of (47), and (48*a*) and (48*b*) as readings of (48), Graff's delivers only (readings equivalent to) the (*a*) readings. There is a hefty tradition in modal logic of taking both (*a*) and (*b*) readings seriously; but perhaps the tradition is wrong. If Graff's Gricean explanation of the "illusion" of (53*b*) could be transposed to explain the "illusions" of (47*b*) and (48*b*), then her position might look more attractive.

But there is also the matter of (49) and (51). Graff's analysis of sentences containing "the *F*" after the copula is not meant to be ad hoc; it is meant to flow directly from a comprehensive account of "the *F*". To this extent, it should declare (50) and (51) equivalent, but it should declare (55) and (56), in which the descriptions occur in subject position, ambiguous (unless some sort of implicature defence is to be mounted again):

(55) The winner is not Cicero
(56) Necessarily, the number of planets is nine.

In the absence of strong evidence to the contrary, I shall continue with the traditional policy of seeing the descriptions as capable of taking large scope in the examples just examined.[32] I should stress,

---

[31] See Grice (1989), who has a variety of interesting things to say about implicatures involving negation and descriptions in the chapter "Presupposition and Conversational Implicature".

[32] A final point about Graff's proposal. If "is" is to be treated identically in (49)–(51) and (53), (55), and (56)—one of the advantages the proposal is meant to

however, that nothing of consequence for the main argument of the book will turn on this assumption, as I shall never need to appeal to the existence of the large-scope readings Graff disputes. As far as I can ascertain, the purported non-existence of those readings touches on the issues I am addressing only tangentially in Chapter 11, where the existence of the large-scope readings is mentioned as something friends of facts and causal logics might wish to explore in order to avoid certain difficulties.

have over a straightforward Russellian proposal is avoiding the multiplication of meanings of the copula in verb phrases—the semantics of, say, "is Cicero" ought to be deducible by the theorist from the semantics of "Cicero" and Graff's semantics for "is the *F*", and it should declare (i) and (ii) logically equivalent:

   (i) Necessarily, Cicero is Tully
   (ii) Necessarily, Tully is Cicero.

But it is not obvious how the proposal as it stands can succeed in doing this. Graff informs me that her position should be viewed as tentative and that a more detailed or modified version may appear in future work.

5

Gödel: Facts and Descriptions

5.1 ELIMINATION

According to Quine, ordinary (constant) singular terms are ultimately redundant: any sentence containing an ordinary singular term is replaceable (without loss and in a manner suggested by the Theory of Descriptions) by a sentence that is term-free. Ordinary singular terms, e.g. names, are no more than "frills" (1970: 25) or practical "conventions of abbreviation" (1941a: 41); contextual definition is our "reward", as Quine sees it, "for recognising that the unit of communication is the sentence not the word" (1981: 75).

Eliminating certain linguistic expressions or forms can certainly facilitate attempts to dispense with entities of one form or another, or with specific entities belonging to an otherwise acceptable category. But the tight connection between semantics and ontology does not justify equating linguistic and ontological elimination. In connection with Russell's Theory of Descriptions, Gödel (1944), Quine (1966), and no doubt others have evinced a tendency to run the two together. The difference is most clearly seen in connection with Russell's views about classes, on the one hand, and descriptions, on the other. By contextually defining class *expressions*, Russell defined away *classes* themselves (so to speak). In contrast, by contextually defining descriptions, he defined away entities (so to speak) purporting to belong to the category of objects (e.g. the king of France and the round square); but he did not define away the relevant *category*. In the form Russell presents it—which is constrained by notation and the choice of primitive symbols—the Theory of Descriptions eliminates a class of apparent singular terms, sentences containing them being replaced by sentences containing variables, unrestricted quantifiers, connectives, and the identity sign. (Using devices of restricted quantification, the same class of apparent singular terms is eliminated, sentences containing them being replaced by sentences containing variables and restricted quantifiers.) There is no direct ontological elimination because the entities the variables range over are not eliminated.

Russell certainly deployed his Theory of Descriptions to onto-logical benefit, but it was not an integral feature of the theory that certain types of entity could be defined away contextually. The chief ontological benefit for Russell was that it allowed him to treat certain sentences as true or false without seeing their grammatical subjects (or grammatical direct objects, for that matter) as standing for things that don't exist, an idea he rightly came to regard with repugnance. This gave him a basic ontology of particulars, univer-sals, and facts.

Russell's theory ought to be very attractive to those who laud the virtues of "extensionalism" and first-order logic. Besides its evident success as an account of the semantics of descriptive phrases, (i) the theory requires the postulation of no new entities, (ii) it avoids problematic existence assumptions and truth-value gaps, (iii) it provides a treatment of descriptions within first-order quantifica-tion theory with identity, and (iv) it captures a range of inferences involving descriptions as a matter of first-order logic, for example the fact that "the F is G" entails "there is at least one F", "there is at most one F", "there is at least one G", "some F is G", and "every F is G". As Gödel (1944) puts it, by defining the meaning of sentences involving descriptions in accordance with *14.01 and *14.02, Russell "avoids in his logical system any axioms about the particle 'the,' *i.e.*, the analyticity of the theorems about 'the' is made explicit; they can be shown to follow from the explicit defin-ition of the meaning of sentences involving 'the' " (p. 130).

These evident virtues have led to numerous examinations of its potential application to noun phrases other than phrases of the form "the F", for example possessive noun phrases ("Socrates' wife", "Socrates' death"), ordinary proper names ("Socrates"), *that*-clauses ("that Socrates died in prison"), demonstratives ("that", "this vase"), indexical pronouns ("I", "you"), anaphoric pronouns ("it" as it occurs in, for example, "John gave Mary a vase; he had purchased it at Sotheby's").[1]

---

[1] Russell (1905) treated possessive noun phrases as subject to the Theory of Descriptions. He also argued that from certain perspectives ordinary proper names should be analysed in terms of definite descriptions (a handful of logically proper

Why is this? There are two reasons, I believe. The first stems from a somewhat *a priori* desire to eliminate singular terms, a desire that appears to be a reflex of the linguistic counterpart of a principle of ontological parsimony. The second is more empirical in nature. In the course of providing an adequate semantics of natural language and an account of many logical features of natural language, the possibility of analysing problematic noun phrases in terms of Russellian descriptions has promised instant solutions to nagging logical and ontological problems.

Quine has interesting ideas about the elimination of singular terms in connection with Russell's Theory of Descriptions. As an account of descriptive phrases, he sees only logical and philosophical good coming from the theory. Part of the appeal for Quine is that on this account descriptions are analysed in terms of the well-understood devices of first-order extensional logic. Secondly, he is happy with the idea that ordinary proper names can be "trivially" reconstrued as descriptions—and thereby analysed in accordance with Russell's theory. Names are "frills", he says, and can be omitted, "a convenient redundancy" (1970: 25). Following Wittgenstein in the *Tractatus* (5.441, 5.47), he says that *Fa* is "equivalent" to (1):

(1) $\exists x (Fx \bullet a=x)$.

So the name *a* need never occur in a formula except in the context *a =*; but *a =* can be rendered as a simple one-place predicate *A*, uniquely true of the object picked out by *a*; so *Fa* can, in fact, be rendered as

(2) $\exists x (Fx \bullet Ax)$,

which contains no occurrence of *a*; indeed all occurrences of *a*—or any other name—are everywhere replaceable by combinations of quantifiers, variables, connectives, and predicates.

Two minor issues arise here. The first concerns the nature of the predicate *A*. It must hold uniquely of the referent of *a*, and it is not entirely clear whether such a predicate can be drummed up without reintroducing *a* or implicitly appealing to some principle of

---

names (basically, "this" and "that", and in some moods "I") resisting analysis). The precise content of this claim and its relevance to semantics, as opposed to pragmatics, are matters of debate.

linguistic, metaphysical, or ostensive essentialism (e.g. ostension under conditions understood as securing uniqueness). Like Church and Carnap, Quine (1947, 1962) baulks at the idea that co-referring names are synonymous; now suppose $a = b$ is true; a and b should be intersubstitutable *salva veritate* (*s.v.*), at the very least in truth-functional contexts; thus A must be uniquely true of the referent of b (i.e. the referent of a). But what if a drops out of use leaving only b as a name of this entity? And what if a had never come into being in the first place, b being the only name of the entity in question? Unless the existence of A is ontologically dependent upon the existence of a (rather than the entity a refers to), in both scenarios A would still be true of that entity. Thus Quine's claim that (2) is equivalent to Fa seems to commit him to some form of essentialism, but this may turn out to be harmless if grounded in ostension.

Secondly, the Quinean "paraphrase" of Fa might be questioned on the following grounds: it is in the nature of an occurrence of a name that it is understood as applying to a single object; but it is not in the nature of an occurrence of a predicate that it is understood as satisfied by a single object; so the "paraphrase deprives us of an assurance of uniqueness that the name afforded" (1970: 25). Quine's response to this point is straightforward: if we are worried about uniqueness we can import it explicitly in the way Russell does in his analyses of sentences containing definite descriptions. That is, (2) can give way to the following,

(3) $\exists x (\forall y (Ay \equiv x=y) \bullet Fx)$,

which is the Russellian spelling out of $F\iota x Ax$ (i.e. $F\iota x(x=a)$). So anything that can be said using names, Quine assures us, can be said using formulae like (2) or (3) because the objects that names name are the values of variables. Moreover: "names can even be restored at pleasure, as a convenient redundancy, by a convention of abbreviation. This convention would be simply the converse of the procedure by which we just now eliminated names" (1970: 25–6). A predication such as Fa is an abbreviation of (2)—or (3) if the uniqueness condition is cashed out elsewhere. "In effect," Quine adds, "this is somewhat the idea behind Russell's theory of singular descriptions" (p. 26).

So, (i) Quine envisions a language in which the devices of quantification, variation, identity, truth-functional connection, and predication do the work that we normally associate with names; and (ii) he sees this idea as essentially a refinement of, or a twist on, Russell's idea that ordinary proper names can be analysed in terms of definite descriptions. One point about Quine's use of descriptions should be noted, however. Quine (1969: 326–7) uses Russell's *iota*-notation only if the description has minimal scope; when he wants to express something that requires larger scope for the description, he uses the unabbreviated form.

The "theoretical advantages" of analysing names as descriptions are "overwhelming" says Quine: "The whole category of singular terms is thereby swept away, so far as theory is concerned; for we know how to eliminate descriptions. In dispensing with the category of singular terms we dispense with a major source of theoretical confusion, to instances of which I have called attention in ... discussions of ontological commitment" (1953d: 167). As Russell stressed from the outset, endorsing the Theory of Descriptions has interesting and far-reaching consequences for logical issues involving substitutivity. But, as we shall soon see, in certain settings Quine's use of examples involving the substitution of descriptions has had the unfortunate consequence of creating almost as much confusion as it has eradicated.

Quine's quantificational analysis of names is an attempt to push Russell's Theory of Descriptions to its limit, to eliminate *all* constant singular terms. Russell resisted this extreme for epistemological reasons that were alien to Quine: he wanted to anchor singular thoughts about particulars in sense data, and to provide a means of capturing such thoughts in language using the simplest of demonstrative expressions. The Quinean extreme is out of favour today, but so is Russell's half-way house at which ordinary names are analysed descriptively. In the light of Kripke's (1971, 1980) work, it is now widely held that it is not possible to provide an adequate semantical analysis of ordinary proper names by treating them either as *synonymous* with definite descriptions or as having their *references fixed* by description. Henceforth, I propose to view Russell's Theory of Descriptions as a theory of descriptions only and treat names as singular terms. Nothing actually turns on this—if, by some chance, names were to require descriptive analyses, the conclusions drawn here would only be stronger—but it makes exposition easier.

5.2 FACTS AND DESCRIPTIONS

The Theory of Descriptions intersects with Russell's theory of facts in interesting ways. For a start, since definite descriptions are treated quantificationally sentence (4) stands for a *general* fact, one whose conditions of individuation make no reference to any particular individual:

(4) The king is mortal.

The syntactic and semantic similarities between "the" and other quantificational determiners noted in the previous chapter suggest using van Fraassen's notation to represent the general fact for which (4) stands as (5):

(5) {⟨⟨THE, KING⟩, MORTAL ⟩}.

We can think of this fact having as its components (i) the logical complex composed of (*a*) the property of being king, and (*b*) the THE-relation (a relation that holds between pairs of properties ⟨P, Q⟩—here represented as ⟨⟨—, P⟩, Q⟩—if and only if there is exactly one thing that has P and there is nothing that has P but does not also have Q), and (ii) the property of being mortal.

We have in place only the barest outline of a Russellian account of facts, stripped of many of the features that were of importance to Russell himself (e.g. the existence of "negative facts" and a sense datum epistemology). But it is only a pared-down account we shall need in what follows. A Russellian account of facts is meant to be committed neither to the view that every true sentence stands for a *distinct* fact nor to the view that they all stand for the *same* fact.

As Davidson (1984) points out, the challenge for the friend of facts is to come up with something between these poles: if all true sentences stand for the *same* fact, the notion is useless; if every true sentence stands for a *distinct* fact, then, as Strawson (1950a) argues, facts can shed no light on truth as they are individuated in terms of true sentences (or statements).

It is within the spirit of a Russellian account of facts that a true sentence might be reorganized or converted into a related sentence that stands for the same fact (in order, say, to highlight a particular expression for some purpose). Suppose (6) is true and stands for the fact given by (7):

    (6) Cicero denounced Catiline
    (7) {⟨CICERO, ⟨DENOUNCED, CATILINE⟩⟩}.

Then the following sentences (obtained from (6) by "passivization" and "topicalization" respectively) are likely to be viewed as standing for (7) too:

    (8) Catiline was denounced by Cicero
    (9) It was Cicero who denounced Catiline.

A more interesting case involves co-referring singular terms. If the fact for which a true sentence stands is determined by, and only by, its syntax and its parts, then two true sentences $\Sigma[\alpha]$ and $\Sigma[\beta]$ will stand for the same fact if they differ in just the following way: the position occupied by a singular term α in $\Sigma[\alpha]$ is occupied by a co-referring singular term β in $\Sigma[\beta]$. For example, taking 'Cicero' and 'Tully' to be co-referring singular terms, (6) and (10) both stand for (7):

    (6) Cicero denounced Catiline
    (10) Tully denounced Catiline.[2]

By contrast, although Cicero is the author of *De fato*, on Russell's account

    (11) The author of *De fato* denounced Catiline

stands for a quite different fact, the *general* fact that (i) exactly one individual authored *De fato* and (ii) every individual who authored *De fato* also denounced Catiline, i.e. it corresponds to the fact given by (12):

    (12) {⟨⟨THE, ⟨AUTHORED, *DE FATO*⟩⟩, ⟨DENOUNCED, CATILINE ⟩⟩}.

Cicero is no more a component of this fact than I am. If Russell had treated 'the author of *De fato*' as a singular term that referred to Cicero, (11) would stand for (7). And, according to Gödel (1944), this would have had a surprising and devastating consequence because there is an important connection between theories of facts and theories of descriptions: if a true sentence stands for a fact,

---

[2] It is usually held that Russell's final semantics treats ordinary proper names like "Cicero" and "Tully" as disguised definite descriptions to which his Theory of Descriptions applies. As I pointed out above I shall treat ordinary proper names as singular terms.

then in order to avoid the collapse of all facts into one, the friend of facts must give up either (*a*) an intuitive and straightforward Fregean Principle of Composition or (*b*) the idea that definite descriptions are expressions that purport to stand for things. Russell, as Gödel sees it, is able to avoid the troublesome conclusion that all true sentences stand for the same fact by denying that descriptions stand for things, i.e. by treating them as incomplete symbols.

5.3 IDENTITIES IN THE MATRIX

As we saw in the previous chapter, although descriptions are not singular terms on Russell's account, they may still contain *parts* that are. The name "France" is a singular term, but neither "the capital of France" nor "the king of France" is—although the matrix of the former, unlike the latter, is uniquely satisfied. It would be a mistake, as we have seen, to claim that if a description "the *F*" contains a *part* that is a singular term then the description itself must be a singular term, a mistake on a par with the claim that if "every *F*" contains a part that is a singular term then the noun phrase itself must be a singular term (if the claim were true, "the king of France" and "the author of *Waverley*" would not have been Russell's stock examples).

Nothing of consequence is altered when a description contains a singular term that happens to be an indexical or demonstrative. The description "the man who gave me this" is not a singular term but the occurrences of "me" and "this" are (Russell (1905, 1959) uses "my son" and "the *present* king of France" as examples).

The general point is that a Russellian description ιxRxa is not automatically a singular term merely because *a* is a singular term. This fact raises some interesting points. First, what if *R* expresses the identity relation?[3] The expression *ix*(*x* = *a*) is *technically* a Russellian description, but there is some inclination, even among the staunchest Russellians, to view it as a verbose form of *a*, which

---

[3] I am somewhat sceptical of the idea that identity is a genuine relation, and I suspect we could manage without an identity predicate because it can be viewed as a piece of context-sensitive and ambiguous shorthand that never involves what is meant to be expressed by =. However, I do not want anything in the present essay to be tainted by this idea.

126 Gödel: Facts and Descriptions

technically it is not (since it is an incomplete symbol). Nevertheless, there is an itch here that needs scratching. Attaching a one-place predicate F to a yields Fa, while attaching it to $ix(x = a)$ yields (13), which, on Russell's account, is merely shorthand for (14):

(13) $Fix(x = a)$
(14) $\exists x(\forall y(x=a \equiv y=x) \bullet Fx)$.

And while *technically* (14) expresses a general proposition, one feels that it differs only in some ephemeral way from the singular proposition expressed by Fa. In short, one feels that if there is a real difference between Fa and (13) it can manifest itself only in the context of an explicit metaphysics allied to a precise account of the relation between language and reality. Much the same might be said about the difference between Fa and (15),

(15) $\exists x(Fx \bullet a=x)$,

which, as noted earlier Wittgenstein and Quine see as equivalent.

It has already been noted that Russell allows for distinct true sentences to stand for the same fact. Officially Russell must say that Fa and $Fix(x = a)$, if true, stand for distinct facts, because the former stands for a singular fact and the latter a general fact (assuming no intersection of singular and general facts). But at the same time he would surely say that Fa stands for a fact just in case $Fix(x = a)$ does, and that there is no conceivable way the world could be in which only one of them stands for a fact. Fa and $Fix(x = a)$, understood as (14), are in fact logically equivalent in standard systems, but one feels that this fact does not get to the heart of the matter, that Fa and $Fix(x = a)$ are more tightly bound to one another than *that*, that there is a more interesting semantic (and perhaps syntactic) relation that holds between them, a relation that does not hold between Fa and, say, (16), to which it is also logically equivalent:

(16) $Fa \bullet (Gb \lor {\sim}Gb)$.

The obvious difference is that (16) contains a *predicate* and a *singular term* not present in Fa, expressions that contribute what we might call "material content". This is enough to start one thinking about special subclasses of the class of pairs of sentences that are logically equivalent to one another. Consider the following:

(17) ~~Fa
(18) Fa • Fa
(19) (λxFx)a.

Each of these sentences is logically equivalent to Fa; but they seem to have more in common with it than that. Ramsey (1927) thought it incomprehensible that Fa and ~~Fa should stand for distinct facts, and made his case, in part, by appeal to the doctrine that the conclusion of a formal inference must be "in some sense contained in the premises and not something new" (p. 48). From the existence of the single fact that Fa one should not be able to infer the existence of an infinite number of different facts, such as the fact that ~~Fa and the fact that (Fa • ~~Fa); at best, says Ramsey, we have here distinct linguistic forms that stand for the same fact.[4]

Fa and (19) are related by *lambda*-conversion, and they might be viewed as sharing material content (at least on some ways of reading λx). This feeling of equivalence of material content seems to be what Gödel (1944) is responding to when he argues for the dependence of Russell's Theory of Facts upon the Theory of Descriptions. For it seems to be Gödel's thought that one would struggle in vain to explain how Fa and (20) could stand for distinct facts (assuming the identity sign to be part of the logical vocabulary):

(20) $a = \iota x(x{=}a \bullet Fx)$,

where the molecular description $\iota x(x{=}a \bullet Fx)$ is read as "the unique x such that x is identical to a and x is F" and a is a singular term (for example, a name), as in the previous chapter. This matter will be taken up in detail shortly. Right now, I want only to point out that Gödel's molecular description differs in material content from a—or, if we want to reserve the expression 'material content' for whole sentences, Ga and (21) differ in material content because (21) contains a predicate, F, that Ga does not:

(21) $G\iota x(x{=}a \bullet Fx)$.

And, importantly, (21) differs in material content from (22) for the same reason:

(22) $G\iota x(x = a)$.

---

[4] To the extent that the fact-theorist is happy with "conjunctive" facts, much the same point could be made using sentences of the forms "*Fa and Gb*", "*Gb and Fa*", "*Fa but Gb*", etc. Using van Fraassen's notation, such a theorist might say that each of these sentences stands for, or is made true by, {⟨F, a⟩ ⟨G, b⟩}.

Unlike $\iota x(x = a)$, on a Russellian treatment Gödel's description $\iota x(x=a \cdot Fx)$ is not even a *contender* for being cast aside as a verbose rendering of a.

5.4 THE ELEATIC ONE

Gödel (1944) argues that there is an important connection between theories of facts and theories of descriptions: if a true sentence stands for a fact, then in order to avoid the collapse of all facts into one, the friend of facts must give up either (i) an intuitive and straightforward Fregean Principle of Composition or (ii) the idea that definite descriptions are expressions that purport to stand for things:

An interesting example of Russell's analysis of the fundamental logical concepts is his treatment of the definite article "the." The problem is: what do the so-called descriptive phrases (*i.e.*, phrases as, e.g., "the author of *Waverley*" or "the king of England") denote or signify [footnote omitted] and what is the meaning of sentences in which they occur? The apparently obvious answer that, e.g., "the author of *Waverley*" signifies Walter Scott, leads to unexpected difficulties. For, if we admit the further apparently obvious axiom, that the signification of a complex expression, containing constituents which have themselves a signification, depends only on the signification of these constituents (not on the manner in which this signification is expressed), then it follows that the sentence "Scott is the author of *Waverley*" signifies the same thing as "Scott is Scott;" *and this again leads almost inevitably to the conclusion that all true sentences have the same signification (as well as all the false ones).* (pp. 128–9; my italics)

The argument for this extraordinary conclusion—which I shall examine shortly—is given in a footnote appended to the last sentence of this passage. Gödel appears to think Frege brought more or less the same considerations to bear in arguing that sentences refer to truth-values: "Frege actually drew this conclusion; and he meant it in an almost metaphysical sense, reminding one somewhat of the Eleatic doctrine of the 'One.' 'The True'—according to Frege's view—is analysed by us in different ways in different propositions; 'the True' being the name he uses for the common signification of all true propositions" (p. 129). As Gödel points out, Russell says nothing explicit about the Principle of Composition, but it is reasonable to suppose that he took it as seriously as Frege did. So

Russell takes the other way out: his Theory of Descriptions denies that descriptions stand for things, and it is this, says Gödel, that is meant to save his Theory of Facts from collapse.

As the reader goes through the argument I am about to attribute to Gödel, it is possible that orthogonal but ultimately irrelevant worries about Semantic Innocence and Direct Reference will come to mind at various points (see Chapter 3). Their irrelevance will become clear once I construct a deductive proof, based on Gödel's argument, which patently does not presuppose either Semantic Innocence or Direct Reference (or their denials), any particular theory of descriptions, or any metaphysical claims about facts. For the moment, I simply ask the reader to bear with me as I attempt to reconstruct Gödel's reasoning, which I find inconclusive as it stands because it contains a few loose ends and perhaps even an outright inconsistency.

Why does Gödel think a treatment of descriptions as singular terms will precipitate a collapse of all facts into one Great Fact? Consider the following complex description containing an identity in its matrix:

(23) $\iota x(x=a \bullet Fx)$.

From a formal point of view such a description is unremarkable because its matrix $(x=a \bullet Fx)$ is a well-formed formula. So on Russell's account, (24) is simply shorthand for the well-formed formula (25):

(24) $G\iota x(x=a \bullet Fx)$
(25) $\exists x(\forall y((Fy \bullet y=a) \equiv y=x) \bullet Gx)$.

The notation of restricted quantification makes the content of (25) clear:

(26) $[the\ x\colon x=a \bullet Fx]\ Gx$.

Gödel's claim boils down to this: if true sentences stand for facts and if an expression of the form $\iota x\phi$ is viewed as a genuine singular term standing for the unique object satisfying ϕ, then by invoking minimal logical principles in connection with formulae containing descriptions of the form of (23) it is possible to demonstrate that all true sentences must stand for the same fact.

In the footnote omitted from the quotation above Gödel hints at a proof of this claim:

The only further assumptions one would need in order to obtain a rigorous proof would be: [G1] that "φ(*a*)" and the proposition "*a* is the object which has the property φ and is identical to *a*" mean the same thing and [G2] that every proposition "speaks about something," i.e. can be brought to the form φ(*a*). Furthermore one would have to use the fact that for any two objects *a . b* there exists a true proposition of the form φ(*a,b*) as, e.g., *a≠b* or *a=a • b=b.* (1944: 129).

[G1] The first assumption is less worrying than Gödel's wording might suggest. The footnote does not reveal what he intends by saying that *Fa* and (27) "mean the same thing":

(27) $a = \iota x(x=a • Fx)$.

An examination of the main text quoted above might suggest that he intends "signify the same thing". Whatever Gödel's intention, for the purposes of the argument I shall attribute to him it is both sufficient and necessary that if descriptions are singular terms that simply stand for things, then *Fa* and (27) stand for the same fact.

[G2] Gödel's second assumption is that any sentence that stands for a fact can be put into predicate-argument form. Without this assumption, his slingshot will show only that all true *atomic* sentences stand for the same fact—of course, this conclusion would be every bit as devastating for most friends of facts, but Gödel thinks the more comprehensive conclusion can be proved. (Presumably he would say that "Socrates snored and Plato snored" can be rendered as "Socrates is *an x such that x snored and Plato snored*", and that "all men snore" can be rendered as something like "Socrates is *an x such that all men snore*" (harmlessly assuming a non-empty universe). If such conversions are found repugnant, one can still follow Gödel's reasoning through in connection with atomic sentences.)

[G3] A third assumption—mentioned not in the footnote but in the earlier quotation from the main text—is the Principle of Composition: "the signification of a composite expression, containing constituents which themselves have a signification, depends only on the signification of these constituents (not on the manner in which this signification is expressed)". This Gödel takes to be an "apparently obvious axiom" (I shall return to its interpretation).

It would seem that Gödel's proof that all true sentences stand for

the same fact is meant to proceed as follows. Assume the following
three sentences are all true:

(I) Fa

(II) $a \neq b$

(III) Gb.

Then each stands for some fact or other; call the facts in question
f_I, f_{II}, and f_{III} respectively. By [G1], since (I) stands for f_I so does

(IV) $a = \iota x(x = a \bullet Fx)$.

By the same assumption, since (II) stands for f_{II}, so does

(V) $a = \iota x(x = a \bullet x \neq b)$.

If a definite description $\iota x \phi$ stands for the unique thing satisfying ϕ,
then the descriptions in (IV) and (V) both stand for the same thing,
namely a. So, by [G3], sentences (IV) and (V) stand for the same
fact, i.e. $f_I = f_{II}$. By [G1], since (III) stands for f_{III}, so does

(VI) $b = \iota x(x = b \bullet Gx)$.

And by the same assumption, since (II) stands for f_{II} so does

(VII) $b = \iota x(x = b \bullet x \neq a)$.

Again, on the assumption that a definite description $\iota x \phi$ stands for
the unique thing satisfying ϕ, the descriptions in (VI) and (VII) stand
for the same thing, namely b. So, by [G3], sentences (VI) and (VII)
stand for the same fact, i.e. $f_{III} = f_{II}$. Thus $f_I = f_{II} = f_{III}$, i.e. Fa and
Gb stand for the same fact. *Mutatis mutandis* where $a = b$ (rather
than $a \neq b$) is true. So all true sentences stand for the same fact.[5]

---

[5] I have benefited from comparing my reconstruction of Gödel's proof—a
preliminary version of which first appeared in a paper I published in *Mind* in
1995—to those offered by Olson (1987), Wallace (1969), and Wedberg (1966,
1984). My reconstruction is considerably leaner and better suited to the tasks at
hand than its predecessors; moreover, I feel confident its leanness captures Gödel's
intentions precisely.

The first published discussion of this argument is by Bernays (1946), who seems
to miss its point entirely. Bernays suggests that Gödel reaches this conclusion
because he fails to separate the sense (*Sinn*) and reference (*Bedeutung*) of a sentence
despite mentioning Frege during his discussion of Russell's Theory of Descriptions.
Bernays's point seems to be that Fa and $a = \iota x(x = a \bullet Fx)$ have different senses. But this
is irrelevant. Gödel's argument concerns the relationship between descriptions and
facts, not descriptions and *modes of presentation* of facts (which Russell did not
have in any case). Bernays's mistake is repeated by Oppy (1997).

Gödel's argument is certainly valid; but it is unclear whether [G1]–[G3] and the assumption that definite descriptions are singular terms form a consistent set, and so unclear whether the argument is valid only in a boring sense. If descriptions are singular terms and if, as [G3] requires, what a description stands for depends only on what its constituents stand for (and not on the manner in which this is expressed), then it is not obvious that (I) and (IV) should be viewed as standing for the same fact:

(I) Fa
(IV) $a = \iota x (x = a \bullet Fx)$.

For (IV), granting [G3] and the assumption that descriptions are singular terms, looks like an identity statement; so one might think it should stand for the same fact as (VIII), at least by the lights of *some* theories that treat descriptions as singular terms:

(VIII) $a = a$.

But unless one *already* holds that all true sentences stand for the same fact, it is implausible in the extreme to hold that (I) and (VIII) stand for the same fact. In short, it is not clear that assumption [G1] sits well with the assumption that descriptions are singular terms; and this may seem to rob Gödel's argument of immediate interest. However, as I shall demonstrate in Chapter 8, it is possible to produce a blemish-free, operator-based version of Gödel's argument that makes no contentious semantical or meta-

---

That Gödel's proof does not overtly invoke the notion of logical equivalence—the notion central to the Church–Quine–Davidson slingshot—is recognized by Wedberg, Wallace, Parsons, Olson, Neale, Neale and Dever, Perry, and Oppy. Burge and Davidson recognize that Gödel's argument is different in form from Church's, but they do not discuss the nature of the difference. The possibility of a modification of the Church-style proof that differs from the original in the crucial respect in which Gödel's does is mentioned by Dale (1978), Taylor (1976, 1985), and Widerker (1983)—though only Widerker actually mentions Gödel in this connection. There is no explicit acknowledgement in these articles of the fact that an argument of the modified form can be stated in such a way that it relies on strictly weaker premisses. Dale remarks, correctly, that claims about logical equivalence are easier to justify within the context of the modified proof. In his discussion of Quine's (1960) slingshot, Sharvy (1969) notes that the argument could be reformulated using a weaker premiss, i.e. by appealing to a tighter notion than the purported logical equivalence of ϕ and "the number x such that $((x = 1) \bullet \phi)$ or $((x = 0) \bullet \sim\phi)$", the purported equivalence that does the work in Quine's slingshot. Føllesdal (1983) notes in passing that not all versions of the slingshot involve the interchange of logical equivalents, but does not mention Gödel in this connection.

physical assumptions and has a considerable bearing on theories of facts.

Returning to Gödel's own discussion, if definite descriptions are treated not as singular terms but in accordance with Russell's Theory of Descriptions—which, as we have seen, has independent motivation—then matters are meant to be somewhat different. The threatened collapse of facts is supposed to be straight-forwardly avoided. Gödel's main point here is that, on Russell's account, since descriptions do not stand for things (they are not singular terms), neither (IV) nor (V) can be obtained from the other by the replacement of expressions that stand for the same thing,

(IV) $a = \iota x(x = a \bullet Fx)$
(V) $a = \iota x(x = a \bullet x \neq b)$,

therefore it does not follow from [G3] that (IV) and (V) stand for the same fact.[6] *Mutatis mutandis* for (VI) and (VII). Hence Russell avoids the "Eleatic" conclusion, Gödel suggests, because he is a Russellian about definite descriptions.

However, it looks as though the collapse Gödel envisages can be blocked by Russell before we get as far as examining the relationship between (IV) and (V). If descriptions are treated in accordance with Russell's theory and if facts are individuated, as they are for Russell, by their components, then (I) and (IV) do not seem to stand for the same fact:

(I) Fa
(IV) $a = \iota x(x{=}a \bullet Fx)$.

The former stands for a singular fact, the latter for a general fact. But at the same time, as we saw in the previous section, there must be a very tight connection between these facts. It is a fact that (I) if and only if it is a fact that (II), and not just in a material sense of 'if and only if'. And since (I) and (IV) share material content, one might be inclined to say that (IV) corresponds to the fact that *Fa*.

Fortunately, for my purposes here I do not need to pronounce on such matters. I am seeking a knock-down constraint on theories of facts, and that is something we cannot obtain solely from

---

[6] This corresponds to the fact that, on a Russellian account, (IV) and (V) stand for different general facts with different components: the property of being *F* is a component of the fact corresponding to (IV) but not the fact corresponding to (V).

the argument I have attributed to Gödel as it stands. At this point we can draw the following moral from Gödel's discussion: anyone who wishes to maintain that descriptions are singular terms and hence stand for (signify, refer to, designate) things, and at the same time hold (in accordance with the Principle of Composition) that sentences stand for facts (or anything else) determined by what their parts stand for, must hold that (I) and (IV) stand for different facts or else accept that all true sentences stand for the same fact.

Russell, as Gödel sees it, is able to avoid the conclusion that all true sentences stand for the same fact by denying that descriptions stand for things, i.e. by denying that they are singular terms, and hence denying that (IV) and (V) stand for the same facts. There is no need to worry, then, about whether Russell could be badgered into accepting that (I) and (IV) stand for the same fact.

But Gödel was not entirely convinced that Russell was off the hook: "I cannot help feeling that the problem raised . . . has only been evaded by Russell's theory of descriptions and that there is something behind it which is not yet completely understood" (1944: p. 130). Gödel is silent on the nature of his worry, but I hazard he was reacting to a superficial feature of Russell's theory that the use of, for example, restricted quantifiers has shown to be dispensable. Russell's own implementation of his theory involved defining descriptions contextually in such a way that they "disappear on analysis" in primitive notation; and Gödel must have thought that excluding descriptions from the primitive notation was a formal manoeuvre that created only an *illusion* of a solution by masking the real philosophical issue. This seems to be borne out by Gödel's next (and final) paragraph on the topic:

There seems to be one purely formal respect in which one may give preference to Russell's theory of descriptions. By defining the meaning of sentences involving descriptions in the above manner, he avoids in his logical system any axioms about the particle "the," *i.e.*, the analyticity of the theorems about "the" is made explicit; they can be shown to follow from the explicit definition of the meaning of sentences involving "the." Frege, on the contrary, has to assume an axiom about "the," which of course is also analytic, but only in the implicit sense that it follows from the meaning of the undefined terms. Closer examination, however, shows that this advantage of Russell's theory over Frege's subsists only as long as one interprets definitions as mere typographical abbreviations, not as

introducing names for objects described by the definitions, a feature which
is common to Frege and Russell. (pp. 130–1)[7]

The final sentence of this passage is instructive. First, it is important to realize that on Russell's Theory of Descriptions *14.01 and
*14.02 *are* typographical abbreviations and that descriptive
phrases are *not* introduced as names for the objects described by
the definitions.[8] Secondly, Gödel thought some of the central difficulties of *Principia* arose precisely because Russell refused to
admit classes and concepts as real objects. I suspect Gödel's
worries about defining away classes by contextually defining the
expressions that purport to refer to them may have clouded his
thinking about contextually defining descriptions. There is an
important ontological difference: contextually defining class
expressions gave Russell a way of defining away *classes* themselves
(so to speak); contextually defining descriptions gave him a way of
defining away the king of France and the round square (so to
speak) but it did not give him a way of defining away *objects*.
Thirdly, in 1943–44 it was not obvious how descriptions, if
analysed in such a way that sentences containing them are
assigned the quantificational truth-conditions assigned by
Russell's theory, should fit into a general account of quantification. As Gödel's final sentence reveals, the possibilities that
presented themselves to him at that time were just two in number:
(i) descriptions are mere typographical abbreviations that disappear on analysis, or (ii) they are terms that have their references
fixed quantificationally (by, for example, overlapping satisfac-
tions). But subsequent work on quantification and on the syntax
and semantics of natural language has revealed a superior possibility: (iii) a description "the *F*" is a quantified noun phrase on an
equal footing with "every *F*", "some *F*", "no *F*", etc. The fact that
Russell's theory can be implemented within a theory of restricted
quantification ought to dispel worries about the artificial banish-

[7] Towards the end of the paper Gödel discusses "whether (and in what sense) the
axioms of *Principia* can be considered to be analytic" (p. 150). In Gödel's *Nachlass*
an annotated page of an offprint of his 1944 paper (p. 150) has the remark "Th. der
natürlichen Zahlen nachweislich nicht analytisch im Kantschen Sinn" ("The theory
of natural numbers [is] demonstrably not analytic in Kant's sense"). See Gödel
(1990: ii. 314).
[8] For reasons given by Kripke (1980), the abbreviations would be *rigid* if this
were the case, and (typically) descriptions are not.

ment of descriptions and also confusions about "incomplete symbols" (see the appendix).

In Chapter 8 I am going to show that we can construct from Gödel's slingshot a deductive proof that demonstrates all sorts of interesting facts about facts, about the semantics of descriptions, and about the limits of purportedly non-extensional logics. But there is a little more work to be done before that.

6

Extensionality

6.1 EXTENSIONS AND SENTENCE CONNECTIVES

A good deal of contemporary philosophy involves manoeuvring within linguistic contexts governed by modal, causal, deontic, and other purportedly non-extensional operators. If this sort of manoeuvring is to be effective, it must respect the logical and other semantical properties of the contexts within which it takes place. It is an unfortunate fact about much of today's technical philosophy that the relevant logico-semantical groundwork is not properly done (if it is done at all), and this is one reason why so much work in metaphysics, ethics, the philosophy of mind, and the philosophy of language reduces to utter nonsense. Great progress has been made in the last fifty years in understanding the logic, structure, and use of language; technical philosophy in the absence of logical grammar in this age barely deserves the name "philosophy". In due course I am going to argue that a formal proof based on Gödel's slingshot places an exacting constraint on non-extensional connectives. But first let us be clear what is meant by "extensional" and "extensionality".

The occurrence of the name "Helen" in the sentence "Helen left voluntarily" might be said to refer to, or stand for, Helen. But pre-theoretically it is much less usual—indeed it is unnatural—to say that the sentence itself or the occurrences of "left", "voluntarily", and "left voluntarily" refer to things. It might seem futile, then, to search for parts of the world to correspond to all the parts of sentences. However, many philosophers interested in constructing theories of meaning for natural languages have assigned entities to serve as the referents of expressions other than names and other devices of singular reference.

I avoid controversy here by adopting some well-defined theoretical vocabulary and stipulating that terms, predicates, sentences, and sentence connectives all have *extensions*. Consider a simple formal language L that contains just names (individual constants), predicates, and truth-functional connectives. The extensions of the various types of expression are stipulated as follows: (i) the extension of a name is simply its referent (for immediate concerns let us agree to exile names that fail to refer, if there are such expressions); (ii) the extension of an n-place predicate is the set of n-tuples of which the predicate holds; (iii) the extension of a sentence is its truth-value;[1] (iv) the extension of an n-place connective is a function from n-tuples of truth-values to truth-values (such functions are *truth-functions*; hence the idea that connectives having truth-functions as their extensions are *truth-functional*). An extensional semantics for L will assign to every complex expression ζ of L an extension based on ζ's syntax and the extensions of ζ's parts. (For atomic sentences: $\text{Ext}(`\Re\alpha') = \text{Truth iff } \text{Ext}(\alpha) \in \text{Ext}(\Re)$, $\text{Ext}(`\Re\alpha\beta')$ $= \text{Truth iff } \langle\text{Ext}(\alpha), \text{Ext}(\beta)\rangle \in \text{Ext}(\Re)$, etc. where $\Re$ is a predicate. Non-atomic sentences: $\text{Ext}(`{\sim}\phi') = \text{Truth iff } \text{Ext}(\phi) = \text{Falsity, Ext}$ $(`(\phi \bullet \psi)') = \text{Truth iff } \text{Ext}(\phi) = \text{Truth and } \text{Ext}(\psi) = \text{Truth, etc.})$

As far as L is concerned, the class of so-called "extensional entities" is simply the class consisting of objects, sets of n-tuples of objects, the two truth-values, and functions from n-tuples of truth-values to truth-values, i.e. the class consisting of all and only those entities capable of serving as the extensions of names, predicates, sentences, or connectives of L. There is nothing deep or mysterious about this class: it is determined *by stipulation* because the class of entities capable of serving as the extensions of terms, predicates, sentences, and connectives of L has been determined by stipulation. Any entity that is not in this class is, by definition, a non-extensional entity as far as L is concerned. (I shall not use "non-extensional" and "intensional" interchangeably; it is useful to reserve the term "intensionality" for a restricted type of non-extensionality.)

---

[1] Given (ii), (iii) is not entirely arbitrary: two n-place predicates $\Re$ and $\Re'$ have the same extension if and only if $(\forall x_1 \ldots x_n)(\Re(x_1 \ldots x_n) \equiv \Re'(x_1 \ldots x_n))$ is true; if a sentence can be viewed as a o-place predicate (i.e. an expression that combines with zero terms to form a sentence), then two sentences ϕ and ψ have the same extension if and only if $(\phi \equiv \psi)$ is true; so, as Carnap (1947: 26) points out, on such an account it seems "natural" to regard the truth-values of sentences as their extensions.

6.2 SCOPE

Although the concept of scope is present in earlier work, the word "scope" itself is first used in the way that has become current by Whitehead and Russell in *Principia* (replacing Russell's earlier talk of (primary, secondary, tertiary, . . .) "occurrences" of symbols. But it is surprising how much confusion there is among philosophers about the *concept* of scope and about why we say that the scope of such-and-such is so-and-so. Anyone who has studied basic logic can tell you the scopes of the occurrences of ~, and • in (1), construed as a sentence of the language L used above:

(1) ~ (~*Fa* • *Ga*).

The scope of the first occurrence of ~ is the whole of (1); the scope of the second occurrence is ~*Fa*; and the scope of • is (~*Fa* • *Ga*). Let us reflect, for a moment, on why we say these things, on how scope is related to compositionality, and on what it would mean for expressions in natural language to have scopes.

Scope is a primitive syntactico-semantic notion: it concerns how semantic evaluation is driven by composition. In any interesting language there are molecular expressions, where the latter are expressions whose ultimate constituents are atomic expressions. It is the way a complex expression in a formal language is put together—its syntax—that tells us the scope of any part of the expression that may interest us. It betrays a fundamental misunderstanding of this concept when people claim, for example, that "only operators have scopes".[2]

The limitations of L are well reflected in the fact that it contains only one type of complex expression: the sentence. This fact tends to make us lazy, accepting the first characterization of scope that seems to get us what we want. We might begin by saying that, in L,

---

[2] See e.g. Patton (1997), who uses precisely these words. Of course, with some ingenuity any expression can be made to function as an operator, in which case it would be true to say that "only operators have scopes". But this is not what Patton has in mind. He is chastizing Kripke and Dummett: "People, Kripke and Dummett for two, freely ascribe *scopes* to singular terms, which is incoherent since only operators have scopes" (p. 251). Unlike Dummett and Kripke, Patton hasn't reflected upon what scope *is*. I don't mean to suggest he is alone in this; indeed, I hesitated to pick on Patton here because the failure is so widespread, but his statement has the virtue of being exceptionally clear.

(S1) the scope of an n-place sentence connective ❽ ("ball") occurring in a sentence S is simply the sentence that has resulted from combining ❽ with n sentences $\phi \ldots \phi_n$, i.e. the smallest sentence in S containing both ❽ and $\phi \ldots \phi_n$ as constituents, i.e. the smallest sentence in S containing ❽ as a constituent.

(S1) is true; but we should resist the temptation to see it as providing a *definition* of scope. If we stop at this traditional and unreflective stopping place we fail to do justice to the generality and fundamental simplicity of the concept of scope. We are on the way to a better understanding of scope (but not yet a definition) when we observe that, in L,

(S2) the scope of an n-place sentence connective ❽ occurring in a sentence S is the smallest sentence in S containing ❽ as a *proper* constituent.

Of course adding "proper" makes no discernible difference where we are asking after the scope of a sentence connective, but it would be a mistake to conclude from this that we are making no progress and simply adding a redundancy.

The linguistic idea at the heart of the concept of scope is simply that of two or more constituents combining to form a larger constituent. We might say that, in L,

(S3) the scope of a constituent α—*any constituent*—of a sentence S is the smallest sentence in S containing α as a proper constituent.

So in ~Fa, the scope of ~ is ~Fa, and the scope of Fa is also ~Fa. The scope of F is Fa, and the scope of a is also Fa. Nothing changes when we examine more complex expressions. In (~Fa • Ga) the scope of • is the whole sentence, and this is also the scope of both ~Fa and Ga. In Rab the scopes of R, a, and b are all Rab. We now see that there was nothing ad hoc or arbitrary in our answers to the questions about the scopes of the occurrences of ~, and • in (1) above. To ask for the scope of a constituent is to ask for information about any constituents with which it combined directly to form a larger constituent, i.e. it is to ask for that larger constituent.

Thus we are lead into a general definition, applicable not only to L, whose only complex constituents are whole sentences, but to languages containing other forms of complex constituents (e.g. restricted quantifiers or complex noun phrases):

(S4) the scope of a constituent α—*any constituent*—of a sentence S is the smallest *constituent* of S containing α as a proper constituent.

(The ambiguity in "Bill bought ripe figs and nectarines" might then be seen as a scope ambiguity that can be resolved when it is made clear (whether by syntactic analysis or translation into a formal version of English) whether the adjective "ripe" combines with "figs" or with "figs and nectarines".)

In this way (and construing "sentence" as "formula" so as to include the open sentences of those languages that make use of such devices) it is evident that scope is a concept that applies to *any* compositional language, be it formal or natural, but a concept *whose semantic utility depends on whether the language being investigated is like standard formal languages in using scope to make semantic relations transparent.* And seen this way it is evident that scope is semantically imperfect as far as the *surface* grammar of natural language is concerned, witness familiar "ambiguities of scope" ("a doctor examined every victim", "no one has met the king of France", "bring your aunt or come alone and drink lots of Scotch". It is, however, an interesting question, one being investigated by the more respectable strains of theoretical linguistics, whether there is a level of linguistic representation, the level relevant to semantic interpretation, at which scope does, in fact, play the desired role.[3]

---

[3] With respect to multiple quantifications, the original motivation in logic for allowing permutations of quantifier scope was the desire to capture readings with distinct truth-conditions. But, as is well known, permuting quantifiers does not always result in such a difference. For example, the truth-conditions of neither (i) nor (ii) are sensitive to which quantifier has larger scope:

(i) every philosopher respects every logician
(ii) some logician respects some philosopher.

But there is no getting round the fact that scopes must still be assigned in providing translations of (i) and (ii) in standard first-order notation, and all intelligible work in that strain of theoretical linguistics which is attempting to characterize a syntactical level of "logical form" respects this fact, declaring each of (i) and (ii) the surface manifestation of two distinct but logically equivalent underlying structures. This might strike some as introducing an unnecessary redundancy, but the perception is

There is one obvious mismatch between the syntax of the elementary formal languages just sketched and the syntax of English. Consider (2)

(2) ~(*Fa* • ~*Gb*).

illusory. First, theorists should be striving after the most general and aesthetically satisfying theory, and the fact that no truth-conditional differences result from scope permutations in *some* simple sentences is of no moment by itself. Secondly, contrary to what some people have claimed, in order to produce such examples, it is neither necessary nor sufficient to use the same quantificational determiner twice. This is easily seen by adopting restricted quantifier notation. That sameness of determiner is not *necessary* is clear from the fact that the pairs of readings for (iii) and (iv) are equivalent:

> (iii) the queen owns a bicycle
> [the_1: $queen_1$] [a_2: $bicycle_1$] x_1 owns x_2
> [a_2: $bicycle_2$] [the_1: $queen_1$] x_1 owns x_2.
> (iv) every outlaw talked to the sheriff
> [$every_1$: $outlaw_1$] [the_2: $sheriff_2$] x_1 talked to x_2
> [the_2: $sheriff_2$] [$every_1$: $outlaw_1$] x_1 talked to x_2.

(In effect, this was pointed out by Whitehead and Russell in *Principia*.) That sameness of determiner is not *sufficient* follows from the fact that (e.g.) "most" is not self-commutative; the two readings of (v) are not equivalent (a point I believe was first made by Nicholas Rescher):

> (v) most outlaws shoot most sheriffs
> [$most_1$: $outlaw_1$] [$most_2$: $sheriff_2$] x_1 shoot x_2
> [$most_2$: $sheriff_2$] [$most_1$: $outlaw_1$] x_1 shoot x_2

The real moral that emerges from reflecting on (i)–(v) is that a theory of logical form is rather more than a theory that associates a sentence of a well-behaved formal language with each sentence of a natural language. If the best syntax and semantics we have both say (or jointly entail) that there are two distinct "logical forms" associated with some particular string, then it would be preposterous to claim that the string in question is not the surface form of two distinct sentences just because the two purported "logical forms" are logically equivalent. My point here is not the familiar one that truth-conditions are not fine-grained enough to serve as propositions or meanings. This matter is irrelevant to the point at hand. (Notice that although the pairs of readings of (i)–(iv) are equivalent, the axioms of a truth-definition will apply in a different order, and to that extent there is still room for the truth-conditional semanticist to say that the sentences (construed, as pairs of "logical" and "surface" forms) differ in an interesting *semantic* respect; on this matter, see Larson and Segal 1995). My point is much simpler. We all accept that the string "visiting professors can be a nuisance" is the surface manifestation of two distinct sentences with distinct truth-conditions, and we don't mind saying this even though the two sentences are written and sound alike. Equally, we all accept that "Bill sold Mary a car" and "Mary bought a car from Bill" are the surface manifestations of two distinct sentences with the same truth-conditions. So neither the "surface sameness" nor the "truth-conditional sameness" of two purported sentences is sufficient to demonstrate that a single sentence is actually under scrutiny. There is no reason to think that the *combination* of surface sameness and truth-conditional sameness demonstrates it either. So there is no reason to reject the view that each of (i)–(iv) is

The scope of the first negation sign ~ is the whole sentence, the scope of the conjunction sign • is the subsentence (*Fa* • ~*Gb*), and the scope of the second negation sign is the sub-sub-sentence ~*Gb*. All of this is readily seen by looking at the phrase structure tree for (3), readily extractable from the standard syntax we would write for *L*:

(3)

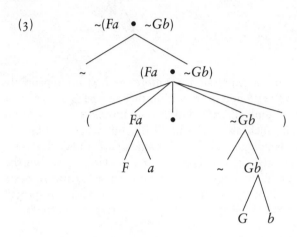

In terms of tree-geometry, the scope of an expression (as already defined) is simply the first node properly dominating it (similarly in the languages of propositional logic, first-order logic, and modal extensions thereof).[4] Following logical and philosophical tradition, in *L* a syntactic and semantic distinction was drawn between one- and two-place predicates. In terms of tree-geometry, the syntactic

the surface manifestation of a pair of sentences. At times we must let the theory decide. If the best syntax and semantics we have say there are two distinct sentences corresponding to a single string, so be it.

It has been argued by Hornstein (1984) that the absence of a difference in truth-conditions for the pairs associated with (iii) and (iv) lends support to his view that descriptions are *not* regular quantified noun phrases that admit of various scope assignments but are always interpreted as if they took maximal scope, something he sees as explicable on the assumption that descriptions are more like referential than quantificational noun phrases. As argued in detail by Soames (1987) and Neale (1990), Hornstein's arguments and his position are beset with philosophical and technical problems so severe that they are unintelligible where they are not plain wrong.

⁴ When considering scope in natural language, the scope of an expression is the first *branching* node properly dominating it. This is because of the possibility (in some theories) of non-branching nodes in connection with, e.g., nouns and intransitive verbs. This need not concern us here.

difference between a sentence containing a one-place predicate and a sentence containing a two-place predicate manifests itself clearly in (4) and (5):

(4)   *Fa*   (5)   *Rab*

            F   a   R   a   b

Since the scope of an expression is simply the first node properly dominating it, in (4) *F* and *a* are within one another's scopes, just as "Alfie" and "fumbled" are within one another's scopes in an English analogue such as "Alfie fumbled". But when it comes to (5), our formal language and English come apart. In (5) *R*, *a*, and *b* are all within each other's scopes; in particular, *a* is within the scope of *R*. But in an English analogue such as "Alfie respects Bertie", "Alfie" is not within the scope of the verb "respects" (though it is within the scope of *verb phrase* "respects Bertie"):

(6)

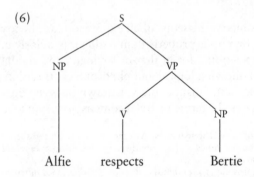

In (6) "respects" combines with the singular term "Bertie" to form an expression (a verb phrase) that combines with the singular term "Alfie" to form a sentence. That is, 'respects' functions as a one-place, one-place-predicate-former. It does no harm to say it functions as a two-place predicate as long as it is kept in mind that the syntactic relations it bears to the two singular terms that function as its "arguments" are quite different.

The situation is strikingly similar when we turn to purported connectives, about which Quine (1953*a*, *c*, 1960) and Davidson (1980) have worried. The English words "and" and "or" seem to be, on at least one of their uses, two-place connectives. Thus a sentence of the form of "φ and ψ" would seem to have the following tree:

(7) φ and ψ

φ and ψ

With the syntactic simplicity of philosophers' favourite formal languages in mind, very often expressions such as "if", "only if", "unless", "before", "after", "because", "although", "when", and "while" are treated as two-place connectives, and for purposes of this book I shall adopt this (naive) policy. From the perspective of providing a syntactic theory of English, these expressions should almost certainly be treated in a more complex fashion, perhaps as constituents of complex one-place connectives. On such an account, the basic syntactic structures of, say, "φ because ψ" and "because ψ, φ" are given by (8) and (9) respectively:

(8)   φ because ψ

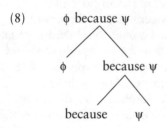

φ   because ψ

because   ψ

(9)   because ψ φ

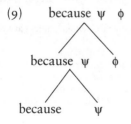

because ψ   φ

because   ψ

Similarly for "φ if ψ" and "if φ, ψ", "φ before ψ" and "before ψ, φ", and so on.[5]

On this account, expressions such as "if Helen left", "before Helen leaves", "because Helen left" and so on are complex expressions that combine with a sentence to form another sentence. In other words, they are complex sentence connectives. Much of what I have to say henceforth is concerned with certain logical properties of connectives and of expressions that form *parts* of connectives such as "if", "only if", "before", "after", "because", "when", and "while". But to keep things simple, I shall partake of the common fiction that these expressions are two-place connectives on a par with "and" and "or" (just as we often partake of the common fiction that transitive verbs are two-place predicates). This will make it easier to focus on the important logical and semantic issues at hand. Any accidental damage that results could easily be repaired if everything were transposed into a format that does justice to a more adequate syntax.

6.3 EXTENSIONAL AND NON-EXTENSIONAL CONNECTIVES

Extensional operators map *extensions* into extensions, i.e. they operate on the *extensions* of their operands. Consider an expression $\otimes(\phi \ldots \phi_n)$ composed of an *n*-place operator $\otimes$ and operands $\phi \ldots \phi_n$. $\otimes$ is an extensional operator if and only if the extension of $\otimes(\phi \ldots \phi_n)$ depends upon no features of $\otimes$ and $\phi \ldots \phi_n$ other than their *extensions* (the syntactic structure of the whole expression $\otimes(\phi \ldots \phi_n)$ supplying anything else that is required). Among those operators that operate on formulae and yield formulae, let us distinguish between those capable of binding variables (e.g. quantifiers) and those that are not (e.g. the truth-functional connectives, on their standard construal). Let us call the latter group *connectives*. Since

---

[5] It is as if such structures may "swivel" at the dominant sentence node, at least in English. Interestingly, infants master "φ before ψ" and "after φ, ψ" before they master "before ψ, φ" and "ψ after φ" (see Clark 1971 and Johnson 1975). This would appear to comport with—and perhaps ultimately underpin—Grice's (1989) views about utterances of "φ and ψ" giving rise, *ceteris paribus*, to suggestions that the event described by φ preceded the event described by ψ (where φ and ψ describe events that can be temporally ordered), a fact Grice attributes to a (contextually defeasible) submaxim of conversation enjoining orderliness.

they take us from the *extensions* of expressions to the *extensions* of larger expressions, the class of *extensional* connectives is a subclass of the class of extensional operators: an *n*-place connective ❸ is extensional if and only if the extension of ❸($\phi \ldots \phi_n$) depends upon no features of ❸ and $\phi \ldots \phi_n$ other than their extensions. Thus a connective ❸ is extensional if and only if any sentence with the same extension (i.e. truth-value) as the sentence ϕ_k (where $1 \le k \le n$) can be substituted for ϕ_k in the sentence ❸($\phi \ldots \phi_n$) to produce a sentence with the same extension (i.e. truth-value) as ❸($\phi \ldots \phi_n$). Since the extension of a sentence has already been stipulated to be a truth-value, the class of *extensional* connectives is the same thing as the class of *truth-functional* connectives.

A sentence ϕ is *extensional* if and only if its extension is determined by its syntax and the extensions of its parts. If $\phi \ldots \phi_n$ are extensional sentences and ❸ is an extensional connective, then any part of ❸($\phi \ldots \phi_n$) can be replaced by a coextensional expression (of the same syntactic category) to produce a sentence that has the same extension (i.e. truth-value) as ❸($\phi \ldots \phi_n$). Thus an extensional (i.e. truth-functional) connective ❸ with large scope permits the substitution *salva veritate* (henceforth *s.v.*) within its scope of coextensional terms, predicates, and sentences (assuming, of course, that the term, predicate, or sentence being replaced is not within the scope of any non-extensional expression).

The issues I want to address require that we entertain the possibility of connectives (in English or formalized languages designed to mirror parts of English) that are non-extensional. Quine and Davidson have used slingshot arguments to cast doubt upon the viability of such connectives. I want to bracket such worries for a short while; all that is required for immediate purposes is a grasp of the *intended* difference between extensional and (purportedly) non-extensional connectives.

The following are sometimes treated as non-extensional connectives (on some of their uses): "necessarily" ($\square$), "possibly" ($\lozenge$), "probably", "provably", "since", "because", "before", "after", "sometimes", "usually", "today", "yesterday", "intentionally", "voluntarily", "freely".[6] For the moment it is sufficient to appreciate that if such expressions are connectives, their *non-extensional*

---

[6] Of course it is possible to treat (e.g.) "necessarily" and "possibly" as quantifiers (over "possible worlds") rather than connectives in my sense.

nature is easily established: sentences with the same extension may not always be substituted for one another *s.v.* within their scopes. For example, if □ were extensional, then □φ and □ψ would have the same truth-value whenever φ and ψ had the same truth-value. But this is not so. The sentences "9 > 7" and "Socrates died in 399 BC" have the same truth-value, but (10) and (11) do not:

(10) □(9 > 7)
(11) □(Socrates died in 399 BC).

Hence □ is not extensional. As we might say, the truth-value of □φ depends upon features of φ other than its truth-value (see below). The intended difference between extensional and non-extensional connectives is clear: extensional connectives permit the substitution *s.v.* of coextensional sentences; non-extensional connectives do not. (Equivalently, a connective ❽ is extensional if and only if it has a complete truth-table.)

In order to keep things as simple as possible and avoid digressions on semantical issues orthogonal to those being discussed here, let us bracket the existence of any purportedly non-extensional operators that are not connectives (e.g. adjectives and verbs such as "fake", "alleged", "fear", and "want"). Where *X* is a particular occurrence of an expression, we can now say that (i) *X* occupies an *extensional position*, and (ii) *X* occurs in an *extensional context* if and only if (iii) *X* is not within the scope of any non-extensional connective.

6.4 INTENSIONAL CONNECTIVES

If ❽ is an *n*-place extensional connective, then the extension of ❽(φ ... φ$_n$) is determined by the extensions of ❽ and φ ... φ$_n$. But suppose ❽ is a *non-extensional* connective; what properties of ❽ and φ ... φ$_n$ determine the extension of ❽(φ ... φ$_n$)? Inspired by Frege's distinction between *sense* and *reference*, many philosophers have attempted to answer this question, for particular values of ❽, by postulating a second level of "semantic value" to supplement extensions. For example, Carnap (1947) and those he has influenced have suggested that each expression has an *intension* as well as an extension, and that for certain interesting non-extensional connectives ❽, the extension of ❽ together with the *intensions* of φ ... φ$_n$ determine the extension of ❽(φ ... φ$_n$).

Consider the modal connectives □ and ◇ (where □φ is understood as ~◇~φ). Allowing ourselves talk of so-called "possible worlds" for a moment, one common idea is to regard the intension of an expression as *a function from possible worlds to extensions*. On such an account, (i) the intension of a singular term is a (possibly partial) function from possible worlds to *objects*;[7] (ii) the intension of an *n*-place predicate is a function from possible worlds to *sets of ordered n-tuples of objects*; and (iii) the intension of a sentence is a function from possible worlds to *truth-values*.

As far as □ and ◇ are concerned, the answer to our original question—"if ❽ is a non-extensional connective, what properties of ❽ and φ . . . $φ_n$ determine the extension of ❽(φ . . . $φ_n$)?"—is now within sight. The extension of, say, □φ is determined (in part) by the extension of □. And the extension of □ must be a function from something ξ to the potential extensions of □φ, i.e. a function from ξ to truth-values. Clearly ξ cannot be the potential extension (i.e. truth-value) of φ, for otherwise □ would be an extensional connective. But if ξ is the potential *intension* of φ, everything fits together perfectly. The extension of □ is simply a function from intensions to truth-values, i.e. a function *from* functions from possible worlds to truth-values *to* truth-values. Thus the extension of □φ is determined by (*a*) the *extension* of □, and (*b*) the *intension* of φ. We say that □ and ◇ are *intensional* connectives because they operate on the *intensions* of their operands.

Where *X* is a particular occurrence of an expression, we can say that (i) *X* occupies an *intensional position*, and (ii) *X* occurs in an *intensional context*, if and only if (*a*) *X* is within the scope of an intensional connective, and (*b*) any connective within whose scope *X* lies is either intensional or extensional.

Carnap (1947) was very clear in his use of "extensional" and "intensional", recognizing that the class of non-extensional contexts does not collapse into the class of intensional contexts. However, many philosophers and linguists use "intensional" and "intensionality" in ways that are much looser, thereby encouraging talk of the "intensionality of propositional attitude reports", and talk of attitude constructions involving "intensional operators", and so on.

---

7 If all singular terms are "rigid designators" in Kripke's (1980) sense, then the extension of a singular term will be a *constant* (but, again, possibly partial) function.

(This surely has something to do with the fact that "intensional" and "intentional" are homophonic.) Such talk muddies already cloudy waters and can lead to philosophical mistakes engendered by running together modal and psychological contexts. There is no obvious reason to think of the logical or metaphysical modalities and psychological attitudes as sharing a logic—they *don't*—nor is there any reason to think that talk of "possible worlds" is of any help in thinking about the semantics of propositional attitude reports—it *isn't*. If we need a technical word to use in connection with attitude reports and constructions, we can settle for "atensional", applied uniformly to contexts, constructions, and operators (including connectives). To the extent that we want to group non-extensional contexts, constructions, and operators together, there is already a perfectly good word: "non-extensional". There is only misery in store for those who would too easily lump together constructions involving the attitudes and those involving logical or metaphysical modality.

At this point we do well to recall how possible worlds and intensions have been related to several other notions in the literature. (1) Whereas some philosophers have been inclined to view possible worlds as primitive, others have been tempted to view them as sets of (consistent) states of affairs. Still others, such as Fine (1982), have been tempted to see them as "very large facts". (2) A common idea is to equate the intension of a sentence with the *proposition* it expresses and characterize the notion of a proposition in terms of *possible worlds*. The basic idea is this: if the intension of a sentence is a function from possible worlds to truth-values, then (assuming an extensional characterization of functions) the intension of a sentence can be viewed as a set of possible worlds, namely those at which the sentence is true. And this set of worlds can be called a "proposition". This notion of a proposition corresponds to the common philosophical notion of the *truth-condition* of a sentence, i.e. the condition under which it is true. Thus we reach the familiar positions that (i) the intension of a sentence is its truth-condition, and (ii) the truth-value of the intensional sentence $\Box \phi$ depends upon ϕ's *truth-condition* (whereas the truth-value of the extensional sentence $\sim\phi$ depends only upon ϕ's *truth-value*). This will suggest to some—for example, those who view the notion of the truth-condition of a sentence as more basic than the notion of a possible world—that we can talk perfectly well about the intensions of expressions without invoking possible worlds at all.

7

Inference Principles

7.1 INTRODUCTORY REMARKS

There is an elegant strategy, essentially due to Quine (1953*e*, 1960), for investigating non-extensional constructions: (i) take an arbitrary *n*-place sentence connective ⊛, an arbitrary truth-functional sentence φ, and an arbitrary compound sentence ⊛(... φ ...); (ii) examine the deductive consequences of replacing the occurrence of φ in ⊛(... φ ...) by another sentence φ′ obtained directly from φ using inference principles that are valid in truth-functional contexts. Importantly, on this strategy the inference principles are applied *not* to ⊛(... φ ...) itself but to an occurrence of the extensional sentence φ occurrence within such a sentence, i.e. an occurrence of φ within the scope of ⊛. With this in mind, I want to set out, in a rather unorthodox way, and with some unorthodox terminology, various inference principles common in extensional logic.

7.2 A PRINCIPLE OF SUBSTITUTIVITY FOR MATERIAL EQUIVALENTS

Principles of inference are meant to preserve truth. Two philosophically useful inference principles that can be employed in extensional contexts concern the substitution of coextensional sentences and coextensional singular terms.

The Principle of Substitutivity for Material Equivalents (PSME) can be put thus:

PSME: $\phi \equiv \psi$

$\Sigma(\phi)$

$\Sigma(\psi)$.

For present purposes this should be read as saying that if two sentences φ and ψ have the same truth-value and Σ(φ) is a true sentence containing at least one occurrence of φ, then Σ(ψ) is also true, where Σ(ψ) is the result of replacing at least one occurrence of φ in Σ(φ) by ψ.

A *context* is extensional if and only if it permits the substitution *salva veritate* (*s.v.*) of coextensional terms, predicates, and sentences. So it is a truism that PSME is a principle that validly can be used on a sentence φ occurring in an extensional context. As shorthand for this, let us say that extensional contexts are +PSME (as opposed to –PSME).

By an unproblematic and extremely useful extension of terminology, let us say that any extensional connective ⊗ is +PSME in the sense that ⊗ permits the use of PSME on any sentence φ within its scope (assuming, of course, that φ does not occur within the scope of any non-extensional connective). To avoid confusion, let me spell out the idea precisely:

> An *n*-place connective ⊗ is +PSME if and only if for any true sentence ⊗(... Σ(φ) ...) in which Σ(φ) is an extensional sentence occurring as an operand of ⊗, if φ and ψ are sentences with the same truth-value, then replacing the contained sentence Σ(φ) by Σ(ψ) in ⊗(... Σ(φ) ...) yields a true sentence ⊗(... Σ(ψ) ...).

7.3 A PRINCIPLE OF SUBSTITUTIVITY FOR SINGULAR TERMS

The Principle of Substitutivity for Singular Terms (PSST) can be put thus:

PSST: α = β   or: Σ(α)
         Σ(α)   ~Σ(β)
        ─────   ──────
         Σ(β).   α ≠ β

This just says that if two singular terms α and β have the same extension (i.e. if α=β is a true identity statement) and Σ(α) is a true sentence containing at least one occurrence of α, then Σ(β) is also true, where Σ(β) is the result of replacing at least one occurrence of α in Σ(α) by β.

There is a manifest difficulty in applying PSST: it presupposes a clear answer to the question *which noun phrases that occur in the grammatical singular are singular terms?*[1] Let us suppose, provisionally, the class of singular terms to comprise just the following: (i) ordinary proper names (assuming they are not truncated descriptions); (ii) the simple demonstratives "this" and "that"; (iii) complex demonstratives such as "this man" and "that man"; (iv) the first- and second-person singular pronouns "I", "me", and "you"; and (v) at least some occurrences of the third-person singular pronouns "he", "him", "she", "her", and "it" (including those occurrences that Quine (1960) argues function as variables hooked up to quantifiers). In order to get things moving, I simply stipulate that a description such as "the prince" is Russellian, hence *not* a singular term but a quantificational noun phrase along with its syntactic siblings "a prince", "one prince", "no prince", "some prince", "each prince", etc., reserving the right to redraw the boundary of the class of singular terms should this provisional characterization prove to be lacking in any way.

A context is extensional only if it permits the substitution *s.v.* of coextensional singular terms. So it is a truism that PSST is a valid rule of inference for terms occurring in extensional contexts. As shorthand for this, let us say that extensional contexts are +PSST (as opposed to –PSST).

In accordance with the convention introduced in connection with PSME, let us say that any extensional connective ❽ is +PSST in the sense that ❽ permits the use of PSST on any sentence φ within its scope (assuming, of course, that φ does not occur within the scope of any non-extensional connective). More precisely:

> An *n*-place connective ❽ is +PSST if and only if for any true sentence ❽(... Σ(α) ...) in which Σ(α) is an extensional sentence occurring as an operand of ❽, if α and β are coextensional singular terms, then replacing the contained sentence Σ(α) by the sentence Σ(β) in ❽(... Σ(α) ...) yields a true sentence ❽(... Σ(β) ...).

Of course, a context or connective that is +PSME is also +PSST; but

---

[1] There is no *syntactical* criterion for being a singular term. "Socrates", "he", "that prince", "the prince", "a prince", "one prince", "only one prince", "no prince", "no one prince", "some prince", "each prince", and "every prince" are all grammatically singular: we need to make a decision based on *semantic* arguments or judgements.

nothing on the table guarantees the converse (an argument would be needed to demonstrate it).[2]

7.4 A PRINCIPLE OF SUBSTITUTIVITY FOR LOGICAL EQUIVALENTS

Following Tarski, and common practice, let us say that ϕ and ψ are logically equivalent if, and only if, ϕ and ψ have the same truth-value in every model. We can now state another rule of inference, the *Principle of Substitutivity for Logical Equivalents* (PSLE):

PSLE: $\phi \models \dashv \psi$
$$\frac{\Sigma(\phi)}{\Sigma(\psi)}$$

For present purposes this should be read as saying that if two sentences ϕ and ψ are logically equivalent and $\Sigma(\phi)$ is a true sentence containing at least one occurrence of ϕ, then $\Sigma(\psi)$ is also true, where $\Sigma(\psi)$ is the result of replacing at least one occurrence of ϕ in $\Sigma(\phi)$ by ψ.

PSLE is, of course, a rule that validly can be used on a sentence ϕ occurring in an extensional context (i.e. a context that is +PSME). As shorthand for this, let us say that extensional contexts and extensional connectives are +PSLE (as opposed to –PSLE).

Continuing with the useful extension of terminology introduced earlier, let us say that any extensional connective ❽ is +PSLE in the sense that ❽ permits the use of +PSLE on any sentence ϕ within its scope (assuming, of course, that ϕ does not occur within the scope of any non-extensional connective). More precisely:

---

[2] Similarly, no argument for the conclusion that intensional connectives are PSST has emerged. In earlier work (1995) I argued that intensional connectives are readily proved +PSST by the following argument: If α and β are terms that both refer to x, and $\Re$ is a one-place extensional predicate, then $\Re\alpha$ and $\Re\beta$ have the same truth-condition: $\Re\alpha$ and $\Re\beta$ are both true if and only if x is $\Re$. If ❽ is an intensional operator, then by definition the truth-value of ❽$\Re\alpha$ depends upon no feature of $\Re\alpha$ but its the truth-condition; and the truth-value of ❽$\Re\beta$ depends upon no feature of $\Re\beta$ but its truth-condition. But $\Re\alpha$ and $\Re\alpha$ have the same truth-condition (they are both true if and only if x is $\Re$). Hence ❽$\Re\alpha$ is true if and only if ❽$\Re\beta$ is true. Hence ❽ is +PSST. Unfortunately the argument either trades on an equivocation in connection with 'truth-condition' or else presupposes its own conclusion.

An n-place connective ⊗ is +PSLE if and only if for any true sentence ⊗(... $\Sigma(\phi)$ ...) in which $\Sigma(\phi)$ is an extensional sentence occurring as an operand of ⊗, if ϕ and ψ are logically equivalent sentences, then replacing the contained sentence $\Sigma(\phi)$ by $\Sigma(\psi)$ in the original sentence ⊗(... $\Sigma(\phi)$ ...) yields a true sentence ⊗(... $\Sigma(\psi)$ ...).

The modal connectives □ and ◇ are +PSLE when understood as expressing logical or analytic modalities; when understood as expressing metaphysical modalities, it is common to see them as +PSLE (although, this being philosophy, there are dissenters).

7.5 AN INFERENCE PRINCIPLE INVOLVING "EXPORTATION"

The inference principles examined hitherto involve replacing one expression in a formula by another, though it is not necessary to characterize the principles in that way. I want now to set out an inference principle that cannot be characterized in terms of such a simple substitution, a principle often known as EG, "existential generalization". In view of the unorthodox way I am setting out inference principles, some care must be taken here. For present purposes, I want to state what *I* shall call "EG" as follows,

EG: $\dfrac{\Sigma(x/\alpha)}{\exists x\Sigma(x)}$

where $\Sigma(x)$ is any extensional formula containing *at least one* occurrence of the variable x and $\Sigma(x/\alpha)$ is the result of replacing *every* occurrence of the variable x in $\Sigma(x)$ by the (closed) singular term α (there may be other occurrences of α in $\Sigma(x)$ as well).

EG is a valid inference principle when applied to extensional sentences. An extensional connective ⊗ is +EG in the sense that ⊗ permits the use of EG on any formula ϕ within its scope (assuming, of course, that ϕ does not occur within the scope of any non-extensional connective). More precisely:

An n-place connective ⊗ is +EG if and only if for any true sentence ⊗(... $\Sigma(x/\alpha)$ ...) in which $\Sigma(x/\alpha)$ is an extensional sentence occurring as an operand of ⊗, $\exists x⊗($... $\Sigma(x)$ ...) is also true.

Questions about propositional attitude contexts in connection with EG are notoriously complex, as Quine (1943, 1953c, 1956, 1960) has stressed. For the sake of argument, assume that (1) is true and (2) is false:

(1) Philip is unaware that Tully denounced Catiline
(2) Philip is unaware that Cicero denounced Catiline.

To use Quine's terminology, the difference in truth-value indicates that attitude contexts are "referentially opaque" in the sense of being –PSST. (There is a wrinkle here because Quine sometimes uses examples involving definite descriptions to exemplify referential opacity, especially when considering modal contexts). Quine's main worry is the intelligibility of an example such as (3), the truth of which should be inferable from (1) if attitude contexts are +EG:

(3) ∃x(Philip is unaware that x denounced Catiline).

Now Quine asks his famous question: "What is this object, that denounced Catiline without Philip yet having become aware of the fact? Tully, i.e., Cicero? But to suppose this would conflict with the fact that [2] is false" (1943: 118).[3]

---

[3] Quine notes that we should not confuse the seemingly unintelligible sentence "∃x(Philip is unaware that x denounced Catiline)" with the false sentence "Philip is unaware that ∃x(x denounced Catiline)". This remark raises an interesting issue. Notice that the following inference is valid:

(i) Philip believes that Cicero denounced Catiline
  _____
  Philip believes that ∃x(x denounced Catiline).

But attempting to capture its validity in terms of an inference principle meant to function as a "smaller scope" version of EG has obvious pitfalls, not least of which is the existence of elements that import negation, as Quine's (1943: 148) observation about the invalidity of the following brings out:

(ii) Philip is unaware that Tully denounced Catiline
  _____
  Philip is unaware that ∃x(x denounced Catiline).

The contrast between the validity of (i) and the invalidity of (ii) is obviously connected to the negation imported by "is unaware"—we find the same with "doubts", "is sceptical", "does not believe", etc. And of course the invalidity of (ii) mirrors that of (iii):

(iii) ~ Tully admired Catiline
  _____
  ~ ∃x(x admired Catiline).

7.6 A PRINCIPLE OF SUBSTITUTIVITY FOR DEFINITE DESCRIPTIONS

I turn now to two substitution rules that are less familiar. If definite descriptions are treated in accordance with Russell's theory—or any other theory that does not treat such devices as singular terms—then, as Russell and others have pointed out, substitutions involving descriptions are not licensed directly by PSST.[4] This matter merits some attention as philosophers who appeal or profess allegiance to Russell's Theory of Descriptions often fail to do justice to the point and thereby run into logical difficulties of a type that will soon concern us.

On Russell's account, what might look like an identity statement involving one or two descriptive phrases is really no such thing. An identity statement has the general form α=β, where α and β are singular terms. The way PSST was stated, it is the truth of a statement of this form that licenses its applications. But, on a Russellian analysis of descriptive phrases, the logical forms of sentences of the superficial grammatical forms "*a* = the *F*" and "the *G* = the *F*" are given by the following quantificational formulae:

(1) $\exists x(\forall y(Fy \ldots y=x) \bullet \underline{x=a})$
(2) $\exists x(\forall y(Fy \ldots y=x) \bullet \exists u(\forall v(Gv \ldots v=u) \bullet \underline{u=x}))$.

And neither (1) nor (2) is an identity statement; each is a quantificational statement that *contains* an important identity statement (underlined) as a proper part.

The real force of this point emerges once we reflect on the nature of derivations in first-order logic with identity. The inference in (3) is obviously valid (on the standard definition of validity):

(3) [1] Cicero = Tully
[2] Cicero snored

[3] Tully snored.

Similarly, in modal systems one wants to be able to infer from $\Diamond Fa$ to $\Diamond \exists x Fx$, but not from $\sim\Diamond Fa$ to $\sim\Diamond \exists x Fx$. There are difficult issues here which, to my mind, have not been satisfactorily resolved in the literature.

[4] See in particular Russell (1905, esp. pp. 47 and 51–2), Whitehead and Russell (1925, *14), Church (1942), Smullyan (1947, 1948), and Fitch (1949, 1950).

In order to provide a formal derivation of the conclusion from the premisses, we can use PSST, which sanctions a direct move from [1] and [2] to [3]:

1　　[1] $c = t$　　　　　　　　　　　　　premiss
2　　[2] Sc　　　　　　　　　　　　　　premiss
1,2　[3] St　　　　　　　　　　　　　　1, 2, PSST.

Now consider (4), which looks like a very similar argument.

(4) [1] Cicero = the greatest Roman orator
　　[2] Cicero snored
　　―――――――――――――――――――――
　　[3] The greatest Roman orator snored.

Clearly this is valid. But—and this is the important point—*if* definite descriptions are Russellian, then they are not singular terms, so we cannot use PSST to move *directly* from lines [1] and [2] to line [3] in the formal analogue of this argument in first-order logic with identity. Reading Rx as "x is greatest Roman orator", it might be tempting to set out a derivation as follows:

1　　[1] $c = \iota x R x$　　　　　　　　　　premiss
2　　[2] Sc　　　　　　　　　　　　　　premiss
1,2　[3] $S\iota x R x$　　　　　　　　　　　1, 2, PSST.

The Russellian accepts that the conclusion follows from the premisses, but rejects this particular derivation: it is illegitimate because PSST can be invoked only where we have an identity statement, and an identity statement has *singular terms* on either side of the identity sign. As Church (1942) points out (in the course of scolding Quine (1941*a*) for employing this sort of direct inference in a purportedly non-extensional context): "On the basis of *Principia* or of Quine's own *Mathematical Logic* . . . any formal deduction must refer to the unabbreviated forms of the sentences in question" (p. 101). Premiss [1] is not an identity statement; on Russell's account it is, to use Quine's (1941*a*) wording again, "mere shorthand" for a complex quantificational statement; indeed, the purported derivation is just shorthand for the following illegitimate derivation:

1　　[1] $\exists x(\forall y(Ry \equiv y=x) \bullet x=c)$　　premiss
2　　[2] Sc　　　　　　　　　　　　　　premiss
1,2　[3] $\exists x(\forall y(Ry \equiv y=x) \bullet Sx)$　　1, 2, PSST.

To say that the derivation is illegitimate is to say that PSST does not sanction a direct move from line [2] to line [3] on the basis of the truth of the entry on line [1]; it is *not* to say that the argument is invalid—it *is* valid—nor is it to say that one cannot *derive* the entry on line [3] from the entries on lines [1] and [2] using standard rules of inference, which include, of course, PSST. Indeed, it is a routine exercise—the logical and philosophical importance of which is stressed in better introductory logic texts—to provide the relevant derivation:

1	[1]	$c = \imath x R x$	premiss
2	[2]	Sc	premiss
1	[3]	$\exists x (\forall y (R y \equiv y{=}x) \bullet c{=}x)$	1, def. of $\imath x$
4	[4]	$(\forall y (R y \equiv y{=}\alpha) \bullet c{=}\alpha)$	assumption
4	[5]	$c = \alpha$	4, $\bullet$ –ELIM
2,4	[6]	$S\alpha$	2, 5, PSST[5]
4	[7]	$\forall y (R y \equiv y{=}\alpha)$	4, $\bullet$ –ELIM
2,4	[8]	$(\forall y (R y \equiv y{=}\alpha) \bullet S\alpha)$	6, 7, $\bullet$ –INTR
2,4	[9]	$\exists x (\forall y (R y \equiv y{=}x) \bullet S x)$	8, EG
1,2	[10]	$\exists x (\forall y (R y \equiv y{=}x) \bullet S x)$	3, 4, 9, EI
1,2	[11]	$S \imath x R x$	10, def. of $\imath x$.

Within a purely extensional system it would be tedious to proceed in this way every time one wanted to prove something involving one or more descriptions, and it would be practical to have a fool-proof method of shortening such proofs. Whitehead and Russell recognized this and reduced their workload by demonstrating that, although descriptions are not genuine singular terms (in their system), if a predicate F applies to exactly one object (i.e. if it has exactly one thing in its extension), in truth-functional contexts the description $\imath x F x$ can be treated *as if* it were a singular term for derivational purposes. As noted earlier, the following theorem to this effect is proved by them for truth-functional contexts:

$$^*14.15 \quad (\imath x \phi = \alpha) \supset \{\Sigma(\imath x \phi) \equiv \Sigma(\alpha)\}.$$

(Recall Whitehead and Russell's convention that absence of the

---

[5] This particular application of PSST assumes that variables and temporary names function as genuine singular terms. I am fully at ease with this assumption, as, in effect, were Whitehead and Russell. It is not obvious how it might be contested, but it is an assumption nonetheless.

scope indicator [ιxφ] signals that the description has minimal scope.) *14.15 says that if the individual that α stands for is the unique object satisfying a formula φ, then one can, as Whitehead and Russell sometimes put it, "verbally substitute" α for the description ιxφ, or vice versa (in truth-functional contexts). (Obviously the derivation given above can be recast to provide a proof of the same thing.) If descriptions are treated in accordance with Russell's theory, it is a mistake to think that when one performs a "verbal substitution" of this sort, one is simply making a direct application of PSST. *14.15 is *not* PSST; it is a *derived rule of inference* that can be used in truth-functional contexts, a rule that licenses certain substitutions when the referent of a particular singular term is identical to the unique object satisfying a particular formula. Naturally, Whitehead and Russell prove the analogue of *14.15 where both noun phrases are descriptions:

$$14.16 \quad (\iota x\phi = \iota x\psi) \supset \{\Sigma(\iota x\phi) \equiv \Sigma(\iota x\psi)\}.$$

This says that if the unique object satisfying a formula φ is identical to the unique object satisfying a formula ψ, then one can "verbally substitute" the description ιxφ for the description ιxψ, or vice versa (in truth-functional contexts).

On the basis of *14.15 and *14.16, we can add a fourth inference rule (actually, a triple of rules) to our collection, ι–SUBSTITUTION:

ι–SUBS:	$\iota x\phi = \iota x\psi$	$\iota x\phi = \alpha$	$\iota x\phi = \alpha$
	$\Sigma(\iota x\phi)$	$\Sigma(\iota x\phi)$	$\Sigma(\alpha)$
	$\Sigma(\iota x\psi)$	$\Sigma(\alpha)$	$\Sigma(\iota x\phi).$

ι–SUBS is a valid rule of inference when the description ιxφ occurs in an extensional context. As shorthand for this, let us say that extensional contexts are +ι-SUBS (as opposed to −ι-SUBS). Continuing with our useful extension of terminology, let us note that any extensional connective ❽ is +ι-SUBS in the sense that ❽ permits the use of ι-SUBS on any sentence φ within its scope (assuming, of course, that φ does not occur within the scope of any non-extensional connective). More precisely:

An *n*-place connective ❽ is +ι-SUBS if and only if for any true sentence ❽(... Σ(ιxφ) ...) in which Σ(ιxφ) is an extensional sentence occurring as an operand of ❽, if $\iota x\phi = \iota x\psi$, then replacing the contained sentence $\Sigma(\iota x\phi)$ by the sentence $\Sigma(\iota x\psi)$ in the original sentence ❽$(\ldots \Sigma(\iota x\phi) \ldots)$ yields a true sentence ❽$(\ldots \Sigma(\iota x\psi) \ldots)$.

(There is no need to build in the second and third allomorphs of ι-SUBS here.) No residual issues concerning scope arise here in connection with those theories of descriptions for which matters of scope are important (e.g. Russell's): scopes remain constant with respect to ❽. Of course, if descriptions are treated as singular terms, ι-SUBS is redundant, its work already done by PSST.

It is surely only *because* truth-functional contexts are +ι-SUBS that Whitehead and Russell introduce descriptive terms in *Principia* (and through them condensed expressions of the form $R'x$): they simplify both formulae and proofs. Adding such rules to an extensional deductive system, we can now formally capture the inference from "Cicero = the greatest Roman orator" and "Cicero snored" to 'the greatest Roman orator snored':

1	[1]	$c = \iota x R x$	premiss
2	[2]	Sc	premiss
1,2	[3]	$S\iota x R x$	1, 2, ι-SUBS.

As far as truth-functional contexts are concerned, there are no interesting reflexes of the formal differences between PSST and ι-SUBS for the Russellian. Only in so far as there are linguistic contexts and connectives that are +PSST but –ι-SUBS does the distinction come alive. It is common for Russellians to view the one-place modal connectives □ and ◇ as +PSST and –ι-SUBS, at least when these devices are understood as expressing necessity and possibility in the metaphysical sense expounded by Kripke (1971, 1980).[6] It is clear that □ and ◇, so understood, are -ι-SUBS. Consider the following argument:

---

[6] Kripke's metaphysical conceptions of necessity and possibility are certainly *not* the strict (logical or analytic) conceptions Quine (1941*a*, 1943, 1947, 1953*a*, *c*) was originally attacking. However Quine (1953*c*, 1960, 1961, 1962) does seem to see that a move from logical to metaphysical modality is what will be needed to restore substitutivity. There are many delicate issues here. I made a preliminary attempt to straighten out the logical and semantic issues in Neale (2000). A more detailed examination will be included in *Possibilities*.

(5) $\Box(9 > 7)$
    9 = the number of planets
    ───────────────────────────
    $\Box$(the number of planets > 7).

There is certainly a way of reading the conclusion of this argument
in such a way that it is false, and hence reading the argument as
invalid (its premisses are true). Rendering the argument as follows
makes this clear:

1   [1] $\Box(9 > 7)$ premiss
2   [2] $9 = \iota x P x$ premiss
1,2 [3] $\Box(\iota x P x > 7)$ 1, 2, $\Box$+ι-SUBS

where (i) the description $\iota x P x$ does duty for "the number of planets" and (ii) "$\Box$+ι-SUBS" is shorthand for "the assumption that $\Box$ is
+ι-SUBS", and (iii) the absence of any scope indicator [$\iota x P x$] signals
that the description has small scope, in accordance with Whitehead
and Russell's convention, discussed earlier. On Russell's account,
the conclusion $\Box(\iota x P x > 7)$ is just shorthand for (6):

(6) $\Box \exists x (\forall y (P y \equiv y = x) \bullet x > 7)$.

But (6) is not true, so the argument, thus rendered, is invalid. This
is enough to show that $\Box$ is −ι-SUBS; if $\Box$ were +ι-SUBS, the description "the number of planets", $\iota x P x$, could replace "9" *s.v.* within
the scope of $\Box$.

The fact that the conclusion of (5) is ambiguous in respect of
scope does not impinge in any way on the point just made, which
was simply that $\Box$ is not +ι-SUBS. The ambiguity in question is
captured very nicely by a Russellian analysis of descriptions. If the
description has small scope, as in (6) (which spells out $\Box \iota x P x > 7$),
we get a falsehood; but if it has large scope as in (7) (which spells
out [$\iota x P x$]$\Box(\iota x P x > 7)$), we get a truth:

(7) $\exists x (\forall y (P y \equiv y = x) \bullet \Box(x > 7))$.

Notoriously, Quine has raised worries about the unintelligibility of
(7); but this matter need not detain us either. Neither the alleged
unintelligibility nor the alleged *truth* of (7) plays any role in establishing that, upon a Russellian treatment of descriptions, $\Box$ is −ι-
SUBS. (In fact, (7) *is* derivable from "$\Box(9 > 7)$" and "$9 = \iota x P x$"
assuming $\Box$ is +PSST. See below.)

As long as descriptions are treated in accordance with Russell's theory, the failure of □ to be +ι-SUBS does not mean that □ is –PSST. Indeed, it is plausible to suppose that □ is +PSST. As Kripke has argued, proper names refer *rigidly*—an expression refers rigidly to an object X if and only if it refers to X in every (metaphysically) possible world in which X exists. Hence co-referring names, since they are rigid, are intersubstitutable within the scopes of □ and ◇ *s.v.*:

(8) □ Cicero is human
  Cicero = Tully
  _____
  □ Tully is human.

We can set out (8) as follows, where "□+PSST" is short for "the assumption that □ is +PSST":

1	[1]	□ Cicero is human	premiss
2	[2]	Cicero = Tully	premiss
1,2	[3]	□ Tully is human	1, 2, □+PSST.[7]

Kaplan (1989*a*) has argued that simple demonstratives and indexicals such as "this", "that", "he" (on some of its uses), "I", and "you" also refer rigidly (relative to the setting of contextual parameters). To claim that □ and ◇, understood metaphysically, are

---

[7] The validity of (8) and the invalidity of (5) (on the intended reading) raise interesting issues for Frege. Since (8) is valid, "Cicero" and "Tully" refer to their customary references in "□ Cicero is human" and "□ Tully is human". But Frege is surely precluded from saying that "Cicero is human" and "Tully is human" refer to their customary references (Truth) as they occur in these modal sentences, for otherwise *any sentence* with the same reference (i.e. any true sentence) would be substitutable *s.v.* for e.g. "Cicero is human" when it is subordinate to □ in this way, making □ truth-functional. It seems that Frege must say at this point that names have their customary references when they occur within the scope of □, while *n*-place predicates in the same environments refer to neither their customary references nor their customary senses, but to functions from *n*-tuples of objects to thoughts (i.e. to functions from *n*-tuples of customary references of singular terms to customary senses of sentences). Given the identity conditions for thoughts suggested by Frege's letter to Husserl (discussed in Ch. 3), this looks like a promising approach. But the invalidity of (5) shows that there is still more work for Frege to do: he must give up the idea that descriptions are singular terms. For if descriptions are singular terms and singular terms refer to their customary references in modal contexts, then (5) should be just as valid as (8). Accepting Russell's position that descriptions are not singular terms would be genuine progress on Frege's part. Not only would it allow Frege to deal with modal contexts, it would also provide him with the means of explaining the very real scope ambiguities involving descriptions in modal and attitude contexts in natural language, something that appears to elude him if descriptions are treated as singular terms. Of course, it is debatable how much Frege cared about the semantics of natural language.

+PSST is to claim that *all* singular terms refer rigidly; and once descriptions are removed from the class of singular terms, as the Russellian insists, the case looks plausible.

Notice that if $\Box$ is +PSST, then the validity of the following is explained:

(9) $9 = \iota x P x$
  $\Box(9 > 7)$
  _____
  $[\iota x P x]\ \Box(\iota x P x > 7)$.

This is readily seen by examining (i) the unabbreviated form of the argument, and (ii) a proof set out in the unabbreviated language.

(i) On a Russellian account of descriptions, the argument in (9) is just shorthand for the following:

(10) $\exists x(\forall y(Py \equiv y=x) \bullet x=9)$
  $\Box 9 > 7$
  _____
  $\exists x(\forall y(Py \equiv y=x) \bullet \Box\ (x > 7))$.

Notice that no descriptive material has been inserted within the scope of $\Box$ in the move from line [2] to line [3]. What *has* been inserted, in place of "9", is a *variable*. What licenses this? The assumption that $\Box$ is +PSST.

(ii) This becomes thoroughly transparent when the full proof—which does not rely on the derived inference principle ι-SUBS—is set out:[8]

1	[1]	$\exists x(\forall y(Py \equiv y=x) \bullet x=9)$	premiss
2	[2]	$\Box\ (9 > 7)$	premiss
3	[3]	$(\forall y(Py \equiv y=\alpha) \bullet \alpha=9)$	assumption
3	[4]	$\alpha = 9$	3, −ELIM
2,3	[5]	$\Box(\alpha > 7)$	2, 4, $\Box$+PSST
3	[6]	$\forall y(Py \equiv y=\alpha)$	3, −ELIM
2,3	[7]	$(\forall y(Py \equiv y=\alpha)\ \Box(\alpha > 7))$	5, 6, −INTR
2,3	[8]	$\exists x(\forall y(Py \equiv y=x)\ \Box\ (x > 7))$	7, $\Box$+EG
1,2	[9]	$\exists x(\forall y(Py \equiv y=x)\ \Box\ (x > 7))$	2, 3, 8, $\Box$+EI.

_____

[8] Let me stress that I am just making an observation: *if* (i) descriptions are Russellian, and *if* (ii) $\Box$ is +PSST, then (iii) the conclusion of (10) is straightforwardly deducible from its premisses; the *intelligibility* of such a quantification (which Quine has contested) is something that is still *sub judice*.

Analogously, a proof can be constructed where □ is replaced by, for example, "George IV wondered whether", thereby capturing the analogous points made by Russell concerning contexts of propositional attitude. Indeed, it was surely this fact about Russell's Theory of Descriptions in connection with propositional attitude reports that tipped off modal logicians in the first place. Moreover, this explanation of how the adoption of Russell's Theory of Descriptions removes any threat to the claim that □ is +PSST is intimately connected to Gödel's explanation of how adopting the same theory instantly removes any threat that Russellian facts will collapse. This will become clear once a generalized, operator-version of Gödel's slingshot is on the table.

8

Logical Equivalence

8.1 INTRODUCTORY REMARKS

The proof implicit in Gödel's (1944) paper, which I discussed in Chapter 5, is certain to call to mind a better-known collapsing argument that appears in Church's (1943a) review of Carnap's (1942) book *Introduction to Semantics*. Carnap had broken with Frege by taking sentences to designate *propositions*—which he viewed as something like *states of affairs*—rather than truth-values. Church's argument was meant to show that sentences could not designate propositions in Carnap's system on pain of entailing that all true sentences designate the same one. (It seems likely that Carnap (1947) accepted Church's argument, now taking the referents of sentences to be truth-values rather than propositions.)

Although he appeals to what Kaplan (1964: 13) calls the "seemingly gratuitous assumption" that logically equivalent sentences have the same reference, Church sees his argument as a "reproduction in more exact form by means of Carnap's semantical terminology" of Frege's argument in support of the view that a sentence designates a truth-value (p. 301). Versions of Church's argument have been deployed to various philosophical ends. Quine (1953c, 1960) uses a version to undermine appeals to non-extensional sentence connectives; Davidson (1980, 1984) uses versions to undermine appeals to causal sentence connectives and to undermine appeals to facts and thereby correspondence theories.

A superficial difference between the arguments of Church (1943a) and Gödel (1944) is that Church uses the abstraction operator λx—where $\lambda x \phi$ is read as "the class of all x such that ϕ"—while Gödel (implicitly) uses the definite description operator ιx. (For the moment I shall adopt a syntax that respects Church's own use of the λ-operator, rather than the one that has come to be preferred in contemporary linguistic theory and which I shall use later to state rules of abstraction and elimination.) This superficial difference should not obscure the fact that Gödel and Church are in complete harmony on the matter of the elimination (by means of contextual definition) of purported term-forming devices such as ιx, λx, μx, Kx, etc. As already noted, Gödel points out that if ιx does not belong to the primitive symbols and receives a Russellian contextual definition, then it will not be possible to use his slingshot to demonstrate that if true sentences stand for facts, all true sentences stand for the same fact. Similarly, Church (1943a: 302–3) points out that if λx does not belong to the primitive symbols and receives a contextual definition such as the following,

(1) $\lambda x Fx = \lambda x Gx =_{df} \forall x(Fx \equiv Gx)$,

then it will not be possible to use his slingshot to demonstrate that if sentences designate propositions, all true sentences designate the same proposition.

An alternative to the contextual definition in (1) would be to view $\lambda x Fx$ as a definite description ("the set of things that are F") that can be analysed in accordance with Russell's theory. This suggestion has been made by Quine (1941a), who offers (2), and by Smullyan (1948) who offers (3), in which α is a class variable and $[\lambda x Fx]$ is a scope marker just like Whitehead and Russell's $[\iota x Fx]$:

(2) $\lambda x Fx =_{df} \iota\alpha(\forall x(Fx \equiv x \in \alpha))$
(3) $[\lambda x Fx] G\lambda x Fx =_{df} \exists\alpha(\forall x(Fx \equiv x \in \alpha) \cdot G\alpha)$.

Church, Quine, and Davidson recognize that it makes no difference whether descriptions or class abstracts are used in setting up the basic slingshot. For epistemological reasons, I have a preference for (first-order definable) description over abstraction, so I will examine only versions that make use of descriptions.

The *important* difference between the slingshots of Gödel and Church is that the latter draws upon purported *logical equivalences*, such as those between (4) and (5),

(4) ϕ
(5) $a = \iota x(x=a \cdot \phi)$

or those between (4) and (6),

(6) $\iota x(x=a) = \iota x(x=a \bullet \phi)$.

The net effect of this is that Church, Quine, and Davidson make use of a more permissive logical manoeuvre than Gödel.

8.2 THE QUINEAN STRATEGY

We are now ready to begin investigating the logic of purportedly non-extensional connectives using the following Quinean strategy: (i) take an arbitrary n-place connective $\textcircled{8}$, an arbitrary extensional sentence ϕ, and an arbitrary compound sentence $\textcircled{8}(\ldots \phi \ldots)$; and then (ii) examine the deductive consequences of replacing the occurrence of ϕ in $\textcircled{8}(\ldots \phi \ldots)$ by another sentence ϕ' obtained directly from ϕ using inference principles known to be valid in truth-functional contexts. The inference principles are applied *not* to $\textcircled{8}(\ldots \phi \ldots)$ itself but to an occurrence of the extensional sentence ϕ within such a sentence, i.e. a sentence ϕ within the scope of $\textcircled{8}$.

I now ask the reader to put out of mind thoughts about any particular non-extensional connective. I want to proceed in the most abstract way possible so as to avoid being distracted by prejudicial thoughts about the semantics of this or that connective, which may have something to do with one's views about, say, necessity, causation, time, facts, or states of affairs, or orthogonal semantic worries about such things as rigidity, direct reference, or semantic innocence.[1]

The Quinean proof I am about to set out is going to be the central component of various deductive arguments meant to show that an inconsistency results when one posits a non-extensional connective that freely permits the use of ι-SUBS (or its analogue for class abstracts) together with some other inference principle within its scope. The inconsistency arises because (roughly) descriptions and abstracts contain *formulae* as proper parts; permitting the interchange of such devices when their contained formulae are satisfied by the same object is tantamount to permitting the interchange of formulae themselves; and once some weak additional inference principle is assumed—and it is in the precise character of the additional principle that the proof hinted at by Gödel (1944) is

---

[1] On the value of keeping apart logical and non-logical issues in explorations of the non-extensional, see Kaplan (1986).

more interesting than those proposed by Church, Quine, and Davidson—the formulae in question can be drawn out of their *iota*-governed contexts to make purportedly non-extensional connectives provably extensional.

As Quine pointed out in his earliest complaints about modal logic, substitutions involving descriptions in modal contexts do not seem to preserve truth (the inference from "□ nine exceeds seven" and "nine = the number of planets in our solar system" to "□ the number of planets in our solar system exceeds seven" seems invalid). In one respect, to notice this is to notice very little; but in another respect, it is to catch the glimmer of something important: an argument that might be used to derive an outright inconsistency from the following assumptions: (i) □ is a non-truth-functional connective, and (ii) □ is +ι-SUBS. It is not exactly an inconsistency that flows from the example involving "the number of planets"— just a sentence that seems false ("□ the number of planets in our solar system exceeds seven") from premises that are true ("□ nine exceeds seven" and "nine = the number of planets in our solar system"). What Quine conjectured was that if one could saddle □ with one more plausible inference principle, perhaps one could derive an outright inconsistency; and if one could make the additional inference principle sufficiently innocuous, perhaps the inconsistency would generalize to *all* non-extensional connectives, not just the modal ones. Following Church (1943*a*), he appealed to an inference principle for interchanging logically equivalent sentences.

Quine (1953*c,e*, 1960) gives three versions of the argument I want to set out, but all three have the same essential ingredients, structure, and purported conclusion: any connective ❽ that (i) permits what he calls "the substitutivity of identicals" and (ii) is +PSLE is, in fact, an extensional connective. For expository convenience and dialectical continuity, I shall take the 1960 version.[2] But before setting out the argument, it will prove useful to set out a simpler version, which contains an interesting gap.

---

[2] Quine chooses to use an attitude construction when formulating his 1960 version of the argument, but (*a*) nothing in the 1960 version turns on any particular non-extensional construction, (*b*) Quine's *formal* target is non-extensional connectives quite generally, (*c*) his main *philosophical* targets were modal connectives, and (*d*) Quine's (1953*c,e*) versions do not use an attitude construction and are, moreover, formulated in ways that are meant to show that they generalize to *all* non-extensional connectives. For explicit confirmation of the generality, see the last paragraph of Quine (1961, 1980) and also Quine's (1941*a*) earliest worries about

8.3 AN INCOMPLETE CONNECTIVE PROOF

Let ❽ be an arbitrary connective that is +PSLE and +ι-SUBS. Let "❽+PSLE" and "❽+ι-SUBS" be shorthand for "the assumption that ❽ is +PSLE" and "the assumption that ❽ is +ι-SUBS" respectively. From the premisses ϕ, ψ, and ❽ϕ, it looks as though we can prove ❽ψ:

1	[1]	ϕ	premiss
2	[2]	ψ	premiss
3	[3]	❽ϕ	premiss
3	[4]	❽$(a = \iota x(x{=}a \bullet \phi))$	3, ❽+PSLE
1	[5]	$\iota x(x = a \bullet \phi) = \iota x(x{=}a \bullet \psi)$	1, 2, def. of ιx
1,2,3	[6]	❽$(a = \iota x(x{=}a \bullet \psi))$	4, 5, ❽+ι-SUBS
1,2,3	[7]	❽ψ	6, ❽+PSLE.

Philosophical consequences of the purported validity of this proof are meant to be drawn by interpreting ❽ as e.g. "the fact that ϕ = the fact that ( )" or "the statement that ϕ corresponds to the fact that ( )" or "the fact that ϕ caused it to be the case that ( )", "it is a moral (/legal/constitutional) requirement that ( )", or any other connective that, prima facie, someone might be tempted to view as +PSLE and +ι-SUBS. Alternatively, since the proof can be

the very idea of non-truth-functional logics. Indeed Quine was the first person to propose a general, connective-based slingshot, his intention being to argue on purely formal grounds without getting embroiled in the semantics of this or that connective. It would be a poor scholar who complained that he used a slingshot only against logical modality, and a poor philosopher who saw an illicit running together of modal and attitude contexts in any attempt to set out a general slingshot using Quine's (1953c,e 1960) versions. I suppose it could be pedantically argued that Quine's slingshots are strictly speaking less ambitious than those of Church, Gödel, and Davidson because they were intended to apply only to languages containing quantifiers construed as binding variables across purportedly non-extensional connectives. That is, if (a) Quine's official formulation of his slingshots is understood as involving not connectives imagined as +ι-SUBS but connectives imagined not to create "referentially opaque" contexts, and (b) his official definition of "referential opacity" *for the purposes of his slingshots* is not in terms of substitution but in terms *of the miscarriage of quantification* (as is suggested in several places), then *trivially* his slingshots were officially intended to apply only to languages that attempt quantification into non-extensional contexts. Of course, this would make Quine's slingshots *officially* less interesting than is usually thought. Quine held that anyone intending to get work out of a purportedly non-extensional language *would*, in fact, want quantifiers in that language, so the whole point is ultimately of no interest, philosophically or historically. In this footnote I am greatly indebted to Quine for discussion.

reformulated in such a way that ❽ is a two- (three-, . . .) place connective, it could be interpreted as "the statement that ( ) corresponds to the fact that ( )" or "the fact that ( ) = the fact that ( )" or "the fact that ( ) caused it to be the case that ( )".[3]

It will not do to object to the proof on the grounds that a description $\iota x \phi$ is not well-formed or not interpretable unless every atomic formula in its matrix contains at least one occurrence of x that ιx can bind. Even if it would normally be odd to use anything like the analogue of such a description in ordinary or theoretical talk, there is no formal difficulty involved in making sense of such a description.

The argument does have a weakness, however. If it is to be taken seriously, it must be supplemented with a precise semantics for definite descriptions. First, lines [4] and [6] both contain definite descriptions, and the notion of *logical equivalence* is invoked in getting from line [3] to line [4] and from line [6] to line [7]: on some treatments of descriptions the logical equivalences obtain, but on others they do not.[4] Secondly, line [5] is meant to be justified by the semantics of descriptions assuming ϕ and ψ are both true. (It should also be noted that the treatment of descriptions assumed by the argument will determine whether or not PSST should replace ι-SUBS as the rule of inference invoked in getting from lines [4] and [5] to line [6].)

If descriptions are analysed in accordance with Russell's theory, then the proof is valid. First, on such an account, (7) is just shorthand for the first-order sentence (8):

(7) $a = \iota x(x=a \bullet \phi)$
(8) $\exists x(\forall y((y=a \bullet \phi) \equiv y=x) \bullet x=a)$.

And (8) agrees in truth-value with ϕ in all models. Secondly, on such an account, if ϕ and ψ are both true, then so is (9), which is just shorthand for (10):

---

[3] To reiterate briefly a point made earlier (see Ch. 2) in connection with Davidson's argument against facts, it is not necessary for every atomic formula inside the matrix of a description $\iota x \phi$ to contain an occurrence of x; so it would be futile to complain that connective proofs based of Church's slingshot (unlike those based on Gödel's in the next chapter) make use of descriptions that are illicit by virtue of containing closed sentences in their matrices.

[4] As Church's remarks about contextual definitions of class abstracts reveal, if the argument is restated using class abstracts, the analogous point arises concerning logical equivalence and the precise semantics for class abstracts.

(9) $\iota x(x=a \bullet \phi) = \iota x(x=a \bullet \psi)$

(10) $\exists x(\forall y((y=a \bullet \phi) \equiv y=x) \bullet \exists z(\forall w((w=a \bullet \psi) \equiv w=z) \bullet x=z))$.

So the argument is valid and the proof perfectly legitimate. We know, then, that *if* descriptions are Russellian and if ❽ is +PSLE and +ι-SUBS, then ❽ permits the substitution *s.v.* of truths for truths. Philosophical consequences for theories of facts emerge if one attempts to read ❽ as, e.g., "the fact that ϕ = the fact that ( )". Certainly some philosophers have been tempted to read such an expression as both +PSLE and +ι-SUBS, but the consequences of such a move are now seen to be dire: for any two true sentences ϕ and ψ, "the fact that ϕ = the fact that ψ" will be true, so all facts collapse into one.

Do we also know that ❽ permits the substitution of falsehoods for falsehoods, i.e. that ❽ is +PSME (i.e. truth-functional) when descriptions are Russellian? The premises in the proof above are ϕ, ψ, and ❽ϕ, and the conclusion is ❽ψ. That is, the proof seems to show that ❽ϕ leads to ❽ψ when ϕ and ψ are true. What we want to know is whether ❽ϕ leads to ❽ψ when ϕ and ψ are *materially equivalent*, not just when they are both true. That is, we want to know whether there is a valid proof from the premises $(\phi \equiv \psi)$ and ❽ϕ to the conclusion ❽ψ. (We cannot assume that this has already been proved because it is not true *in general* that if $\phi,\psi,\chi/\zeta$ is a valid proof, then so is $(\phi \equiv \psi),\chi/\zeta$. If so, then ❽ permits the substitution *s.v.* of material equivalents, so it is +PSME.

The following proof will not quite do as it stands:

1　　[1]　$\phi \equiv \psi$　　　　　　　　premiss
2　　[2]　❽ϕ　　　　　　　　premiss
2　　[3]　❽$(a = \iota x((x=a \bullet \phi) \vee (x=b \bullet \sim\phi)))$　　2, ❽+PSLE
1,2　[4]　$\iota x((x=a \bullet \phi) \vee (x=b \bullet \sim\phi))$
　　　　　$= \iota x((x=a \bullet \psi) \vee (x=b \bullet \sim\psi))$　　1, def. of 'ιx'
1,2　[5]　❽$(a = \iota x((x=a \bullet \psi) \vee x=b \bullet \sim \psi)))$　　3, 4, ❽+ι-SUBS
1,2　[6]　❽ψ　　　　　　　　5, ❽+PSLE

It will not do because, on the Russellian semantics for descriptions we are assuming, the entry on line (10), which is shorthand for [4], is *false* when ϕ and ψ are both false:

(10) $\exists x(\forall y((y=a \bullet \phi) \equiv y=x) \bullet \exists z(\forall w((w=a \bullet \psi) \equiv w=z) \bullet x=z))$.

8.4 A COMPLETE CONNECTIVE PROOF

Quine (1960) anticipated this problem (which is frequently missed), and in his own version of the slingshot he uses descriptions designed to circumvent it. The method is cumbersome but effective; instead of the description $\iota x(x=a \bullet \phi)$, he uses one *guaranteed to be uniquely satisfied*: $\iota x((x=a \bullet \phi) \lor (x=b \bullet \sim\phi))$.[5] Putting this description in place of $\iota x(x=a \bullet \phi)$, and putting $\iota x((x=a \bullet \psi) \lor (x=b \bullet \sim\psi))$ in place of $\iota x(x=a \bullet \psi)$, we get the following valid proof:

1	[1]	$\phi \equiv \psi$	premiss
2	[2]	$\mathbf{8}\phi$	premiss
2	[3]	$\mathbf{8}(a = \iota x((x=a \bullet \phi) \lor (x=b \bullet \sim\phi)))$	2, $\mathbf{8}$+PSLE
1,2	[4]	$\iota x((x=a \bullet \phi) \lor (x=b \bullet \sim\phi))$	
		$= \iota x((x=a \bullet \psi) \lor (x=b \bullet \sim\psi))$	1, def. of 'ιx'
1,2	[5]	$\mathbf{8}(a = \iota x((x=a \bullet \psi) \lor (x=b \bullet \sim\psi)))$	3, 4, $\mathbf{8}$+ι-SUBS
1,2	[6]	$\mathbf{8}\psi$	5, $\mathbf{8}$+PSLE.

The move from line [2] to line [3] is justified because, on the Russellian account of descriptions we are presupposing at this point, (11) is shorthand for (12), which is logically equivalent to ϕ:

(11) $a = \iota x((x=a \bullet \phi) \lor (x=b \bullet \sim\phi))$

(12) $\exists x(\forall y(((y=a \bullet \phi) \lor (y=b \bullet \sim\phi)) \equiv y=x) \bullet x=a).$[6]

And, unlike line [4] in the previous proof, line [4] in *this* proof, which is shorthand for (13),

(13) $\exists x(\forall y(((y=a \bullet \phi) \lor (y=b \bullet \sim\phi)) \equiv y = x) \bullet$
$\exists z(\forall w(((w=a \bullet \psi) \lor (w=b \bullet \sim\psi)) \equiv w=z) \bullet x=z))$

will be true not only when ϕ and ψ are both true, but also when

---

[5] Actually $\iota x((x=1 \bullet \phi) \lor (x=0 \bullet \sim\phi))$ which, "following Kronecker", Quine abbreviates as $\delta\phi$ (1960: 148). Note the similarity with Carnap's (1937) K-operator: for Carnap $(Kx)m(x > 7)$ is read as "the smallest positive integer x up to and including m such that '$x > 7$' is true, and 0 if there is no such integer". An alternative way of fixing things would be to use class abstracts instead of descriptions: $\hat{x}(x=a \bullet \phi) = \hat{x}(x=a \bullet \psi)$ will be true when ϕ and ψ are false because both abstracts will pick out the null class. This is the road Quine took in his (1953a,c) slingshots.

[6] Using Quine's (1936) criterion, on a Russellian treatment of descriptions, ϕ and (12) have the same truth-value for all interpretations of their non-logical vocabulary. (Equivalently, following Tarski, the sentences are true in exactly the same models; equivalently, they are interdeducible.) Very likely it was this fact that prompted Quine to claim that $\delta p = 1$ and p are logically equivalent.

they are both false, i.e. whenever line [1] is true. So we have reached the conclusion that *if* descriptions are Russellian, then *if* ❸ is +ι-SUBS and +PSLE, ❸ is also +PSME, i.e. truth-functional.[7] To put matters another way, the following combination of features for a connective ❸ is inconsistent:

(14) −PSME   +PSLE   +ι-SUBS.

But this result, incontrovertible as it is, will not worry all proponents of non-extensional logics. *Individual systems and their interpretations need to be investigated.*

It is doubtful that today's modal logician working with a metaphysical conception of necessity will be troubled. Modal logicians are antecedently predisposed to think that □ is −ι-SUBS, largely because of examples brought up by Quine in connection with an analytic conception of necessity, examples which, as Kripke (1971, 1980) saw, carry over to a metaphysical conception. Consider the following argument, where the description "the number of planets in our solar system" is substituted for "nine" within the scope of □:

(15) □(9 > 7);
      9 = the number of planets in our solar system
      _____
      □ (the number of planets > 7).

The fact that (15) is invalid (when □ has large scope) shows that □ is not +ι-SUBS. (The purported existence of a separate (true) reading

---

[7] Using Quine's abbreviatory convention (see previous two footnotes), the proof can be restated thus:

1	[1] $p \equiv q$	premiss	
2	[2] ❸p	premiss	
2	[3] ❸($\delta p = 1$)	2, ❸+PSLE	
1	[4] $\delta p = \delta q$	1, def. of δ	
1,2	[5] ❸($\delta q = 1$)	3, 4, ❸+ι-SUBS	
1,2	[6] ❸q	5, ❸+PSLE.	

Incidentally, it will not do to object to *Quine's* use of slingshot proofs using descriptions (as e.g. Oppy (1997) does) on the grounds that the use of such proofs is incompatible with Quine's elimination of such devices (recall Quine wants to reduce sentences containing singular terms to sentences containing quantifiers, variables, the identity sign, predicates, and truth-functional connectives). Quine's reinterpretation of the argument when singular terms are eliminated is straightforward: (i) ι-SUBS is interpreted as shorthand for an inference principle in which the descriptions it contains are given their Russellian expansions, in accordance with *Principia* *14.01, *14.02, *14.15, and *14.16.

of the conclusion upon which the description has large scope is irrelevant to this point.) The upshot of all this is that if Quine treats descriptions as Russellian, (*a*) the logical equivalences he needs for his slingshot are guaranteed, but (*b*) the conclusion of the argument is one that today's modal logicians will endorse, namely that $\square$ does not possess the set of features given in (14).

None of this has a bearing on whether or not $\square$ is +PSST. (Of course, in the 1940s and 1950s Quine gave other arguments for thinking that $\square$ is –PSST when it is interpreted as expressing analytic or logical necessity; but these arguments do not carry over directly to the metaphysical interpretation favoured by many modal logicians today, an interpretation Quine assails on other grounds.) So no argument against the possibility of treating $\square$ as a non-extensional sentence connective emerges from the Quinean slingshot just examined. To the extent that $\square$ is treated as +PSLE, it is the combination given in (16) that many modal logicians seem to want to ascribe to it these days:

(16) –PSME +PSLE +PSST.

And the Quinean proof has no bearing on the viability of *this* combination when descriptions are provided with a Russellian treatment.

The only way to convert Quine's slingshot into an argument against non-extensional sentence connectives (and thereby an argument against the viability of $\square$) would be to articulate a treatment of descriptions as singular terms and ensure that it licenses the purported logical equivalences. In order to demonstrate that more interesting conclusion, one would need (i) to restate line [5] of the proof just given as

1,2 [5′] ❽$(a = \iota x(x=a \bullet \psi))$ 3, 4, ❽+PSST

i.e. with ❽+PSST replacing ❽+ι-SUBS in the move from lines [3] and [4] to the fifth line, and (ii) provide a semantics for definite descriptions that not only treats them as singular terms and validates the entry at line [4], but at the same time validates the purported logical equivalences that justify the move from line [2] to line [3], and the move from line [5] to line [6]. On the Russellian analysis of descriptions, all is clear and automatic; but on a referential treatment, difficult choices must be made about the truth-theoretic contributions of improper descriptions, choices that bear crucially on claims of logical equivalence—$\iota x((x=a \bullet \phi) \vee (x=b \bullet \sim\phi))$ will never be improper but one wants the semantics of this description to flow from a general semantics for descriptions which provides a viable semantics for those that *are* improper.

Of course an explicit appeal to a referential treatment of descriptions would be a strikingly odd move for *Quine* to make: as noted earlier, it is his view that a Russellian Theory of Descriptions can be used to eliminate names and other singular terms in favour of devices of quantification, predication, identity, and truth-functional connection and he has championed this elimination on ontological, semantic, and logical grounds. But there is no guarantee that Quine is right about this, so in the interests of a comprehensive examination of the connective slingshot just constructed, we must explore the consequences of referential treatments of descriptions. And of course this is something we should do in any case as we might stumble across a theory that is superior to Russell's. But, as I shall illustrate later, it is far from clear that there is an antecedently plausible referential theory that simultaneously (*a*) licenses the logical equivalences Quine needs, (*b*) provides a plausible account of descriptions whose matrices are unsatisfied, and (*c*) respects the intuitive meaning of the description operator accorded it by the referentialist: if a matrix $\Sigma(x)$ containing at least one occurrence of the variable x (and no free occurrence of any other variable) is uniquely satisfied by A, then the description $\iota x\Sigma(x)$ must refer to A.

9

Gödelian Equivalence

9.1 PRINCIPLES OF CONVERSION FOR DESCRIPTIONS

We are now in a position to set out in Quinean connective format a slingshot proof based on the argument I attributed to Gödel in Chapter 5.[1]

In natural language there appear to be ways of reorganizing a sentence, or converting it into a related sentence, without changing meaning, or at least without changing meaning in any philosophically interesting sense. For example, double negation, passivization, and topicalization will convert (1) into sentences (2)–(4), which seem to have the same truth-condition and which, if true, might be said to stand for the same fact:

(1) Cicero denounced Catiline
(2) It is false that Cicero did not denounce Catiline[2]
(3) Catiline was denounced by Cicero
(4) It was Cicero who denounced Catiline.

(Some will wish to go further, insisting that (1)–(4) are actually synonymous.) Reorganizations and conversions not entirely dissimilar to these grammatical processes are sometimes employed in logic and semantics, perhaps the most common being the inference rule DNN (double negation) and λ-CONV (*lambda*-conversion)

---

[1] I first set out a version of this proof in "The Philosophical Significance of Gödel's Slingshot" (1995); Josh Dever and I set out a cleaner version in "Slingshots and Boomerangs" (1997). Everything is done in more detail and yet more cleanly here. Certain misunderstandings of the 1995 proof that have crept into the literature should now be impossible. I am grateful to Dever for allowing me to draw from our joint work in various places in this and subsequent chapters.

[2] Some logicians have claimed that double negation does not preserve truth. In my view, these people are simply not discussing what the rest of us are discussing when we discuss negation.

in roughly the sense of Church (1940, 1944). On Church's account, $\lambda x\phi$, $\iota x\phi$, $\hat{x}\phi$, $\mu x\phi$, etc. are all singular terms. For purposes of exposition and to avoid distracting side issues about the status of (purportedly) complex singular terms, I want to adopt a use of λx that is found in much contemporary work in semantics and differs in a harmless way from Church's usage: where ϕ is a formula, $\lambda x\phi$ will be a one-place predicate; and where α is a singular term, $(\lambda x\phi)\alpha$ will be a formula. However, I follow Church in introducing *lambda*-conversion by way of inference rules.

For certain purposes the extensional sentence $(Fa \bullet Ga)$ might be rendered as

(5) $(\lambda x(Fx \bullet Gx))a$,

which, depending upon one's taste, can be read as (*a*) "*a* is something that is both *F* and *G*"; (*b*) "the class of things that are both *F* and *G* contains *a*"; or (*c*) "the property of being both *F* and *G* is a property *a* has". For concreteness, let us think of *lambda*-conversions as sanctioned by two rules of inference, *lambda*-INTRODUCTION and *lambda*-ELIMINATION:

λ-INTR: $\dfrac{T[\Sigma(x/\alpha)]}{T[(\lambda x\Sigma(x))\alpha]}$

λ-ELIM: $\dfrac{T[(\lambda x\Sigma(x))\alpha]}{T[\Sigma(x/\alpha)]}.$

Here, α is a (closed) singular term and x is a variable, $\Sigma(x)$ is an extensional formula containing *at least one* occurrence of x, $\Sigma(x/\alpha)$ is the result of replacing *every* occurrence of x in $\Sigma(x)$ by α (there may be additional occurrences of α in $\Sigma(x)$), $T[\Sigma(x/\alpha)]$ is an extensional sentence containing $\Sigma(x/\alpha)$ (it may be just $\Sigma(x/\alpha)$ itself), and $T[(\lambda x\Sigma(x))\alpha]$ is a sentence in which $(\lambda x\Sigma(x))$ has minimal scope.

λ-INTR and λ-ELIM are valid rules of inference in extensional contexts. As λ shorthand for this, let us say that extensional contexts are $+\lambda$-INTR and $+\lambda$-ELIM. Continuing with the useful extension of terminology introduced earlier in connection with principles of substitution, let us say that any extensional connective ❸ is $+\lambda$-INTR and $+\lambda$-ELIM in the sense that ❸ permits the use of λ-INTR and λ-ELIM on any sentence ϕ within its scope (assuming, of course, that φ does not occur within the scope of any non-extensional connective). More precisely:

> An *n*-place connective ❽ is +λ-INTR if and only if for any true sentence ❽(... T[Σ(*x*/α)] ...) in which T[Σ(*x*/α)] is an extensional sentence occurring as an operand of ❽ and containing Σ(*x*/α), replacing T[Σ(*x*/α)] by T[(λ*x*Σ(*x*))α] in ❽(... T[Σ(*x*/α)] ...) yields a true sentence ❽(... T[(λ*x*Σ(*x*))α] ...) (*Mutatis mutandis* for +λ-ELIM.)

No residual issues concerning scope arise: scopes remain constant with respect to ❽. When a connective is both +λ-INTR and +λ-ELIM, let us say that it is +λ-CONV. On the weakest reading of *lambda*-expressions, i.e. (*a*) above, those who make use of such expressions will view extensional connectives as +λ-CONV, just as they will view them as +PSST, +PSME, and +ι-SUBS.

With Gödel's (1944) thoughts about the tight relationship between *Fa* and *a* = ι*x*(*x*=*a* • *Fx*) in mind, I want to draw up two similar inference principles involving the description operator, principles I shall call *iota*-INTRODUCTION and *iota*-ELIMINATION:

ι-INTR: $$\frac{T[Σ(x/α)]}{T[α = ιx(x=α • Σ(x))]}$$.

ι-ELIM: $$\frac{T[α = ιx(x=α • Σ(x))]}{T[Σ(x/α)].}$$

Here Σ(*x*) is an extensional formula containing *at least one* occurrence of the variable *x*, Σ(*x*/α) is the result of replacing *every* occurrence of *x* in Σ(*x*) by the (closed) singular term α (there may be additional occurrences of α in Σ(*x*)), T[Σ(*x*/α)] is an extensional sentence containing Σ(*x*/α) (it may be just Σ(*x*/α) itself), and T[α=ι*x*(*x*=α • Σ(*x*))] is a sentence in which ι*x*(*x*=α • Σ(*x*)) has minimal scope.

Notice that (6) and (7) can *both* be inferred from ~*Fa* (and vice versa):

(6) *a* = ι*x*(*x*=*a* • ~*Fx*)
(7) ~*a* = ι*x*(*x*=*a* • *Fx*).

This is because Σ(*x*/α) is extensional and can be taken as either *Fa* or ~*Fa*.

ι-INTR and ι-ELIM are valid rules of inference in extensional contexts.[3] As shorthand for this, let us say that extensional contexts are +ι-INTR and +ι-ELIM. (Any adequate theory of descriptions, it seems to me, must be compatible with this fact, as Russell's theory is. On Russell's account, the fact that extensional contexts are +ι-INTR and +ι-ELIM follows immediately from the fact that extensional contexts are +PSLE.) Continuing with our useful extension of terminology, let us say that any extensional connective ❸ is +ι-INTR and +ι-ELIM in the sense that ❸ permits the use of ι-INTR and ι-ELIM on any sentence φ within its scope (assuming, of course, that φ does not occur within the scope of any non-extensional connective). More precisely:

> An *n*-place connective ❸ is +ι-INTR if and only if for any true sentence ❸(... T[Σ(*x*/α)] ...) in which T[Σ(*x*/α)] is an extensional sentence occurring as an operand of ❸ and containing Σ(*x*/α), replacing T[Σ(*x*/α)] by T[α = ι*x*(*x*=α • Σ(*x*))] in ❸(... T[Σ(*x*/α)] ...) produces a true sentence ❸(... T[α = ι*x*(*x*=α • Σ(*x*)] ...). (*Mutatis mutandis* for +ι-ELIM.)

Again no residual issues concerning scope arise: scopes remain constant with respect to ❸. When a context or connective is both +ι-INTR and +ι-ELIM, let us say that it is +ι-CONV (it permits *iota-conversion s.v.*).[4]

---

[3] Carnap (1947) and advocates of certain forms of free logic seem to be in the awkward position of having to deny this. See next footnote and Ch. 10.

[4] Mark Sainsbury has pointed out to me that certain forms of so-called free logic must deny that extensional contexts are +ι-CONV. From a model-theoretic perspective, a logic is free if an interpretation is not required to assign an object to every singular term; proof-theoretically, the distinctive feature of free logic is the rejection of the classical inference principles of existential generalization and universal instantiation (extensional contexts are -EG and -UI). The motivation for such logics—see e.g. Burge (1974), Grandy (1972), Lambert (1962), Schock (1968), Scott (1967), and van Fraassen and Lambert (1967)—is the purported existence of names and descriptions that fail to refer, e.g. "Vulcan" (which was introduced as the name of a planet whose orbit was thought to lie between that of Mercury and the sun) or "the king of France". (If descriptions are treated in Russell's way, the existence of descriptive phrases whose matrices are not true of anything provides no motivation for free logic whatsoever. Some advocates of free logic tend to misunderstand Russell's Theory of Descriptions, being antecedently convinced that Russell sought to treat descriptions as singular terms.) Three varieties of free logic are usefully distinguished. In the "Fregean" variety, every sentence containing an empty name

9.2 GÖDEL'S PROOF IN QUINEAN FORMAT

Soon I am going to convert Gödel's hints for constructing a sling-shot into a proof that has interesting consequences for the seman-tics of natural language and for any system that is meant to contain definite descriptions and identity. But first I want to set out a simple proof $\mathfrak{J}_0$ of something that should already be worrying.

$\mathfrak{J}_0$. Let $\otimes$ be an *arbitrary* one-place connective that is +ι-CONV and +ι-SUBS. Let "$\otimes$+ι-CONV" be shorthand for "the assumption that $\otimes$ is +ι-CONV", and so on. From the premisses Fa and $\otimes(Fa)$ we can now derive the startling conclusion that $\otimes(a = a)$:

1	[1]	Fa	premiss
2	[2]	$\otimes(Fa)$	premiss
1	[3]	$a = \iota x(x{=}a \bullet Fx)$	1, ι-CONV
2	[4]	$\otimes(a = \iota x(x{=}a \bullet Fx))$	2, $\otimes$+ι-CONV
1,2	[5]	$\otimes(a = a)$	3, 4, $\otimes$+ι-SUBS.

lacks a truth-value (except in cases where the name occurs in an oblique context, for example within the scope of a verb of propositional attitude). A *positive* free logic allows that certain atomic sentences containing empty singular terms are true, iden-tity statements ("Vulcan = Vulcan" and "the king of France = the king of France" are standard examples). In *negative* free logic atomic sentences containing empty singular terms are all false. (The lack of agreement among free logicians on how to handle empty names is striking given that these are the expressions that motivated and sustain the enterprise.) As Sainsbury has pointed out to me, some advocates of negative free logic (*nfl*) must deny that extensional contexts are +ι-CONV. (i) and (ii) are interderivable using ι-CONV:

(i) $\sim Fa$
(ii) $a = \iota x(x{=}a \bullet \sim Fx)$.

If a is a name that fails to refer, then *nfl* declares (i) true. If descriptions are treated in the favoured way of free logic, as singular terms, then *nfl* also declares (ii) true, so it would seem that extensional contexts are indeed +ι-CONV (although one would want very much to see the particular referential semantics for descriptions proposed by the free logician and the accompanying definitions of logical equivalence and logical truth before one could be more confident). Sainsbury suggests that there is room for a negative free logic that treats descriptions in accordance with Russell's theory (despite treating names as singular terms). On such an account (i) will be true and (ii) false; in the logic so-conceived ι-CONV is not a valid inference principle in extensional contexts. Of course, the advocate of such a logic might decide to embrace this conclusion—just as he might be tempted to allow scope ambiguities involving names to affect truth: (i) can be true while '$[a]\sim Fa$' —or perhaps '$[a]_x\sim Fx$' or something more like (ii) even—is false. I shall continue with the policy (essentially Gödel's) of seeing extensional contexts as +ι-CONV. (Strictly speaking, this will be a ground-floor assumption of my rendering of Gödel's slingshot in Quinean format. To reject it is really to express a lack of interest in arguments involving ι-CONV: to

I say "startling" because this holds of *any* connective that is +ι-CONV and +ι-SUBS and for *any* predicate *F*. $\mathfrak{S}_0$ should worry anyone contemplating treating a *non-extensional* connective ❸ as +ι-CONV and +ι-SUBS. Jumping ahead slightly, notice that if ❸ were to be read as "the fact that *Fa* = the fact that ( )", then if *Fa* is true and stands for a fact—the fact that *Fa*—we obtain the unpromising result that the fact that *Fa* is identical to the fact that *a* = *a*. By parity of argument, if *Ga* is true and stands for a fact—the fact that *Ga*—then the fact that *Ga* is also identical to the fact that *a* = *a*. And by transitivity of identity we reach the deeply worrying conclusion that the fact that *Fa* = the fact that *Ga*. So there is only one fact about *a* (or at least only one *atomic* fact about *a*).[5] For the fact-theorist who

claim that extensional contexts are –ι-CONV is to claim that truth-functional sentence connectives are –ι-CONV; and if one holds that not even truth-functional connectives are +ι-CONV, one is surely not going to think there are philosophically interesting *non-*truth-functional connectives that are +ι-CONV. (It is not hard to concoct an artificial connective that is +RULE despite truth-functional connectives being –RULE, but such connectives are of little interest to logic or semantics.) So the advocate of free logic who rejects ι-CONV for extensional contexts is expressing a lack of interest in any arguments of the type under consideration on the grounds that it concerns an *arbitrary* one-place connective ❸ that is +ι-CONV and +ι-SUBS, and the free logician in question denies that any philosophically interesting connective is +ι-CONV. (I am here, and in n. 6, indebted to Mark Sainsbury and Josh Dever for fruitful discussion.)

Are modal contexts +ι-CONV? Inferences of some of the following forms seem intuitively valid to many people, on some popular interpretations of □ (the absence of scope markers indicating smallest scope for the descriptions), but questions about varying domains in connection with certain interpretations are apt to complicate matters:

(iii) $\dfrac{\Box Fa}{\Box a = \iota x(x{=}a \bullet Fx)}$ (iv) $\dfrac{\Box\ a = \iota x(x{=}a \bullet Fx)}{\Box\ Fa}$

(v) $\dfrac{\Box Fa}{a = \iota x(x{=}a \bullet \Box Fx)}$ (vi) $\dfrac{a = \iota x(x{=}a \bullet \Box\ Fx)}{\Box Fa.}$

The advocate of a negative free logic containing modal operators might be inclined to deny similar inferences containing negation, for example, (vii):

(vii) $\dfrac{\Box{\sim}Fa}{\Box a = \iota x(x{=}a \bullet {\sim}Fx).}$

At this point matters become extraordinarily complex: choices in free logic, theory of descriptions, modal system, interpretation of □, and domain specification conspire to produce a dizzying array of possibilities.

[5] An argument along more or less these lines is presented by Rodriguez-Pereyra (1998*a*) in connection with Searle's (1995) theory of facts.

accepts that "the fact that Fa = the fact that ( )" is +ι-CONV and +ι-SUBS the following sentences will provably stand for the same fact:

(1) Cicero denounced Catiline
(2) Cicero wrote *De fato*
(3) Cicero = Cicero.

And this is surely a catastrophe for anyone hoping to get philosophical work out of facts.[6]

The full generality and magnitude of the problem comes out clearly in a longer but only slightly more complex proof, $\mathfrak{I}$, of what I shall call the *Descriptive Constraint*, a proof based on Gödel's slingshot. Basically, $\mathfrak{I}$ ends up showing that (i) there is only one fact about a (as above) and (ii) the fact about a = the fact about b. $\mathfrak{I}$ is a proof, in four parts, $\mathfrak{I}_1$–$\mathfrak{I}_4$, from premisses $Fa \equiv Gb$ and ❽ (Fa) to the conclusion ❽(Gb). The general idea should be clear by the end of $\mathfrak{I}_1$.

$\mathfrak{I}_1$: From premisses Fa, $a \neq b$, Gb, and ❽(Fa) to conclusion ❽ (Gb).

1	[1] Fa	premiss
2	[2] $a \neq b$	premiss
3	[3] Gb	premiss
1	[4] $a = \iota x(x{=}a \bullet Fx)$	1, ι-CONV
2	[5] $a = \iota x(x{=}a \bullet x{\neq}b)$	2, ι-CONV
2	[6] $b = \iota x(x{=}b \bullet x{\neq}a)$	2, ι-CONV
3	[7] $b = \iota x(x{=}b \bullet Gx)$	3, ι-CONV

---

[6] The free logician (see n. 4) might consider questioning the five-line proof—so on the grounds that if descriptions are treated in accordance with Russell's Theory of Descriptions (or any other theory of descriptions with an existence assumption), its success will depend upon assuming something free logic rejects, namely that all names (individual constants) in the language of the deduction have referents. But in fact the little argument, as it stands, does *not* presuppose that all names have referents, only that 'a' has a referent (no other name appears in the argument). So the free logician's worry is simply not pertinent to the central issue; from the premisses 'Fa' and '❽(Fa)' we can still infer '❽$(a = a)$' *where 'a' is any name 'a' is that has a referent*. If ❽ were to be read as "the fact that Fa = the fact that ( )", then if Fa is true and stands for a fact, we still obtain the result that the fact that Fa is identical to the fact that $a = a$. By parity of argument, if 'Ga' is true and stands for a fact, then the fact that Ga is identical to the fact that $a = a$. By transitivity of identity we still reach the conclusion that the fact that Fa = the fact that Ga, and still end up with only one fact about a. And by parity of the whole argument, there is only one fact about b, where 'b' is any name with a referent.

1,2	[8]	$\iota x(x = a \bullet Fx) = \iota x(x{=}a \bullet x{\neq}b)$	4, 5, ι-SUBS
2,3	[9]	$\iota x(x{=}b \bullet Gx) = \iota x(x{=}b \bullet x{\neq}a)$	6, 7, ι-SUBS
10	[10]	$\otimes(Fa)$	premiss
10	[11]	$\otimes(a = \iota x(x{=}a \bullet Fx))$	10, $\otimes$+ι-CONV
1,2,10	[12]	$\otimes(a = \iota x(x{=}a \bullet x{\neq}b))$	11, 8, $\otimes$+ι-SUBS
1,2,10	[13]	$\otimes(a \neq b)$	12, $\otimes$+ι-CONV
1,2,10	[14]	$\otimes(b = \iota x(x{=}b \bullet x{\neq}a))$	13, $\otimes$+ι-CONV
1,2,3,10	[15]	$\otimes(b = \iota x(x{=}b \bullet Gx))$	14, 9, $\otimes$+ι-SUBS
1,2,3,10	[16]	$\otimes(Gb)$	15, $\otimes$+ι-CONV

$\mathfrak{J}_2$: *Mutatis mutandis* where premiss [2] is $a = b$ rather than $a \neq b$, though of course a shorter proof can be constructed when $a = b$ is used.[7]

Putting $\mathfrak{J}_1$ and $\mathfrak{J}_2$ together we have a proof $\mathfrak{J}_1\mathfrak{J}_2$: if $\otimes$ is +ι-SUBS and +ι-CONV, then it permits the substitution *s.v.* of (atomic) truths for (atomic) truths within its scope (e.g. *Fa* and *Gb*).

The attraction of $\mathfrak{J}_1\mathfrak{J}_2$ is twofold. First, the two halves of the proof are in Quinean connective format and have as their entries sentences that are meant to be equivalent only in truth-value with their predecessors, and not equivalent in any richer respect (e.g. logically equivalent or synonymous). Secondly, in all crucial respects $\mathfrak{J}_1\mathfrak{J}_2$ is semantically neutral; most importantly, and unlike Quine's connective proof, $\mathfrak{J}_1\mathfrak{J}_2$ *requires no supplementation with a precise semantics for definite descriptions*. This is because (*a*) it nowhere appeals to alleged logical equivalences involving descriptions—on some theories of descriptions *Fa* and $a{=}\iota x(x{=}a \bullet Fx)$ *are* logically equivalent, but no appeal is made to this interesting fact in the course of setting out $\mathfrak{J}_1\mathfrak{J}_2$—and (*b*) the apparent identities

---

[7] For example, by appealing to the fact that if $\otimes$ is +ι–SUBS it is also +PSST, the following will suffice:

1	[1]	*Fa*	premiss
2	[2]	$a = b$	premiss
3	[3]	*Gb*	premiss
1	[4]	$a = \iota x(x{=}a \bullet Fx)$	1, ι-CONV
3	[5]	$b = \iota x(x{=}b \bullet Gx)$	3, ι-CONV
2,3	[6]	$a = \iota x(x{=}b \bullet Gx)$	5, 2, PSST
1,2,3	[7]	$\iota x(x{=}a \bullet Fx) = \iota x(x{=}b \bullet Gx)$	4, 6, ι-SUBS
8	[8]	$\otimes(Fa)$	premiss
8	[9]	$\otimes(a = \iota x(x{=}a \bullet Fx))$	8, $\otimes$+ι-CONV
8	[10]	$\otimes(a = \iota x(x{=}b \bullet Gx))$	9, 7, $\otimes$+ι-SUBS
1,2,3,8	[11]	$\otimes(b = \iota x(x{=}b \bullet Gx))$	10, 2 $\otimes$+PSST
1,2,3,8	[12]	$\otimes(Gb)$	11, $\otimes$+ι-CONV.

involving descriptions—e.g. at lines [8] and [9] of $\Im_1$ are obtained by appeal to ι-SUBS not by any *specific* assumption about the semantics of descriptions.

It should also be noted that $\Im_1\Im_2$ nowhere assumes "direct" (or "indirect") reference, semantic "innocence" (or "guilt"), or any facts about the semantics of ❽ beyond the hypothesis being investigated, namely, that it is a one-place connective that is +ι-SUBS and +ι-CONV. What it shows, without any qualification whatsoever, is that if ❽ is +ι-SUBS and +ι-CONV, then it permits the substitution *s.v.* of (atomic) truths for (atomic) truths within its scope (e.g. *Fa* and *Gb*).

Immediate philosophical consequences of $\Im_1\Im_2$ can be drawn by interpreting ❽(. . .) as, e.g., "the fact that φ = the fact that (. . .)", "the statement that φ corresponds to the fact that (. . .)", "the fact that φ caused it to be the case that (. . .)", or any other connective that, at least prima facie, someone might be tempted to view as +ι-SUBS and +ι-CONV. The friend of facts needs a theory according to which these connectives are either −ι-SUBS or −ι−CONV. This is the *Descriptive Constraint* on theories of facts.

It ought to be clear, intuitively, that we have in fact proved something stronger, namely that if ❽ is +ι-SUBS and +ι-CONV, then it permits not only the substitution *s.v.* of truths for truths within its scope, but also falsehoods for falsehoods, i.e. that if ❽ is +ι-SUBS and +ι-CONV it is extensional. Some commentators have suggested that the stronger conclusion does not follow, so let me complete everything with two more subproofs $\Im_3$ and $\Im_4$.

$\Im_3$: We replace the premisses *Fa* and *Ga* in $\Im_1$ by ~*Fa* and ~*Gb* to produce a proof of ❽(*Gb*) from ~*Fa*, ~*Gb*, $a \neq b$, and ❽(*Fa*):

1	[1] ~*Fa*	premiss
2	[2] $a \neq b$	premiss
3	[3] ~*Gb*	premiss
1	[4] $a = \iota x(x{=}a \bullet {\sim}Fx)$	1, ι-CONV
2	[5] $a = \iota x(x{=}a \bullet x{\neq}b)$	2, ι-CONV
2	[6] $b = \iota x(x{=}b \bullet x{\neq}a)$	2, ι-CONV
3	[7] $b = \iota x(x{=}b \bullet {\sim}Gx)$	3, ι-CONV
8	[8] ❽(*Fa*)	premiss
8	[9] ❽(~~*Fa*)	8, ❽+DNN
8	[10] ❽(~$a = \iota x(x{=}a \bullet {\sim}Fx)$)	9, ❽+ι-CONV
1,8	[11] ❽(~$a = a$)	4, 10, ❽+ι-SUBS

1,2,8	[12]	$\otimes(\sim a = \iota x(x=a \bullet x \neq b))$	5, 11,	$\otimes$+ι-SUBS
1,2,8	[13]	$\otimes(\sim a \neq b)$	12,	$\otimes$+ι-CONV
1,2,8	[14]	$\otimes(\sim b = \iota x(x=b \bullet x \neq a))$	13,	$\otimes$+ι-CONV
1,2,3,8	[15]	$\otimes(\sim b = b)$	6, 14,	$\otimes$+ι-SUBS
1,2,3,8	[16]	$\otimes(\sim b = \iota x(x=b \bullet \sim Gx))$	7, 15,	$\otimes$+ι-SUBS
1,2,3,8	[17]	$\otimes(\sim\sim Gb)$	16,	$\otimes$+ι-CONV
1,2,3,8	[18]	$\otimes(Gb)$	17,	$\otimes$+DNN

$\mathfrak{I}_4$: *Mutatis mutandis* where premiss [2] is '$a = b$' rather than '$a \neq b$', though again a shorter proof can be constructed when '$a = b$' is used.

Putting $\mathfrak{I}_1\mathfrak{I}_2$ and $\mathfrak{I}_3\mathfrak{I}_4$ together, we have our proof $\mathfrak{I}$: if a connective $\otimes$ is +ι-CONV and +ι-SUBS, then it is *extensional*. (Again this assumes, with Gödel, that every sentence can be brought into subject–predicate form. If this is problematic, the argument demonstrates the technically weaker—but equally important—conclusion that if $\otimes$ is +ι-SUBS and +ι-CONV, then it is extensional with respect to *atomic* sentences.) Let us call this the *Descriptive Constraint* on non-extensional logics.

It is important to distinguish this consequence of $\mathfrak{I}$ from any philosophical implications—concerning, say, facts, causation, necessity, or action—that it may have. It ought to be clear that metaphysical issues about (e.g.) whether there are facts or whether there are any general facts, and semantic issues about whether descriptions are singular terms, whether singular terms are directly referential, or whether semantic innocence can be maintained, are *not* issues concerning the proof (which is not to say, of course, that interesting implications for such issues might not emerge from reflecting on the proof in the context of this or that philosophical theory).

The relation between the subproof $\mathfrak{I}_1\mathfrak{I}_2$ and the proof Gödel originally suggested comes into focus if $\otimes(\ldots)$ is interpreted as "the fact that Fa = the fact that $(\ldots)$" or as "the sentence 'Fa' corresponds to the fact that $(\ldots)$".

How worrying is $\mathfrak{I}$ for friends of facts, non-extensional logics, and purportedly non-extensional connectives in natural language? That is something I shall take up in the remaining chapters. But one logical point needs to be made immediately. $\mathfrak{I}$ does *not* show that a connective is extensional if it is both +PSST and +ι-CONV, i.e. it does *not* directly demonstrate that the following combination of features is inconsistent:

(8) +ι-CONV   +PSST   -PSME.

But the inconsistency of (8) *would* be shown if it were possible to prove that any connective that is +PSST is also +ι-SUBS, or prove that any connective with the three features in (8) must also be +ι-SUBS. I know of no attempts to construct such proofs; indeed, if descriptions are Russellian, such proofs cannot be constructed. So anyone hoping to use ℑ as part of an argument against the consistency of (8) needs (i) to provide a viable treatment of descriptions according to which they are (*a*) singular terms (and hence subject to PSST) and (*b*) still the plausible inputs and outputs of ι-CONV, and then (ii) to construct a proof exactly like the one above except that it appeals to PSST (rather than ι-SUBS) in the obvious places. That is the topic of the next chapter.

9.3 A STRONGER SLINGSHOT?

Whitehead and Russell proved that if ❽ is +PSME, then it is also +ι-SUBS (see Chapter 5). But what about the converse, which they do *not* prove? Quine says things that suggest he once thought it true (see below). As far as I am aware, ℑ is as close as anyone has come to confirming it, but there is still a way to go. One way to get all the way would be to show that if ❽ is +ι-SUBS, then it is also +ι-CONV. But I hazard this cannot be proved in a way that is sufficiently neutral on the semantics of definite descriptions to be satisfying.[8]

In his paper "Whitehead and the Rise of Modern Logic", Quine (1941*a*) endorses Russell's Theory of Descriptions and goes on to express doubts about the viability of *any* form of non-truth-functional logic:

In *Principia*, as in Frege's logic, one statement is capable of containing other statements truth-functionally only; i.e., in such a way that the truth value (truth or falsehood) of the whole remains unchanged when a true part is replaced by any other truth, or a false part by any other falsehood. Preservation of the principle of truth-functionality is *essential* to simplicity and convenience of logical theory. In *all* departures from this norm that have to my knowledge ever been propounded, moreover, a sacrifice is

---

[8] Connectives devised by Paul Horwich and Saul Kripke in discussion have reinforced my doubts on this point.

made not only with regard to simplicity and convenience, but with regard even to the admissibility of a certain *common-sense mode of inference*: inference by interchanging terms that designate the same object. (1941*a*: 141–2; my italics)

In the terminology of this book one of the things Quine seems to be claiming at the end of this passage is that any connective he has encountered that is –PSME is also –PSST. In a footnote appended to the passage just quoted Quine mentions two concrete cases of departures from the "norm" of truth-functionality that appear to "sacrifice" the "common-sense mode of inference":

C. I. Lewis and C. H. Langford (*Symbolic Logic*, New York, 1932), e.g., use a non-truth-functional operator '◇' to express logical possibility. Thus the statements:

◇ (number of planets in solar system < 7)
◇ (9 < 7)

would be judged as true and false respectively, despite the fact that they are interconvertible by interchanging the terms "9" and "number of planets in solar system", both of which designate the same object. Similar examples are readily devised for the early Whitehead system [discussed in §III.] On grounds of technical expediency and on *common-sense* grounds as well, thus, there is a strong case for the principle of truth-functionality. (1941*a*: 141–2; my italics)

This is Quine's first published attempt to demonstrate what he later called the *referential opacity* of modal contexts. He expresses no explicit worry about quantifying into modal contexts until 1943: he talks only of a substitution failure. (However, in his 1941 review of Russell's "Inquiry into Meaning and Truth", Quine (1941*b*) expresses concern that Russell does not explain how to interpret sentences in which a quantifier binds a variable across verbs of propositional attitude like "believe", sentences Russell used from 1905 onwards in discussions of scope ambiguities involving definite and indefinite descriptions.) By putting together Quine's footnote and the passage to which it is appended, we dimly discern a general "slingshot" argument forming in Quine's mind—as it must have been forming in the minds of Church and Gödel at about the same time. For one of Quine's claims here seems to be that, as far as he can ascertain, giving up truth-functionality requires giving up a "common-sense mode of inference"—which he will later call *substitutivity*—the implication being that holding onto the common-sense mode of inference requires holding onto truth-functionality. When the formal slingshots of Church (1943a) and Quine (1953c,e, 1960) finally appeared, they involved not just *inference by interchanging terms that designate the same object* but also *inference by interchanging logical equivalents*; Gödel's (1944) slingshot involved *interchanging Gödelian equivalents*, i.e. sentences related via ι-CONV.

Proofs based on slingshots are the central components of watertight deductive arguments; they show that an inconsistency results when one posits a non-extensional connective that freely permits the use of inference principles involving descriptions within its scope. There is a definite constraint on what one can do with descriptions within the scopes of non-extensional operators, the Descriptive Constraint. This much we now know from the connective version of Gödel's slingshot. The relevant inconsistency arises, roughly speaking, because descriptions and abstracts (as standardly understood) contain *formulae* as proper parts; by permitting the interchange of such devices when their contained formulae are satisfied by the same object, one is essentially allowing the interchange of formulae; and once a weak additional inference principle is assumed—and, as I have argued, it is in the precise character of the second principle that proofs based on Gödel's slingshot are superior to those based on Church's—the formulae in question can be drawn out of their *iota*-governed contexts to make the purportedly non-truth-functional connectives provably truth-functional.

10

Description and Equivalence

10.1 INTRODUCTORY REMARKS

Although there are good reasons for thinking that descriptions should be analysed in accordance with Russell's theory, as devices of quantification rather than as devices of singular reference, there are a number of superficially attractive referential treatments of descriptions on the market. For present purposes, it will not be necessary to pronounce on most of the virtues and vices of this or that referential theory: it will be necessary only to examine the commitments of such theories in connection with logical and Gödelian equivalence, for the aim is to uncover the consequences of employing referential theories (satisfying a minimal condition any such theory must satisfy) in connection with slingshot arguments in Quinean format. Quine himself was seeking a stronger conclusion than the one that can be obtained if descriptions are Russellian, and so was Davidson. We owe it to them to see if stronger conclusions are forthcoming on referential treatments; and we owe it to ourselves to see if stronger results can be obtained from a connective version of Gödel's slingshot. The main issue is whether the logical and Gödelian equivalences the respective proofs invoke can be sustained if descriptions are referential. If one is already convinced that a Russellian quantificational treatment of descriptions is adequate, the present chapter is likely to have little more than curiosity value.

If the intuitive meaning of the description operator is to be honoured, one definite condition must be satisfied by any referential treatment: if a formula $\Sigma(x)$ containing at least one occurrence of the variable x (and no free occurrence of any other variable) is uniquely satisfied by A, then the description $\iota x \Sigma(x)$ must refer to A. But the wording of this condition brings out questions that any referential treatment must answer, questions that can be sharpened by reflecting on the logical simplicity afforded by Russell's treatment.

Russell's theory provides straightforward accounts of sentences containing descriptions whose matrices are not uniquely satisfied, so-called "improper" descriptions. Refining our terminology, let us say that a description $\iota x \Sigma(x)$ is *proper* (according to some model M) if, and only if, its matrix $\Sigma(x)$ is (on M's interpretation) true of exactly one item in the domain over which the variables of quantification range, and *improper* otherwise.[1] Let us assume, then, that we are dealing only with referential treatments that generate no serious problems for proper descriptions (if there are such theories): a model M interprets a proper description $\iota x \Sigma(x)$ as referring to the unique object satisfying $\Sigma(x)$.

But what of improper descriptions? An adequate referential treatment must say something about them, and there are various competing approaches in the literature, or else constructible on the basis of existing informal suggestions. A good deal of the relevant work here has been done by Carnap (1947) and Taylor (1985), from whom I shall draw liberally.

10.2 HILBERT AND BERNAYS

In the system of Hilbert and Bernays (1934) a description $\iota x \Sigma(x)$ can be used only after it has been proved proper, i.e. only after (1) has been proved:

(1) $\exists x(\forall y(\Sigma(x/y) \equiv y=x)$.

Although this treatment may be useful for certain mathematical purposes, as Quine (1940), Carnap (1947), and Scott (1967) have

---

[1] Terminology aside, I here follow Taylor (1985). For the sake of simplicity I propose (again with Taylor) to ignore the irrelevant complexities raised by relativized descriptions such as "the woman sitting next to him" where "him" is bound by a higher quantifier. Nothing of any bearing upon the point at hand turns on the existence or interpretation of such descriptions. Russell's theory both predicts the existence of, and provides an automatic and successful interpretation of, such descriptions without any special stipulation or additional machinery. With some work, presumably certain referential accounts of descriptions can also supply what is necessary here; so I propose to ignore any potential problems that relativization creates for the non-Russellian.

pointed out, there are insurmountable problems involved in viewing it as a treatment of descriptions in any interesting fragment of natural language. First, since the class of well-formed formulae will not be recursive, the question of whether a string of symbols containing the substring ιx is a formula will depend not only upon a set of syntactical rules but also on, for example, matters of logic and the "contingency of facts". And secondly, utterances of many sentences of natural language containing improper descriptions (or descriptions not known to be proper) are straightforwardly true or false (e.g. "last night Boris dined with the king of France") or straightforwardly used to conjecture, as even Strawson was finally forced to concede (see below). There would appear to be no prospect, then, of using Hilbert and Bernays's treatment in connection with descriptions belonging to any interesting fragment of natural language.

Furthermore, since the use of a description of the form of (2)

(2) $\iota x(x=a \bullet \Sigma)$

is permitted on Hilbert and Bernays's treatment only if Σ or $\Sigma(x/a)$ is provable, the adoption of this treatment will not bring about stronger results in connection with the connective proofs based on the slingshots of Church–Quine and Gödel. Certainly the reinterpreted proofs would not show that there can be no connective with the combinations of features given in (3) (the Church–Quine-Davidson version) or (4) (the Gödel version):

(3)   +PSST   −PSME   +PSLE
(4)   +PSST   −PSME   +ι-CONV.

The proofs would show only that connectives satisfying (3) and (4) also permit the substitution *s.v.* of logical truths for logical truths.[2]

As far as the proof based on the Church–Quine slingshot is concerned, this result is already a direct consequence of one of its assumptions, namely that the connective is +PSLE, so the new proof is of no interest.

The connective version of Gödel's slingshot would demonstrate something of mild interest: if ❽ is +PSST and +ι-CONV, then it also permits the intersubstitution *s.v.* of logical truths. This is not a

---

[2] Following Tarski, let us say that a sentence ϕ of first-order logic is *logically true* if, and only if, it is true in every first-order model.

direct consequence of any particular assumption made by the argument. On standard Tarskian conceptions of logical truth, logical consequence, and logical equivalence, if ❽ permits the intersubstitution of logical truths *s.v.*, then it must also be +PSLE. Thus it would seem that a mildly interesting result emerges on Hilbert and Bernays's treatment of descriptions, namely that the slingshots of Church–Quine and Gödel are basically equivalent (every Gödelian equivalence being a logical equivalence).

To sum up, on the plausible assumption that any connective that permits the intersubstitution *s.v.* of logical truths is +PSLE, all that can be demonstrated by adopting Hilbert and Bernays's (antecedently implausible) treatment of definite descriptions is that no connective can have the following combination of features:

(5)   +ι-CONV   +PSST   -PSLE.

There would still be no collapse of non-extensional connectives into the class of extensional connectives. (Carried back over to the discussion of facts, the proofs would show only that logically equivalent sentences stand for the same fact. There would still be no collapse of all facts into one.)

10.3 FREGEAN THEORIES

Rather different approaches to improper descriptions have been inspired by Frege, who thought it an imperfection of languages that they contain apparent singular terms that fail to refer. Frege (1892) suggests that a description is a "compound proper name" and, as such, "must actually always be assured a reference, by means of a special stipulation, e.g. by the convention that it shall count as referring to o when the concept applies to no object or to more than one" (p. 71).

Elsewhere Frege (1893) suggests an alternative treatment according to which an improper description refers to *the class of entities satisfying its matrix* (thus all empty descriptions refer to the empty class). Within the context of Frege's overall theory of reference, this looks like an improvement as far as compositionality and extensionality are concerned. The matrix of a definite description, on Frege's account, is a concept expression and, as such, it is paired—though not directly in Frege's semantics—with a class of entities, its extension. In order to respect minimally the intuitive meaning of the definite article, where the extension of a matrix φ is one-membered, that one member qualifies as the referent of the resulting description ιxφ; if the class in question is anything other than one-membered, *the class itself* serves as the referent. So, on this account, there is an extensionality constraint governing *all* definite descriptions: if $\Sigma(x)$ and $\Sigma'(x)$ are satisfied by the same elements, then $\iota x\Sigma(x)$ and $\iota x\Sigma'(x)$ have the same reference.[3] Once the suggestion has been made that empty descriptions refer to the empty class, it would be misleading to say, with Quine (1940: 149), that there is something "arbitrary" about Frege's suggestion that those "uninteresting" descriptions whose matrices are satisfied by more than one entity refer to the class of things satisfying the matrix: for this is *exactly* the suggestion for empty descriptions.

Frege's suggestions have been developed in a number of seemingly promising ways, notably by Carnap (1947), Scott (1967), and Grandy (1972). Carnap's position on improper descriptions might be summarized model-theoretically as follows: in each model M some arbitrary element $*_M$ in the domain (over which the variables of quantification range) serves as the referent (in M) of *all* descriptions that are improper with respect to M.[4]

On this treatment of descriptions, about the only thing that Gödel's slingshot demonstrates is just how bad Carnap's treatment of descriptions is (it was hardly a plausible treatment of descriptions in natural language anyway). Consider a model M in which *Fa* is false and the singular term *a* refers to $*_M$. (The existence of such a model presupposes that *which* element of the domain is functioning as the referent of improper descriptions is one feature (i.e. assignment) used in individuating models. This is surely the way to make sense of the idea that an "arbitrarily" chosen entity in the domain serves as the referent of improper descriptions.) In M (6) is false while (7) is true (for it amounts to the statement that $*_M$ $= *_M$):

---

[3] I am here indebted to Mark Sainsbury and Barry Smith.

[4] It is unclear whether it makes a great deal of sense to attribute to Carnap, as part of his overall account of descriptions—which, as he points out (1947: 8), "deviates deliberately from the meaning of descriptions in the ordinary language"—even the informal analogue of this model-theoretic account of improper descriptions, given the way he characterizes state descriptions. As Carnap points out, his system requires a prohibition on descriptions containing modal operators.

(6) *Fa*

(7) $a = \iota x(x=a \bullet Fx)$.

So on this model-theoretic treatment of descriptions, +ι-CONV is not even truth-preserving in *truth-functional* contexts. To my mind this finishes off Carnap's account once and for all; but even if some die-hard Carnapian semanticist insists on the theory, the fact that it permits (6) and (7) to differ in truth-value means it cannot be used in conjunction with a connective version of Gödel's slingshot to demonstrate any interesting conclusion.

The problem just raised concerning +ι-CONV could be eradicated by an ad hoc stipulation to the effect that only those singular terms that are definite descriptions can be assigned $*_M$ as their reference (that *names* of $*_M$ are not permitted!). If the resulting treatment of descriptions turns out to be the correct one—remember descriptions are still meant to be devices of singular reference on this treatment—then the connective version of Gödel's slingshot would demonstrate that no connective can have the following combination of features:

(8)   +ι-CONV   +PSST   −PSME.

This would be devastating for any theory of facts requiring "the fact that *Fa* = the fact that (. . .)" to have this set of features; but the particular model-theoretic bifurcation of names and descriptions it proposes should make one look askance.

The situation is only slightly different when it comes to the connective version of Church's slingshot. As pointed out by Taylor (1985), on the Carnapian treatment of descriptions (9) and (10) are *not* logically equivalent:

(9) ϕ

(10) $a = \iota x(x=a \bullet \phi)$.

Consider a model *M* in which ϕ is false, and the singular term '*a*' refers to $*_M$. (10) will be true in *M*; so (9) and (10) do not have the same truth-value in all models, hence they are not logically equivalent. So the connective version of the Church–Quine–Davidson slingshot itself collapses if descriptions are treated in the strict Carnapian way. The required logical equivalence could be regained by stipulating that only descriptions can refer, in *M*, to $*_M$; and with this stipulation the connective version of the slingshot would

now produce a result on the modified Carnapian treatment, namely
that no connective can have the following combination of features:

(11)   +PSLE   +PSST   −PSME.

While this will herald the demise of certain theories of facts, it will
not unsettle Barwise and Perry (1983) or Searle (1996) who see
logical equivalence as no guarantee of factual equivalence, i.e. it
will not bother those who deny that "the fact that φ = the fact that
(. . .)" is +PSLE.

The failure of the desired logical equivalence on the original
Carnapian treatment of descriptions suggests to Taylor a modified
slingshot. The idea, put into connective format, is to tack $a \neq \iota x(x$
$\neq x)$ onto φ and derive ❽(ψ • $a \neq \iota x(x \neq x)$) from ❽(φ • $a \neq \iota x(x \neq x)$)
and (φ ≡ ψ) in exactly the same way as ❽ψ is meant to be derived
from ❽φ and (φ ≡ ψ) using the original proof. The beauty of Taylor's
version of the slingshot is that it avoids any special stipulation
concerning which terms can refer to $*_M$, *and* it guarantees the logical equivalence of (9) and (10). This could be viewed as damaging
to some theories of facts and states of affairs because it demonstrates the truth of a statement such as (12):

(12) The fact that (φ • $a \neq \iota x(x \neq x)$) =
      the fact that (ψ • $a \neq \iota x(x \neq x)$).

Taylor's strategy for avoiding this slingshot is to define a
notion of "tight" logical equivalence, and then maintain that tight
logical equivalents stand for the same state of affairs whereas
mere logical equivalents need not. This involves defining a class
of expressions that might be called the "tight" logical constants,
a class that includes the quantifiers and truth-functional connectives but not the description operator or the identity sign. While I
have sympathy with Taylor's view that the standard notion of
logical equivalence is still somewhat murky, I am not sure that he
improves matters by rolling in tight equivalence. More importantly, Taylor's manoeuvres do not, by themselves, allow him to
avoid *Gödel's* slingshot, which makes no appeal to logical equivalence, standard or tight. As far as Taylor's theory of facts (or
states) is concerned, in order to avoid Gödel's slingshot, he would
have to deny, in addition, that *Fa* and $a = \iota x(x=a • Fx)$ stand for
the same fact.

Fregean approaches to descriptions have also been proposed by

Scott (1967) and Grandy (1972). On these treatments, bound variables range over a domain D, but the values of singular terms and free variables may lie in a "pseudo-domain" $D°$ stipulated to be disjoint from D and non-empty. An improper description is assigned a value in $D°$, "thereby emphasising its impropriety" as Scott says.[5] The situation with respect to Gödel's slingshot is much as before. Consider a model M in which Fa is false and the singular term a refers to $*_M°$, the "pseudo-object" selected from $D°$ to be the referent of descriptions that are improper with respect to M. In such a model (9) is false while (10) is true. So, again, we have treatments of descriptions according to which truth-functional contexts are not +ι-CONV. So while these treatments certainly solve some of the problems that taxed Scott and Grandy the fact that they permit (9) and (10) to differ in truth-value ensures that they cannot be used in conjunction with Gödel's slingshot to show anything new about connectives and also suggests strongly that they are inadequate as treatments of descriptions in natural language.

Church's slingshot fares no better because (9) and (10) are *not* logically equivalent. Scott's treatment declares (9) false and (10) true in any model M in which φ is false and a refers to $*_M°$; Grandy's declares (9) false and (10) true in any model M in which φ is false and a refers to the referent of descriptions whose matrix has the *intension* of $(x=a • φ)$. Thus Church's slingshot falls apart if descriptions are treated in the ways Scott and Grandy suggest.

Again, tinkering with the class of expressions that can take $*_M°$ (or anything else in $D°$) as a value would alter things, but such a move would constitute a clear departure from the theories of Scott and Grandy. However, such tinkering may be what Olson (1987) has in mind when he suggests that (9) and (10) are logically equivalent upon a "Fregean" theory of descriptions according to which an improper description refers to "some object outside the universe" (p. 84 n. 9). Assuming that Olson has not simply overlooked models in which a refers to $*_M°$, he must have in mind a semantics quite different from those envisaged by Scott and Grandy (not to mention Frege). It is a feature of the Scott–Grandy systems that the values of singular terms (but not bound variables) may lie

---

[5] According to Grandy, "Not all objects in the pseudo-domain are possible objects for one of them will be the denotation of $(\iota x)(x \neq x)$" (1972: 175).

in $D°$, and it is this feature that legitimizes the selection of an element in $D°$ as the value of a description—a singular term on this proposal—whose matrix is not uniquely satisfied by something in D. So if Olson has in mind a referential semantics according to which (9) and (10) *are* logically equivalent, then he must postulate two distinct classes of singular terms, those that can take values in $D°$ and those that cannot, and he must put descriptions into the former class and proper names into the latter. Treating definite descriptions so differently from other singular terms would make the resulting theory less attractive than the Scott–Grandy theories and raise the question "why treat descriptions as singular terms at all rather than as quantified noun phrases as the Russellian proposes?"

10.4 STRAWSONIAN THEORIES

The final treatment of descriptions I want to consider is the one Taylor produces (but does not overtly endorse) by recasting some of Strawson's (1950*b*) views in model-theoretic terms. (Taylor is well aware that his reformulation cannot capture Strawson's own intentions and that these intentions are not important for the purposes at hand. On Strawson's account it is *speakers* rather than singular terms that refer; and his assault on Russell's Theory of Descriptions is part of a general campaign against the ideas that terms refer and sentences are true or false; thus some distortion of Strawson's views is inevitable in any attempt to recast them model-theoretically; important choices where Strawson is unclear or inconsistent are also necessary.)

The key features of this account are (*a*) the rejection of bivalence: a sentence containing a description that is improper with respect to a model M will lack a truth-value in M; and (*b*) a refinement of the notion of logical equivalence to take into account cases in which sentences lack truth-values: two sentences are *logically equivalent* if and only if they have the same truth-value *in every model in which they both have a truth-value*. (It would be very odd for *Quine* to pursue such an approach as he has consistently opposed truth-value gaps and praised Russell's Theory of Descriptions for eliminating them where descriptions and names are concerned.) On this account, (13) and (14) are logically equivalent:

(13) φ

(14) $a = \imath x(x{=}a \bullet \phi)$.

In any model in which (13) is true, so is (14); in any model in which
(13) is either false or lacks a truth-value, the description $\imath x(x{=}a \bullet \phi)$
is improper and so (14) lacks a truth-value; so every model in which
(13) and (14) both have a truth-value is a model in which they are
both true; thus they are ("Strawsonian") logical equivalents.

On this treatment of descriptions, the Church–Quine–Davidson
slingshot appears to demonstrate that no connective can have the
following combination of features:

(15)   +PSST   +PSLE   −PSME.

But the rejection of bivalence and the subsequent refining of logical equivalence raise important questions. First, logical equivalence
is standardly taken to be tightly, if not definitionally, connected to
other notions, for example *logical consequence*, *logical truth*, and
material equivalence. On the proposed refinement, is there pressure
to redefine the notion of logical truth (from the standard (i) "$\models \phi$
if, and only if, ϕ is true in all models" to (ii) "$\models \phi$ if, and only if, ϕ
is true in all models in which ϕ has a truth-value")? Given that stan-
dardly $\phi \models \dashv \psi$ if and only if $\phi \models \psi$ and $\psi \models \phi$, is there pressure to
redefine the notion of logical consequence? And given that stan-
dardly if $\phi \models \dashv \psi$ then $\models (\phi \equiv \psi)$, should the truth-table for '$\equiv$' be
the one given by Halldén (1949) and Körner (1960) for certain
logics in which bivalence is rejected—"($\phi \equiv \psi$) is true if, and only if,
ϕ and ψ are either both true or both false; without (standard) truth-
value otherwise"—or should it differ in some way? And what of
the truth-table for negation? I do not mean to be insisting that all
of these (and related) questions cannot be answered together to
produce a consistent and attractive package; I simply want to point
out that such questions need to be answered by anyone who wants
to give up bivalence and refine logical consequence in the way
Taylor suggests.[6]

Secondly, and more importantly, even if there is no formal problem with the account, it appears to be inadequate to the task of
providing an account of descriptions in natural language. Put
bluntly, there are just too many (utterances of) sentences of natural

---

[6] I am here indebted to Marcus Giaquinto for fruitful discussion.

language that seem to have clear truth-values despite containing improper descriptions. I have discussed such cases at length elsewhere, so I will be brief here.[7] Utterances of (16)–(18) made today would surely be true, false, and true respectively precisely because there is no king of France:

(16) The king of France does not exist
(17) Gödel is the king of France
(18) The king of France is not bald since there is no king of France.

Perhaps clever theories of negation, existence, identity, and predication could help the Strawsonian here, but they could not help with a sentence like (19):

(19) Last night Blair dined with the king of France.

And appeals to a semantically relevant asymmetry between singular terms in subject position and those that form part of a predicate phrase might help with (19), but they will not help with (20) and (21):

(20) The king of France borrowed Blair's car last night.
(21) The king of France shot himself last night.

Descriptions occurring in non-extensional contexts create similar problems. I may say something true or false by uttering (22) or (23):

(22) The first person to land on Mars in 1990 might have been Dutch
(23) Kurt thinks the largest prime lies between 10^{27} and 10^{31}.

At the very least, then, we must reject the view that the use of an empty description *always* results in an utterance without a (standard) truth-value. Strawson (1964, 1972, 1986) came to realize this; and in an attempt to reduce the number of incorrect predictions made by his earlier theory, he suggests that sometimes the presence of an improper description renders the proposition expressed false, and at other times it prevents a proposition from being expressed at all. Since nothing appears to turn on structural or logical facts about the sentence used, Strawson suggests restrict-

---

7 See Neale (1990, ch. 2).

ing the "truth-value gap" result by appealing to the *topic of discourse*. Once the Strawsonian model-theorist makes this concession, even if a workable semantics can be salvaged, the logical equivalence being sought must surely drift away.

The status of slingshot arguments is clearly a complex matter if definite descriptions are treated as devices of singular reference. On Hilbert and Bernays's treatment Gödel's slingshot demonstrates something of mild interest, but the Church–Quine–Davidson version proves only the truth of one of its own premisses. On Fregean treatments, according to which improper descriptions refer, by stipulation, to some entity in the domain D of quantification or to some entity in a non-empty and disjoint "pseudo-domain" $D°$, both slingshots demonstrate something of significance only if descriptions are treated differently from other singular terms, a move which robs the placement of descriptions into the class of singular terms of its appeal and has formal consequences that still need to be explored. (But a modified slingshot, due to Taylor, appears to hit its target without such a contortion.) The full range of consequences of the model-theoretic Strawsonian treatment (which abandons bivalence) also needs exploration. On the assumption that the treatment is coherent, both slingshots hit their targets, but the treatment itself, even if coherent, does not come at all close to succeeding as an account of descriptions in natural language.

At this juncture it is worth reminding ourselves of the force of slingshot arguments on a standard Russellian analysis of descriptions. The Church–Quine–Davidson slingshot succeeds in showing only that any connective that is +PSLE and +ι-SUBS is also +PSME. Gödel's, by contrast, shows something more worrying: any connective that is +ι-CONV and +ι-SUBS is also +PSME (this is more worrying on the obvious assumption that every "Gödelian equivalence", as given by ι-CONV, is also a logical equivalence, but not vice versa). This fact will be of interest if we find connectives or contexts that are −PSLE, +ι-SUBS, and +ι-CONV: defenders of such connectives will have no recourse to the most common rejoinder to slingshot arguments: denying that the connective in question is +PSLE.

Facts Revisited

11.1 IDENTITY CONNECTIVES

The importance of the proofs examined in the previous three chapters lies in the fact that interesting sentence connectives are common, although often buried, in various forms of philosophical discourse. The pressing question is the degree to which constraints on the logic of connectives place strictures on philosophical theories of, for example, facts, states of affairs, situations, propositions, beliefs, necessity, time, probability, causation, action, explanation, and obligation.[1]

In addition to any syntactically simple connectives we come across, more complex ones can be extracted from sentences that purport to be about facts, propositions, psychological states, or anything else that is naturally expressed sententially. For example, it is a simple matter to construct two-place *entity–identity connectives* from sentences: "$FIC(\phi, \psi)$" for "the fact that ϕ = the fact that ψ"; "$PIC(\phi, \psi)$" for "the proposition that ϕ = the proposition that ψ"; and "$BIC(\phi, \psi)$" for "the belief that ϕ = the belief that ψ". The relevance of this to theories of facts, propositions, and beliefs is straightforward: no theory of facts (propositions, beliefs) can treat

---

[1] Of course if a formal constraint were of such a nature that no one could ever consider putting forward a theory that was later found to violate it, then it would be of no philosophical significance. The claim that any constraint delivered by a slingshot proof would be of this nature is trumpeted by Oppy (1997) in response to my 1995 discussion of Gödel's slingshot. Presumably, in order to verify Oppy's claim, one would need either (i) to examine every theory of facts, states, propositions, probability, causation, action, explanation, obligation, etc. ever postulated (or likely to be postulated) and then show that each satisfies the constraint, or (ii) to discover some precise feature F possessed by every conceivable theory and show that any theory with F trivially and obviously satisfies the constraint. Unsurprisingly, Oppy succeeds in doing neither of these things. For discussion, see Neale and Dever (1997).

FIC (PIC, BIC) as both +ι-SUBS and +ι-CONV for otherwise the fact (proposition, belief) that φ will be identical to the fact (proposition, belief) that ψ, where φ and ψ are replaced any two true sentences, and so all facts (propositions, beliefs)—or at least all *atomic ones*—will collapse into one Great Fact (Proposition, Belief).

As far as beliefs (and other psychological states) are concerned, the constraint is trivially satisfied by practically every theory one might take seriously. To the extent that there is any widespread and sustained agreement about substitutions *s.v.* in contexts of propositional attitude, only perfect synonyms (if there are any) may be swapped (it is maintained by some people that certain singular terms are directly referential and swappable *s.v.* in such contexts); and since the result of applying ι-SUBS to an extensional sentence φ will rarely yield a sentence φ′ that is synonymous with φ, there is no reason to think that BIC(φ) and BIC(φ′) will always be true together. In short, *no theory of belief* is going to treat BIC as +ι-SUBS, and to that extent the connective proof based on Gödel's slingshot will have no impact on such theories. (Since BIC is -ι-SUBS, it is irrelevant whether it is +ι-CONV, as some would maintain.)

11.2 FACT IDENTITY

When we turn to facts (states, etc.) and propositions, matters are considerably more complex and interesting. Facts have been summoned to play diverse philosophical roles, including those of, for example, truth-makers, causal relata, objects of knowledge, objects of perception, slices of possible worlds, and (when big enough) possible worlds themselves. Consequently, the literature contains all sorts of theories of facts.[2] Some philosophers view facts as true propositions, others vehemently deny this; some individuate facts by their constituents and structure, others deny that facts have objectual constituents; some identify facts that necessarily coexist, others treat all facts as necessary existents; some identify facts in terms of spatio-temporal location, others deny that facts have one or other form of location; some posit only atomic facts, others are happy with, for instance, conjunctive, negative, or general facts.

Recall that Gödel's main claim about facts and descriptions was

[2] See Ch. 1 n. 2.

that *Russell's* theory is unscathed by slingshot as long as it is
supported by his Theory of Descriptions (about which Gödel had
confused reservations). Russell held a structuralist theory in the
sense of Fine (1982): (i) facts contain objects and properties as
components; (ii) the structure of a true sentence mirrors the structure of the fact for which it stands. Additionally, Russell held that
(iii) no object in a fact corresponding to "the *F* is *G*" corresponds
to the definite description "the *F*" because such a phrase, along
with "every *F*" or "no *F*", is not a singular term but a device of
quantification. On such accounts, FIC is not +ι-SUBS because two
definite descriptions of the same object will not, in general,
contribute the same descriptive properties to a fact. Secondly, the
structured character of facts guarantees that FIC will not support ι-
CONV since the quantificational nature of descriptions introduces
properties not present in the pre-*iota*-conversion fact. So Russell's
theory of facts is *fine*: even if he takes FIC to be +PSST (which he
does), he assumes his own Theory of Descriptions and takes FIC to
be −ι-SUBS (and also −ι-CONV, given other aspects of the theory).
Gödel appears to have seen all of this.

But of course not all theories of facts are Russellian. The relevant question is whether *every* friend of facts can deny that FIC is
+ι-SUBS and +ι-CONV as easily as Russell can, i.e. without giving up
core components of his or her theory. As Taylor (1985) points out,
there are legitimate philosophical pressures driving the fact-theorist
towards *acceptance* of the inference principles ι-SUBS and ι-CONV in
connection with FIC. Such an acceptance

> embodies two further evident consequences of the traditional conception
> of the descriptum of a sentence as the complex of the entities relevant for
> its truth—that sentences so closely connected as to be guaranteed by logic
> alone to share a truth-value cannot differ in truth-relevant entities, and so
> must share their descriptum; and that sentences which, like "Cicero
> orated" and "Tully orated", differ merely in the manner they choose to
> specify the same truth-relevant entity cannot diverge in the complex of
> such entities they describe. (1985: 30)

Taylor is here suggesting that according to common views of the
role and nature of facts, FIC is *both* +ι-SUBS and +ι-CONV. (To be
precise, the second principle Taylor is concerned with is not ι-CONV
but the more generous PSLE.) And this is surely enough to refute the
claim, voiced by Oppy (1997), that *no* fact-theorist could *ever*

begin constructing a theory of facts which, upon later examination, was found to entail a treatment of FIC as +ι-SUBS and +ι-CONV. The contrast between Taylor and Oppy on this matter is striking. Prima facie, says Taylor, theories of facts will treat FIC as both +ι-SUBS and +ι-CONV. But according to Oppy, every prima facie plausible theory of facts will treat FIC as either –ι-SUBS or –ι-CONV. Taylor and Oppy seem to be pulled in opposite directions by their own ideas of *what facts should look like*. The reasonable thing for a neutral investigator to do is avoid commitment one way or the other: prima facie, philosophers are likely to posit *all sorts* of theories of facts, and it will pay to *examine* a few in connection with ι-SUBS and ι-CONV.

Wittgensteinian theories of facts—by which I mean theories shaped by a number of doctrines in the *Tractatus*—are interestingly different from their Russellian cousins. According to Wittgensteinian theories, at bedrock there are just *atomic, particular* facts because (i) all facts are truth-functions of particular facts, and (ii) the logical constants do not stand for components of facts. (Proposition (i) is a reflex of *Tractatus* 5: "A proposition is a truth-function of elementary propositions"; proposition (ii) is a reflex of *Tractatus* 4.0312: "My fundamental idea is that the 'logical constants' are not representatives; that there can be no representatives of the *logic* of facts.") The positive thought behind these doctrines is that the world is the totality of atomic particular facts. This totality determines everything. The negative thoughts behind the doctrines are reflexes of (*a*) a reluctance to regard universals as components of facts, and (*b*) the purported incomprehensibility of the idea that, for example, ϕ and $\sim\sim\phi$ should stand for distinct facts. Appeal to first-order properties is meant to be finessed by appeals to "arrangements" of objects; appeal to second-order properties (i.e. generality) is meant to be finessed by appeal to truth-functions of atomic, particular facts. The case against ϕ and $\sim\sim\phi$ standing for distinct facts is usually made, in part, by appeal to the doctrine that the conclusion of a formal inference must be "in some sense contained in the premises and not something new" (Ramsey 1927: 48). From the single fact that ϕ one should not be able to infer an infinite number of different facts, such as the fact that $\sim\sim\phi$ and the fact that $(\phi \bullet \sim\sim\phi)$; at best, says Ramsey, we have here distinct linguistic forms that stand for the same fact.

Wittgensteinian theories also hold that tautologies do not stand for facts. (This is a reflex of *Tractatus* 4.462: "Tautologies and contradictions are not pictures of reality. They do not represent any possible situations. For the former admit *all* possible situations, and the latter none.") This invites a question about ($\phi \bullet (\psi \vee \sim\psi)$), where ϕ is true. And the official answer is that this sentence and ϕ stand for the same fact. (This is a reflex of *Tractatus* 4.465: "The logical product of a tautology and a proposition says the same thing as the proposition. This product, therefore, is identical to the proposition.") This is also a consequence of the account of facts proposed by Prior (1948), according to which logically equivalent sentences stand for the same fact. As noted in Chapter 4, Wittgenstein holds that Fa and $\exists x(x=a \bullet Fx)$ are equivalent (*Tractatus* 5.441, 5.47); and both Wittgenstein and Prior commit themselves to the logical equivalence of Fa and $a = \iota x(x=a \bullet Fx)$ via Russellian analyses of descriptions. Hence neither Wittgenstein nor Prior has the means (or inclination) to claim that Fa and $a = \iota x(x=a \bullet Fx)$ stand for distinct facts (where Fa is true).[3] In short, Wittgenstein and Prior are committed to viewing FIC as +ι-CONV, and the sorts of consideration motivating them are surely those behind (i) Taylor's (1985) suggestion that sentences "so closely connected as to be guaranteed by logic alone to share a truth-value" should stand for the same fact, and (ii) Fine's (1982) suggestion that what he calls *empirical* theories of facts identify facts if and only if they "necessarily co-exist", a suggestion that Olson (1987) also finds attractive. For present purposes the moral of all

---

[3] Wittgenstein's position is complicated by his postulation of only particular facts. It is commonly held that he accepts Russell's position that descriptions cannot be taken to stand for things and that the viability of the project of the *Tractatus* presupposes the viability of Russell's Theory of Descriptions—or some other non-referential treatment. (See e.g. Anscombe 1959.) Of course, since he posits only particular facts and does not take universals to be components of facts, Wittgenstein treats quantified sentences very differently from Russell, and his treatment must extend to sentences containing descriptions—or rather to the quantified sentences that sentences containing descriptions abbreviate. It would be a mistake to view Wittgenstein's rejection of Russell's account of quantification as involving a rejection of Russell's Theory of Descriptions. I am inclined to agree with Anscombe that without the Theory of Descriptions (or some other non-referential theory) there could have been no *Tractatus* as we understand it. The main point here, however, is that even if Wittgenstein wants to reduce sentences containing descriptions to sentences containing only primitive notation, this will not guarantee, within his system that FIC is −ι-SUBS. Indeed, it is not at all obvious that he is not committed to the view that FIC is +ι-SUBS. I leave it to those better qualified to comment on the full theory of the *Tractatus* to sort this out, something that needs to be done to establish whether Wittgenstein's theory of facts is even consistent.

this is that, in order to avoid the collapse of all facts into one, Wittgenstein and Prior need to ensure that FIC is –ι-SUBS. And it is unclear whether this comports with the rest of Wittgenstein's system without extensive investigation.

There are Wittgensteinian theories of facts that explicitly treat FIC as +ι-SUBS. For example, Wilson (1959*b*, 1974) holds that (i) the world is the totality of facts, (ii) a true sentence corresponds to a fact, (iii) facts are true propositions, (iv) there are only atomic particular propositions and hence only atomic particular facts. Additionally, Wilson is explicit that (v) FIC is both +PSST and +ι-SUBS. However, it is unclear from his writing whether Wilson takes himself to be following Wittgenstein and Prior in taking FIC to be +PSLE or +ι-CONV. If he is, then his facts provably collapse into one. He does commit himself to this: (vi) the fact that the teacher of Plato is wise = the fact that something is wise and identical to all and only those things which are teachers of Plato (1974: 307). But since he holds that there are only atomic particular facts, it would seem that Wilson will have to treat FIC as +ι-CONV, thus precipitating the aforementioned collapse. The situation is muddied, however, by his claim that (vii) propositions contain individuals, properties, and times as components. It is unclear how he can maintain this while holding that FIC is +ι-SUBS, as he does. At the very least, then, the connective proof obtained from Gödel's slingshot puts unbearable pressure on Wilson's theory of facts. This, of course, is precisely what the proof is *supposed* to do: force the fact-theorist to articulate his or her theory with sufficient precision that it can be evaluated for consistency given that a definite barrier to consistency has been established. The point is not to eradicate talk of facts but to filter out theories of facts that are inconsistent.[4]

Austinian theories of facts are also vulnerable here. Austin construes facts quite broadly: "phenomena, events, situations, states of affairs ... surely of all of these we can say that they are facts" (1954: 156). To the extent that he wants facts as "entities" Austin wants them as truth-makers, and it is this feature of his approach to truth that leads people to view it as a version of the correspondence theory and prompts Davidson to assemble a slingshot argument against facts.

[4] This is something Oppy (1997) fails to appreciate. For discussion, see Neale and Dever (1997).

Austin requires no *structural* correspondence between the words used to make a (true) statement and a fact; he distinguishes himself from Russell and Wittgenstein in no uncertain terms:

> there is no need whatsoever for the words used in making a true statement to "mirror", in any way, however indirect, any feature or component of the situation or event; a statement no more needs, in order to be true, to reproduce the "multiplicity," say, of the "structure" or "form" of the reality, than a word needs to be echoic or writing pictographic. To suppose that it does, is to fall once again into the error of reading back into the world the features of language. (1950: 125)

It is not easy to pin Austin down on the precise status of facts and the way we are meant to distinguish them from one another. Although he voices suspicion of the "fact that" idiom and outlaws questions as to whether a statement fits a particular fact, he does permit questions as to "whether the statement that *S squares with* or '*does justice to*' the fact that *F* ('*F*' ≠ '*S*')" (1954: 160). The phrases that replace '*S*' and '*F*' will be sentences; so, although we cannot extract FIC from Austin's talk, we can extract a two-place connective SQ, where SQ(ϕ, ψ) is read as "the statement that ϕ squares with the fact that ψ".

On Austinian theories, facts are commonplace parts of the world, and this leaves such theories particularly vulnerable to the connective proof based on Gödel's slingshot, particularly if descriptions are treated as singular terms—presumably Austin would not endorse Russell's theory. Consider

(1) The cat has mange.

This squares with a fact, and that fact is just the condition of the cat: "the condition of the cat is a fact, and is something in the world" (1954: 158). However we understand the condition of the cat, the description we use to pick out the cat itself will not affect that condition (that it has mange). Thus the condition of the cat is the very same condition as the condition of the largest feline in the room—if "one" is in a mangy condition, then "both" are.[5] So if the

---

[5] This is at least clear on the assumption that descriptions are interpreted referentially, and thus provide the same object—that cat—in both cases. Matters are less clear when descriptions are taken to be Russellian. Austin says next to nothing to say about the nature of the demonstrative conventions at work in quantified statements, but at one point he does express scepticism about general facts:

condition of the cat is the fact that the cat has mange, then both of the following are true:

(2) The statement that the cat has mange squares with the fact that the cat has mange

(3) The statement that the largest feline in the room has mange squares with the fact that the cat has mange.

So the Austinian connective SQ is plausibly +ι-SUBS. It also seems likely that it will be +ι-CONV, at least if descriptions are treated referentially. The relevant question here is whether the following square with the same fact:

(4) Cicero snores
(5) Cicero is the unique person who is Cicero and snores.

In both cases, the relevant fact is just the condition of Cicero (his snoring condition, if the statements are true). Again, since Austin wants his facts to be just ordinary parts of the world singled out by the demonstrative conventions of the sentence in question, and since—by any reasonable account of what counts as a demonstrative convention—sentences related by Gödelian equivalence share demonstrative content, the Austinian has little room for manoeuvre.[6] It seems likely, then, that the simplest Austinian theories will succumb to the connective proof based on Gödel's slingshot, reducing to the position that there is only one fact.[7]

> Either we suppose that there is nothing there but the true statement itself, nothing to which it corresponds, or else we populate the world with linguistic Doppelgänger (and grossly overpopulate it—every nugget of 'positive' fact overlaid by a massive concentration of negative facts, every tiny detailed fact larded with generous general facts, and so on). (1950: 123)

One plausible interpretation is that, on Austin's account, general statements are demonstratively correlated with the entire world, in which case inter-substitution of (Russellian) definite descriptions will not affect the fact expressed.

[6] Interestingly, Austinian theories appear to avoid Church's slingshot.

[7] In response to my 1995 paper, Oppy (1997) suggests that the constraint imposed on theories of facts by the connective proof based on Gödel's slingshot is no more philosophically interesting than this one: "Oppy's cheapshot says that no theory of facts should allow that it is a fact that the moon is made of green cheese. Oppy's cheapshot is a genuine constraint: no decent theory of facts should violate it" (1997: 127). Apparently realizing the weakness of the comparison as soon as he airs it, Oppy immediately retreats, in a footnote, to a revised cheapshot in order to make the same rhetorical point: "no theory of facts should allow that it is a fact that the greatest prime number is less than 200" (p. 127). The purported advantage of the revised cheapshot is that it imposes a constraint on "what facts there could be,

As I have stressed, Russell's Theory of Facts, according to which facts have properties as components, is safe. It is certainly tempting to draw the moral that if one wants non-collapsing facts one needs properties as components of facts. I have not attempted to prove this here, but I suspect it will be proved in due course.

11.3 EVENTS

The analysis of ordinary talk about causes and effects is taken by many philosophers, including Davidson, to have an important bearing on appeals to *events* and *facts*; and characterizing the logical forms of causal statements, with a view to revealing their semantic properties and ontological commitments, has become something of an industry within contemporary philosophy. Perhaps the most widely accepted view of causation is that, if it is anything interesting at all, it is a relation that holds between *events*, construed as unrepeatable particulars. But there are philosophers who hold that *facts* enter into causal relations, notably Barwise and Perry (1980), Bennett (1988), Searle (1995, 1998) and Vendler (1976). Indeed, causal statements are used directly by some of these authors to motivate ontologies of facts.

Before examining the sorts of causal statements that appear to involve reference to, or quantification over facts, I want to clarify various points about events, for it seems to me that the literature is rife with misunderstandings that we need to eradicate before we can say anything of consequence about facts.

The notion of an event lies at the heart of much contemporary philosophical discussion of causation, scientific explanation, perception, action, freedom, determinism, and the relationship between mind and body. And it seems to loom large in much recent work on the semantics of natural language, and not just in work that addresses talk of causes, explanations, actions, perception, and so on.

and not what facts there are" (p. 127 n. 7). But in both the main text and the foot-note Oppy has simply missed the real point of the proof based on Gödel's slingshot: it imposes a *structural* constraint on theories of facts, a constraint about the *logic* of facts as manifested in the connective FIC, a constraint on fact *identity*. For discussion, see Neale and Dever (1997).

It is largely due to Davidson (1980) that events have attracted so much attention in recent years. He has presented a two-pronged motivation for an ontology of events.

First, he has argued that without events—construed as unrepeatable particulars located in space and time—there is little prospect of making sense of much of our philosophical and daily talk. Talk of causation, for example, appears to be intelligible only if we assume that causes and effects are events and that causation is a relation that holds between events; determinism is best understood as the thesis that every event is causally determined by antecedent events, while materialism is most plausibly construed as the thesis that every mental event is identical with some physiological, hence physical, event; and human actions, according to Davidson, are themselves events, making these entities the primary subject matter of the theory of action.

Secondly, Davidson has led the way in exposing quantification over events in the *logical forms* of certain types of statement; and in the light of this work the notion of an event seems to be playing an increasingly prominent role in work on adverbs, reference, quantification, anaphora, and conditionals. Recall that for Davidson a theory of meaning for a language *L* should take the form of a theory of truth for *L* satisfying certain antecedently specified conditions (see Chapter 2). Such a theory is meant to reveal an ontology of events by virtue of pairing pieces of language (the variables of quantification) with both particular objects and particular events.

It is easy enough, semantically speaking, to motivate an ontology of events without positing hidden quantifications in, for example, action sentences or sentences containing adverbs. Gerunds are often used as common nouns of events, and the syntactic similarities with common nouns of ordinary objects—usually viewed as three-dimensional continuants—is simply too good to ignore, witness the following:

(6) Aristophanes saw a frog
(7) Aristophanes saw a flogging
(8) Aristophanes savoured every frog
(9) Aristophanes savoured every flogging.

In the notation of restricted quantification (see Chapter 4), (10) gives the schematic *logical form* of (6) and (7), (11) the schematic logical form (8) and (9):

(10) [an_x: Fx] Aristophanes saw x
(11) [$every_x$: Fx] Aristophanes saw x.

And it is not only gerunds; as Davidson reminds us, we have ordinary nouns of events too:

(12) Aristophanes saw a (some, one, every, no) storm.

Quantified noun phrases of events appear to function syntactically and semantically just like those of objects. For example, we find ambiguities of scope as in (13), which is the surface manifestation of two distinct logical forms:

(13) Most citizens saw a flogging
    (a) [a_y: flogging y] [$most_x$: citizens x] x saw y
    (b) [$most_x$: citizens x] [a_y: flogging y] x saw y.

And a noun phrase that involves quantification over events may contain a variable bound by a noun phrase with larger scope as in (14):

(14) Every citizen was upset by a flogging he saw
    [$every_x$: citizen x] [a_y: flogging y • x saw y]
    x was upset by y.[8]

As Davidson (1980) points out, it is plausible to suppose that phrases like "the flood", "the short-circuit", "the sinking of the *Titanic*", "the death of Socrates", "Socrates' death", and so on are definite descriptions of events. Consider (15) and (16), the logical forms of which can be provided using restricted quantifiers:

[8] Higginbotham (1983, 1999) has argued that there is at least one more type of perceptual statement that involves quantification over events. On his account, "Aristophanes saw a flogging" and "Aristophanes saw Socrates flog Plato" have similar logical forms in so far as the phrase functioning as the complement of "saw" functions as an indefinite description of an event in both cases. The logical form of the former is given by (i), that of the latter by (ii), which makes use of Davidson's (1980) event variables:

(i) [an_x: flogging x] Aristophanes saw x
(ii) [an_x: flogging(Socrates, Plato, x)] Aristophanes saw x.

Neale (1988) argues against the viability Higginbotham's (1983) original proposal, at least as it was meant to receive support from and dovetail with contemporary syntactic theory in the manner stated. The objections, it now seems to me, are flat-footed and can be met by systematic refinements. For discussion, see Higginbotham (1999).

(15) The death of Socrates upset Phaedo
[*the$_x$*: *death*(*Socrates, x*)] *x upset Phaedo.*[9]

(16) Simmias thinks the death of Socrates upset Phaedo
(a) *Simmias thinks*:
[*the$_x$*: *death*(*Socrates, x*)] *x upset Phaedo*
(b) [*the$_x$*: *death*(*Socrates, x*)]
Simmias thinks: x upset Phaedo.

The usual arguments used by Russell and others to show that noun phrases of the form "the so-and-so" used to describe objects are not referring expressions are equally applicable to noun phrases of the same form when used to describe events, e.g. the noun phrase "the death of Socrates". Assuming "Simmias", "Socrates", and "Phaedo" to be referring expressions, utterances of (15) and (16) would express propositions with perfectly determinate truth-conditions *even if*, at the time of utterance, Socrates is not dead. Moreover, an utterance of (16) may express a *true* proposition even if, at the time of utterance, Socrates is not dead. In summary, the non-occurrence of anything that satisfies the noun predicate "death of Socrates" would not prevent utterances of (15) and (16) from expressing determinate propositions with determinate truth-conditions. (Additionally, negation can be added to (15) with larger or smaller scope than "the death of Socrates", and the usual Russellian facts and reasoning ought to be clear.) So definite descriptions of events, just like descriptions of objects, can be involved in the usual ambiguities of scope as in (16) above, and permit binding from without as in (17):

(17) Every citizen was upset by the execution he saw
[*every$_x$*: *citizen x*] [*the$_y$*: *execution y* • *x saw y*]
x was upset by y.

11.4 EVENTS AND CAUSES

Consider the following sentences:

(18) There was a short-circuit *and* there was a fire
(19) There was a short-circuit *before* there was a fire

[9] I have here made use of Davidson's event variables.

(20) There was a fire *after* there was a short-circuit
(21) There was a fire *because* there was a short-circuit
(22) There was a short-circuit, *which caused it to be the case that* there was a fire
(23) *If* there was a short-circuit *then* there was a fire
(24) *The fact that* there was a short-circuit *caused it to be the case that* there was a fire.

The italicized expressions in these sentences are often seen as two-place connectives, the occurrence of "and" in (18) being the syntactic model for those in (19)–(22), and the (discontinuous) "if ... then" in (23) the syntactic model for the "the fact that ... caused it to be the case that" in (24). The important difference, of course, is that "and" and "if ... then" are meant to be extensional (i.e. truth-functional)—for the sake of argument, let us assume that they *are* extensional (or at least have extensional readings) and that apparent counter-examples can be explained away in a Gricean manner—whereas the proposed connectives in the other sentences are not: they are –PSME, as is readily verified.

According to Davidson (1980), the assumption that "before", "because", "which caused it to be the case that", and "the fact that ... caused it to be the case that" function semantically as connectives leads to the conclusion that they are extensional after all, and thereby heralds the end of such treatments. It is not necessary to examine the formal structure of the argument Davidson uses to reach this conclusion as it is a notational variant of the connective argument based on Church's slingshot, examined in Chapter 8. We have established already that this type of argument demonstrates neither that there are no non-extensional connectives nor that no non-extensional connective can be both +PSLE and +PSST, but only that no non-extensional connective can be both +PSLE and +ι-SUBS.

Whether this conclusion should be worrying to anyone proposing to view the temporal and causal expressions italicized above as connectives is something I shall examine shortly. First, I want to set out Davidson's own analyses of these temporal and causal expressions. For Davidson, the logical form of (18) is given by (25),

(18) There was a short-circuit *and* there was a fire
(25) $\exists x(short\text{-}circuit(x) \bullet \exists y(fire(y)))$,

where x and y are variables ranging over individual events. The logical forms of (19)–(21) are built on this simple model. For example, (19) comes out as (26):

(19) There was a short-circuit *before* there was a fire
(26) $\exists x(short\text{-}circuit(x) \bullet \exists y(fire(y) \bullet preceded(x,y)))$.

While (21) comes out as (27):

(21) There was a short-circuit, *because* there was a fire
(27) $\exists x(fire(x) \bullet \exists y(short\text{-}circuit(y) \bullet caused(x,y)))$.

This proposal is extensional because the work done by the seemingly non-extensional, temporal and causal expressions ("before" and "because") is handled by the extensional connective $\bullet$ and the extensional two-place predicates "preceded" and "caused". Moreover, according to Davidson, (27) also specifies the logical form of (22) and (24):

(22) There was a short-circuit, *which caused it to be the case that* there was a fire
(24) *The fact that* there was a short-circuit *caused it to be the case that* there was a fire.

Notice that since Davidson's account is purely extensional, all of the inference principles that preserve truth in truth-functional contexts should do likewise in the temporal and causal statements we have been examining—once their Davidsonian logical forms are properly specified. For example, suppose that (28) is true:

(28) The best hotel in town = the hotel on Lovers' Lane.

Then by ι-SUBS—an inference principle valid in extensional contexts—the truth of (29) should guarantee the truth of (30)

(29) There was a fire at the best hotel in town because there was a short-circuit
(30) There was a fire at the hotel on Lovers Lane because there was a short-circuit.

This seems correct. Any competing theory must account for data of this sort.

11.5 FACTS AND CAUSES

Strange claims have been made by people who take themselves to
be addressing the question "Are causal contexts extensional?"[10] If
we are to inject clarity into this question, we need to distinguish at
least two brands of purportedly causal locution. Compare the
following:

(31) The short-circuit *caused* the fire at the hotel on Lovers'
 Lane
(32) There was a fire at the hotel on Lovers' Lane *because* there
 was a short-circuit.

In (31) the causal expression is a transitive verb whose arguments
are noun phrases (definite descriptions of events). In (32), by
contrast, the causal expression looks more like a two-place connective whose arguments are *sentences* rather than noun phrases.
Davidson (1980) has argued that this difference is superficial and
that an analysis of the logical form of (32) reveals an occurrence of
the transitive verb "cause" and no occurrence of any causal
connective. Indeed, he uses a slingshot argument against the viability of non-extensional causal connectives.[11]

Putting aside the correct analysis of the logical form of (32) for
a moment, consider (31). On the assumption that nouns such as
'short-circuit' and 'fire' apply to events (rather than objects), and
on the plausible assumption that event descriptions, like object
descriptions, are best treated as Russellian—an assumption that
looks more attractive than ever in the light of the referential theories examined in the previous chapter—the logical form of (31) is
given by (31'):

(31') [the$_x$: *short-circuit x*]
 [the$_y$: *fire y • at-the-hotel-on-Lovers' Lane y*] *x* caused *y*.

---

[10] The question is addressed by, for example, Achinstein (1975, 1979), Anscombe
(1969), Chisholm (1965), Davidson (1980), Føllesdal (1965), Gottlieb and Davis
(1974), Kim (1993), Levin (1976), Lombard (1979), Lycan (1974), Mackie (1965,
1974), Mellor (1995), Pap (1958), Rosenberg and Martin (1979), Stern (1978), and
Vendler (1967a).
[11] Analyses of various causal expressions as non-extensional connectives have
been provided by e.g. Burks (1951), Mackie (1965, 1974), Needham (1994), and
Pap (1958).

So (31) has the same logical structure as (33), whose logical form is given by (33′):

(33) The king kissed the queen
(33′) [*the$_x$*: *king x*] [*the$_y$*: *queen y*] *x* kissed *y*.

The important point here concerns *scope*. On a Russellian analysis the descriptions in (31′) and (33′), unlike the variables they bind, are not within the scopes of "caused" or "kissed". More generally, since the descriptions in (31′) and (33′) do not occur within the scopes of any non-extensional expressions, they occur in extensional contexts.

Since coextensional predicate substitution in extensional contexts will not affect truth-value, any predicate inside any of the descriptions in (31) and (33) can be replaced *s.v.* by any coextensional predicate. Consequently, in an extensional context a description of an object or event may be replaced by any other description of the same object or event (see Whitehead and Russell's derived rule of inference *14.16 (ch. 4) and our ι-SUBS (Chapter 6)). So from (33) and (34),

(34) The queen = the most beautiful woman in the kingdom

we can validly infer (35):

(35) The king kissed the most beautiful woman in the kingdom.

Similarly, from (31) and (36),

(31) the short-circuit *caused* the fire at the hotel on Lovers' Lane
(36) the fire at the hotel on Lovers' Lane = the fire at the best hotel in town

we can validly infer (37):

(37) The short-circuit *caused* the fire at the best hotel in town.

But it would be a grave mistake to package this into the unthinking claim that causal contexts are extensional: we have not been talking about causal contexts here because we have not been talking about substitutions *within* the scopes of causal expressions: we've been talking about *external* substitutions, i.e. substitutions in simple non-causal extensional contexts.

By contrast, when it comes to (32),

(32) There was a fire at the hotel on Lovers' Lane *because* there was a short-circuit,

interesting questions about causal contexts and extensionality do emerge. In particular, if the occurrence of "because" is treated as a two-place connective, we can sensibly ask whether or not it is extensional and then proceed to examine what happens when coextensional expressions are substituted within its scope. And it is clear that the purported connective is *not* extensional: it does not permit the substitution of coextensional sentences *s.v.* Suppose (32) is true; then the contained sentences "There was a fire at the hotel on Lovers' Lane" and "There was a short-circuit" have the same extension (they are both true); but this is not enough to guarantee the truth of (38), which is obtained simply by switching the contained sentences:

(38) There was a short-circuit *because* there was a fire at the hotel on Lovers Lane.

Thus the purported connective is not +PSME.

But two further questions emerge at this point: (i) Is the connective +PSST? (ii) Is it +ι-SUBS?

(i) Let us use © as shorthand for the causal logician's two-place connective that is supposed to capture the semantics of "because" on one of its uses. It is clear that © is +PSST. The following is surely a valid inference:

(39) [1] Catiline fell © Cicero denounced him;
    [2] Cicero = Tully;
—————————————————————————
    [3] Catiline fell © Tully denounced him.

(ii) The connective © also *seems* to be +ι-SUBS, witness the following:

(40) [1] Catiline fell © the greatest Roman orator denounced him
    [2] The greatest Roman orator = the author of *De fato*
—————————————————————————
    [3] Catiline fell © the author of *De fato* denounced him.

But here we must be careful. The situation is reminiscent of Russell's (1905) discussion of George IV's wondering whether Scott was the author of *Waverley* and Smullyan's (1948) discussion of whether the number of planets is necessarily odd. In (40) perhaps the entries on lines [1] and [3] are ambiguous according as the descriptions are given large or small scope. If so, then it might be possible to claim that the purported validity of (40) provides no reason to think that © is +ι-SUBS. The idea would be that (40) is valid on the following interpretation:

(40′) [1] [*the$_x$*: *greatest-Roman-orator x*]
(*Catiline fell* © *x denounced Catiline*)
[2] The greatest Roman orator = the author of *De fato*

---

[3] [*the$_x$*: *author-of-De Fato x*]
(*Catiline fell* © *x denounced Catiline*).

But since there is no ι-substitution within the scope of © here, the intuitive validity of (40) gives us precious little information about the logic of ©. The relevant information must reside in the validity or invalidity of the following reading of (40):

(40″) [1] *Catiline fell* © [*the$_x$*: *greatest-Roman-orator x*]
(*x denounced Catiline*);
[2] The greatest Roman orator = the author of *De fato*

---

[3] *Catiline fell* ©
[*the$_x$*: *author-of-De fato x*] *x denounced Catiline*.

Can (40) can be understood as (40′)? Or does (40″) give the sole logical form of (40) and thereby demonstrate that © is +ι-SUBS? My own suspicion is that lines [1] and [3] of (40′) are not genuine readings of lines [1] and [3] of (40), for reasons that Evans (1977) highlighted in his discussion of anaphora.[12]

---

[12] (i) cannot be understood as either (ii) or (iii):

(i) *Every boy liked it$_1$ because [some car]$_1$ was red.
(ii) [*some$_y$*: *car y*] [*every$_x$*: *boy x*] ((*x liked y*) *because* (*y was red*))
(iii) [*every$_x$*: *boy x*] [*some$_y$*: *car y*] ((*x liked y*) *because* (*y was red*)).

Does this signal that it is not, in general, possible for a quantified noun phrase occurring within one of the "conjuncts" of "because" to be understood with larger scope than "because"? I suspect not, and that it shows only that the constraints on quantifier scope form a proper subset of the constraints on quantifier-variable anaphora.

Suppose © is +ι-SUBS; there is no good reason to think it is also +PSLE. If © is +PSLE, then (41), (42), and (43) all entail one another:

(41)   Catiline fell © Tully denounced him
(42)   (Catiline fell • (φ v ~φ)) © Tully denounced him
(43)   Catiline fell © (Tully denounced him • (φ v ~φ)).

And since there is no compelling reason to think this is the case, Church's slingshot poses no threat to a non-extensional understanding of ©.[13]

Gödel's slingshot is more worrying, however. Again, suppose © is +ι-SUBS. Is it also +ι-CONV? Do (41) and (44), or (41) and (45), entail one another?

(41)   Catiline fell © Tully denounced him
(44)   Catiline = ιx(x = Catiline • x fell) © Tully denounced him
(45)   Catiline fell © Tully = ιx(x = Tully • x denounced him).

If so, then the connective proof based on Gödel's slingshot has definite consequences for the causal logician: it is imperative to deny that © is +ι-SUBS. And obviously the way for the causal logician to do this is to endorse Russell's Theory of Descriptions and maintain that the argument in (40) is being read as (40′) by people who maintain that the inference is valid.

11.6 FACT IDENTITY AGAIN

We can put many statements that purport to make reference to facts into connective format; for example, the following can be rendered as one-place connectives:

(46)   It is a fact that ( )
(47)   the statement that (φ) corresponds to the fact that ( )
(48)   the fact that (φ) caused it to be the case that ( )
(49)   the fact that (φ) = the fact that ( ).

And if the occurrences of φ are removed from (47)–(49), we can view the results as two-place connectives, mirroring our fact identity connective FIC:

---

[13] Neale (1993b) suggests that © is +PSLE. This suggestion, which does not impinge upon the main points of that work, is mistaken.

(50)   the fact that ( ) = the fact that ( ).

Obviously FIC(ϕ, ϕ) is true (for fact-theorists). So we can begin to examine *any* theory of facts by looking at the inferential properties of FIC. If FIC is +PSME, then there is at most one fact. The connective proof based on Gödel's slingshot provides us with an additional piece of information: any fact-theorist who maintains that FIC is +ι-SUBS and +ι-CONV is committed to FIC's being +PSME, and so to the existence of at most one fact. So the task for the fact-theorist is now easy to state: (*a*) articulate a theory of facts according to which FIC lacks one of these properties; and (*b*) provide a semantics for descriptions that is consistent with the logic ascribed to FIC and also viable as an account of descriptions in natural language. (As far as Russell's theory of facts is concerned, Gödel's point is really that Russell manages to do all of this by (i) individuating facts by reference to their components, i.e. objects and properties (construed non-extensionally); (ii) denying that FIC is +ι-SUBS; and (iii)—surprise—subscribing to Russell's Theory of Descriptions.)

I take it that *no* fact-theorist who intends to get some metaphysical work out of facts wants to deny that FIC is +PSST. So the fact-theorist who wants to maintain that descriptions are singular terms has some work to do to avoid Gödel's slingshot. It cannot be avoided by remaining agnostic on the semantics of descriptions and denying that FIC is +PSLE (the principal strategy of Barwise and Perry (1981, 1983), Bennett (1988), and Searle (1995)). For Gödel's slingshot does not make use of PSLE, it makes use of ι-CONV. Denying that FIC is +ι-CONV means taking a definite position—if only disjunctively, with precise disjuncts—on the semantics of descriptions.

The fact-theorist who is a Russellian about descriptions has an easier task, for he or she has the option of simply denying that FIC is +ι-SUBS.[14] This strategy means saying something about the following inference:

---

[14] Searle (1995: 20) seems to want to hold that FIC is +PSST but not +ι–SUBS. This would give him a way of avoiding Gödel's slingshot as well as the Church–Davidson version if he had a theory of descriptions that allowed him to treat descriptions as other than singular terms. The obvious thing for him to do would be to accept Russell's theory. In earlier work Searle (1969) expressed reservations about that theory, but he has recently warmed to it.

(51) [1] The fact that the greatest Roman orator snored
= the fact that the greatest Roman orator snored
[2] The greatest Roman orator = the author of *De fato*

---

[3] the fact that the greatest Roman orator snored
= the fact that the author of *De Fato* snored.

If this is valid, then the fact-theorist who is a Russellian about descriptions will have to say that it does not involve ι-SUBS within the scope of FIC, but a substitution in the truth-functional context outside its scope, the argument being understood as valid only when the descriptions have large scope, i.e. when the argument is understood as (51'):

(51') [1] [the_x: greatest-Roman-orator x]
[the_y: greatest-Roman-orator y]
the fact that x snored = the fact that y snored
[2] The greatest Roman orator = the author of *De fato*

---

[3] [the_x: greatest-Roman-orator x]
[the_y: author-of-*De fato* y]
the fact that x snored = the fact that y snored.

(For simplicity, I have here ignored the quantification resulting from treating "the fact that . . ." as a Russellian description. Nothing turns on this.) So, again, we are faced with the question of determining whether or not the constraints on quantifier scope and variable-binding delivered by the best theory of syntax license (51') line [1] as a reading of (51) line [1]. (Cf. the discussion of (40) in Section 11.5.)

Naturally enough, exactly the same considerations apply when we bring together talk of facts and talk of causes—in the spirit of those fact-theorists who would maintain that facts (as well as, or instead of, events) are causal relata—as in the following inference:

(52) [1] The fact that there was a malfunction in the new sprinkler system caused the water not to flow
[2] The new sprinkler system = the cheap sprinkler system that Bill installed

---

[3] The fact that there was a malfunction in the cheap sprinkler system that Bill installed caused the water not to flow.

There is no knock-down argument against facts in this; but it is now abundantly clear that unless a theory of facts is presented with an accompanying theory of descriptions and an accompanying logic of FIC, there is every reason to treat it with caution. The task for the friend of facts is to put together a theory according to which facts are not so fine-grained that they are unhelpfully individuated in terms of true sentences, and not so coarse-grained that they collapse into one.

Finally, it should be noted that analogous tests can be produced for accounts of truth, statements, and propositions that do not appeal to facts. This is easily seen by viewing the following as connectives:

(53)   the statement that ( ) is true if and only if ( )
(54)   the proposition that ( ) is true if and only if ( )
(55)   the proposition that ( ) = the proposition that ( ).

We have learned several things. First, logical equivalence is not the real issue when it comes to the force of slingshot arguments. Secondly, the power of Gödel's version lies in the fact that it forces philosophers to say something about the semantics of definite descriptions as soon as they step outside the realm of extensional logic and as soon as they posit entities to which sentences are meant to correspond. Thirdly, although no non-extensional connective can be +ι-SUBS and +ι-CONV, this need not spell trouble for advocates of non-extensional logics and connectives who endorse Russell's Theory of Descriptions. Fourthly, Gödel's argument yields an elegant test for examining the logics of purportedly non-extensional contexts. Finally, referential treatments of descriptions have unpleasant consequences that are highlighted by connective proofs based on Gödel's slingshot.

The task for the fact-theorist is clear: provide a logic of FIC that (i) avoids the collapse that Gödel's argument demonstrates will take place if FIC is both +ι-SUBS and +ι-CONV, (ii) does justice to the semi-ordinary, semi-philosophical idea of what facts are, and (iii) permits facts to do some philosophical work.

Appendix

Incomplete Symbols

Russell says that descriptions are "incomplete symbols", that they "have no meaning in isolation", that they must be "contextually defined", that they "disappear on analysis". I suspect no attempt to say what Russell meant by these locutions will be at the same time consistent and satisfactory to all scholars. However, it is certainly possible to untangle much of what Russell says, and doing so can help explain some lingering worries about the Theory of Descriptions, including Gödel's.

What is a contextual definition? Are Russell's specific definitions *14.01 and *14.02 meant to have ontological import, to be reductive? Or are they intended merely to set out the truth-conditional contributions of descriptions? Or is the truth somewhere in between? Do all and only incomplete symbols receive contextual definitions? Upon examination, I think it is clear that requiring a contextual definition, being incomplete, and disappearing on analysis are quite distinct ideas. An important range of expressions, including quantified noun phrases ("denoting phrases") and connectives, are incomplete symbols, and at least some of these require contextual definitions (on at least one construal) yet do not disappear on analysis in any interesting sense. Furthermore, descriptions are incomplete symbols, for a Russellian, even if systems of restricted quantification are used.

At the time Russell was arguing for the Theory of Descriptions, he espoused what is often called a "realist" theory of meaning, according to which the meaning of an expression is some entity or other, the entity for which it *stands*.[1] Other things being equal, singular terms stand for particulars; predicates (common nouns, verbs, adjectives) stand for universals; and true sentences stand for facts. But what about quantified noun phases (denoting phrases) and logical connectives?

Quantified noun phrases do not have meanings in Russell's sense, i.e. they do not *stand for* things in the way names and predicates do. This is made clear as early as "On Denoting":

---

[1] For discussion, see e.g. Sainsbury (1979, 1993). My interpretation of Russell in this appendix is influenced by Sainsbury.

Everything, nothing, and *something* are not assumed to have any meaning in isolation, but a meaning is assigned to *every* proposition in which they occur. This is the principle of the theory of denoting I wish to advocate: that denoting phrases never have any meaning in themselves, but that every proposition in whose verbal expression they occur has a meaning. (1905: 42)

It requires no great effort to construct a semantic theory according to which denoting phrases *do* stand for things, e.g. higher-order functions, as in some versions of the theory of generalized quantification. Given the intimate connection between his theory of meaning and his theory of knowledge—in particular, the link expressed by the Principle of Acquaintance, which states that every proposition which we can understand must be composed wholly of constituents with which we are acquainted—Russell seems to have thought that no symbol should stand for such a function, and he consequently accepted that there are "meaningful" expressions that do not mean, i.e. stand for, anything—namely the logical constants and denoting phrases.[2] Definite descriptions belong to the latter class.

Here are three apparently different things we might say about a symbol *x*: (i) *x* is incomplete (or has no "meaning in isolation"); (ii) *x*'s semantic power is given by a "definition in use" (a "contextual definition"); (iii) *x* disappears on analysis. Many commentators view (i)–(iii) as three ways of expressing the same point, but this is surely incorrect. Let us begin with certain key remarks on pages 66–7 of *Principia* (Whitehead and Russell 1925):

By an "incomplete" symbol we mean a symbol which is not supposed to have any meaning in isolation but is only defined in certain contexts . . . Such symbols have what may be called a "definition in use" . . . we define the *use* of [such a symbol], but [the symbol] itself remains without meaning . . . This distinguishes such symbols from what (in a generalized sense) we may call *proper names*: "Socrates," for example, stands for a certain man, and therefore has a meaning by itself, without the need of any context. If we supply a context, as in "Socrates is mortal," these words express a fact of which Socrates himself is a constituent: there is a certain object, namely Socrates, which does have the property of mortality, and this object is a constituent of the complex fact which we assert when we say "Socrates is mortal."

Where there is talk of descriptions, we must be careful to distinguish those occurring in sentences of English ("the king of France" etc.) from those occurring in Russell's abbreviations of formulae of the language of *Principia* (ιxFx etc.). It is surely clear in Russell's remarks that what makes a

---

[2] The Principle of Acquaintance is stated in more or less the same way by Russell (1905: 56, 1911: 159, 1912: 32). Russell does, on occasion, say that quantifiers and connectives "involve" logical notions and that in order to use these expressions intelligibly we must grasp the notions involved. This does not, of course, entail that the expressions stand for objects.

symbol *incomplete* is the fact that it is not the sort of expression that stands for something. Now certainly there are grammatical, notational, and analytical *repercussions* of a symbol's being incomplete, for example where noun phrases—the sorts of expressions that may occupy the grammatical subject position of a sentence—are concerned:

> Whenever the grammatical subject of a proposition can be supposed not to exist without rendering the proposition meaningless, it is plain that the grammatical subject is not a proper name, *i.e.* not a name directly representing an object. Thus in all such cases, the proposition must be capable of being so analysed that what was the grammatical subject shall have disappeared.

Russell is here using "proposition" in the sense of "sentence", and the passage is fraught with characteristic use–mention sloppiness. When he says that "Whenever the grammatical subject of a proposition can be supposed not to exist" he is trying to avoid saying: "Whenever the grammatical subject of a proposition can be supposed to *stand for something* that does not exist", which is obviously problematic. What Russell means is: "Whenever the grammatical subject of a proposition can be supposed not to *stand for something*". On this account the grammatical subjects in each of the following sentences are not proper names: "The round square does not exist", "It is raining", "There is a fly in my soup". And two things follow from this: (*a*) they are incomplete symbols, and (*b*) if the sentences are to have truth-values, they must be "capable of being so analysed that what was the grammatical subject shall have disappeared". It is important to distinguish these claims. Here is what I think we can extract from Russell's discussions: (i) There are three types of expression that stand for things, namely, proper names, predicates, and sentences (standing for particulars, universals, and facts, respectively). (ii) An expression that does not stand for something is an incomplete symbol. (iii) A definite description is neither a predicate nor a sentence; so if a description stands for something it must be a proper name. (iv) If the grammatical subject of a sentence can be supposed not to stand for something without rendering the sentence incapable of standing for a fact, the grammatical subject is not a proper name. (v) A definite description can be supposed not to stand for something without rendering the sentence incapable of standing for a fact; so a definite description is not a proper name. (vi) So a description is an incomplete symbol. (vii) If the grammatical subject of a sentence can be supposed not to stand for something without rendering the sentence incapable of standing for a fact, then the sentence must be "capable of being so analysed that what was the grammatical subject shall have disappeared". (viii) So a sentence with a definite description as grammatical subject must be "capable of being so analysed that what was the grammatical subject shall have disappeared".

So (*a*) if *x* disappears on analysis, then *x* is an incomplete symbol, but (*b*) it is not the case that if *x* is an incomplete symbol, then *x* disappears on analysis. In particular, quantifiers and connectives are incomplete symbols, but they do not disappear on analysis. Indeed, some of them appear in the analyses of sentences whose grammatical subjects *do* disappear on analysis; for example, in the analysis of sentences whose grammatical subjects are definite descriptions. In abbreviatory notation, (1) is represented as (1′), which is shorthand for (1″):

(1)   the *F* does not exist
(1′)   ~E!$\imath x F x$
(1″)   ~$\exists x (\forall y (F y \equiv y = x))$.

"Here", says Russell, "the apparent grammatical subject [$\imath x F x$] has disappeared; thus in [(1′)] [$\imath x F x$] is an incomplete symbol" (Whitehead and Russell 1925: 66). The point here is that an incomplete symbol cannot appear as a "logical subject", i.e. it cannot appear *logically* as a subject expression—i.e., more generally, it cannot appear as the argument of a predicate in any genuine formula of the language of analysis. (This cannot be definitional because *predicates* also fail to show up in such positions but are not incomplete symbols.) Says Russell: "all phrases (other than propositions) containing the word *the* (in the singular) are incomplete symbols: they have a meaning in use, but not in isolation" (p. 67).

A contextual definition does not seem to be exactly a stipulative or an explicative definition.[3] If we look back at *14.01 and *14.02, there is a stipulative element to them, but this is really because they look as though they are stipulating a certain type of abbreviation, as far as the formal language of *Principia* is concerned. There is also an explicative element because Russell takes his contextual definitions to embody his analysis of definite descriptions in ordinary language, or at least a part (or form) of ordinary language precise or constrained enough to use in philosophical discussion. And I take it when Russell says descriptions are "defined in use", he means that his contextual definitions explicate their semantic powers. So these contextual definitions are real hybrids. Notice also that they involve something "disappearing on analysis", namely, expressions of the form $\imath x \phi$.

The question we need to ask now is whether contextual definitions of this ilk are characteristic of expressions "defined in use". It is usual to call the definition of • in terms of v and ~ a contextual definition. A symbol is introduced as an abbreviation, the semantic power of that symbol is explicated, and the symbol disappears on analysis. If we were so inclined, we could provide contextual definitions for *all* of our logical vocabulary (to

---

[3] As noted by Kaplan (1972), who discusses the notion fruitfully.

deal with negation straightforwardly, add the Scheffer stroke to our set of connectives). But of course this would be unsatisfactory as far as the explication of semantic powers is concerned: we would have an explicative circle with no way in. It is here that notions like analysis and reduction begin to loom large. For Russell, *14.01 and *14.02 are useful contextual definitions because they define new symbols in terms of primitive symbols of his formal language. Similarly for •, ≡, and =, which are not primitive but defined symbols in *Principia Mathematica*. But of course what is primitive for one purpose may not be for another. Rewriting the whole of *Principia* using the Scheffer stroke would certainly *reduce* the number of symbol types in play and so, in one way, simplify the execution of the project. But of course doing this would add insurmountably to comprehension: as Russell himself stressed, negation, conjunction, and alternation are more primitive *psychologically*; and to that extent they are more primitive *semantically* in the sense of "semantics" that most interests people working on the theory of meaning for natural language.

What are we to make, then, of Russell's talk of quantifiers and connectives being "defined in use"? We must, I think, either regard contextual definitions and definitions in use as rather different notions or else accept (more plausibly) that Russell had two closely related notions in mind when he talked ambiguously of contextual definitions, notions he had not cleanly separated. We might think of the truth-tables for ~ and ∨ (or axioms based on those tables) as showing us the semantic powers of these symbols; and since they do this by invoking whole sentences—i.e. fuller expressions in which the symbols are *used*—we might think of these as definitions in use; but these are not what people have standardly understood as "contextual definitions".[4] We must conclude, I think, that when Russell talks of "definitions in use", he has at least two things in mind, and to the extent that there is a common core it is that contextual definitions are invoked for symbols that are *incomplete*; they are ways of explaining the semantic powers of symbols that do not stand for things, i.e. symbols that do not stand for particulars or universals (or facts).

The proposition expressed by "the F is G" is the general proposition that there is one and only one F and everything that is F is also G. That is, the truth-conditions of "the F is G" can be given by a quantificational formula, which contains quantifiers and predicates but no singular term corresponding to the grammatical subject "the F". And this is what Russell means by saying that the *proposition* has no *logical subject*, even though the *sentence* has a *grammatical subject*; and what he means by saying that the sentence's *grammatical form* is not a good indication of its *logical form*

---

[4] The so-called contextual definition that Russell provides for the inverted-comma *of*-notation (see Ch. 4) does not use whole formulae at all: it looks a lot like a very straightforward abbreviation technique.

(or the logical form of the proposition the sentence expresses). The proposition is not about an object at all; it is about the relationship between two properties, *F* and *G*: exactly one thing has *F*, and nothing has *F* while lacking *G*. As we might put it today—but in a way not at all consonant with Russell's aims—"some *F* is *G*" is true if and only if the SOME relation holds between *F* and *G*; and "the *F* is *G*" is true if and only if the THE relation holds between them (this idea has more bite once the Theory of Descriptions is properly located with a theory of quantification in natural language, such as the theory of restricted quantification outlined in Ch 4).

It is sometimes claimed that treating descriptions in terms of restricted quantification involves rejecting Russell's view that descriptions are incomplete symbols.[5] The claim is confused. First a minor point. In the language of restricted quantification I have been using, it is not strictly accurate to say that English descriptions are represented *as* restricted quantifiers— although this is a useful shorthand that captures the spirit of the truth. Strictly speaking, a description functioning as the argument of a predicate *G* in English is represented in the language of restricted quantification by a restricted quantifier within whose scope *G* lies, *together with* a variable that lies within the scope of *G*, *a fortiori* within the scope of the restricted quantifier, which in fact binds the variable. If one insists on putting a notational spin on the idea that descriptions are incomplete symbols, the best thing to say is this: in any standard notation that makes use of quantifiers and variables, the formula representing an English sentence "the *F* is *G*" will contain a variable—rather than a closed singular term—as the argument of *G*. (Of course, there may be better ways of representing quantification than the standard way involving variables, but within the confines of traditional variable-binding systems, the generalization is fair.)

Secondly, although one is at liberty to interpret restricted quantifiers using the resources of generalized quantifier theory so that restricted quantifiers

---

[5] See e.g. Evans (1977, 1982) and B. Linsky (1992, forthcoming). I suppose no account of descriptions can be "truly" Russellian unless it is stated exactly as Russell stated it, but Evans and Linsky are wrong on the matter of what is involved, for Russell, in saying that a symbol is incomplete. According to Evans the use of a "binary" quantification $[the_x](Fx; Gx)$ to represent "the *F* is *G*" is quite compatible with Russell's claim that descriptions are incomplete symbols, whereas the use of a unary restricted quantification $[the_x: Fx]Gx$ is not. (Evans uses "binary" not in the standard sense of binding two distinct variables but in the sense of combining with two formulae to form a formula".) In a curious attempt to support this claim Evans argues that certain facts about donkey anaphora that can be captured using his binary quantifiers cannot be captured using unary restricted quantifiers. On the technical matter, Evans is just wrong: all of the relevant anaphoric facts drop out straightforwardly using unary restricted quantifiers; Evans simply overlooked the fact that a pronoun may go proxy for a relativized description taking smaller scope than another quantified noun phrase. For discussion, see Neale (1990, 1993*a*).

stand for things (typically, higher-order functions), such an interpretation is not forced upon the theorist who uses the notation of restricted quantification any more than a Tarskian or a Fregean or a substitutional interpretation is forced upon a theorist who uses a standard notation for the unrestricted quantifiers ∃ and ∀.[6] Indeed there are recent traditions that provide either Tarskian or Fregean analyses of restricted and binary quantifiers.[7] Thirdly, although Russell's Theory of Descriptions is often put forward as the paradigm case of a theory that invokes a distinction between *grammatical form* and *logical form*, ironically there is a sense in which it preserves symmetry: "the *F*", "every *F*", "some *F*", "no *F*", etc. are alike syntactically in that they are noun phrases that may occupy grammatically subject positions in surface grammar; but they are also *semantically* alike in that they are all incomplete symbols and, as their definitions in use make clear, induce quantification. On neither the account of quantification assumed by Russell nor the Tarskian account I have borrowed here do quantificational noun phrases *stand for* things. And neither the move from unrestricted to restricted quantification nor the use of a systematic *notation* for restricted quantification magically makes quantificational noun phrases start standing for things. In fact, the syntax and semantics of the particular notation I have used to represent restricted quantification might be thought to *highlight* the fact that I am treating quantified noun phrases as incomplete symbols. In the cases that are of any interest to us, the formula ψ with which a description [*the*$_1$: φ] combines to form a formula will contain a variable x_1 that the quantifier binds:

(2) [*the*$_1$: *king* x_1] x_1 *likes Cicero.*

The variable x_1 occupies the "logical subject position" of the formula x_1 *likes Cicero* and, so to speak, marks the position upon which the quantifier has an impact, the position that, in effect, represents the spot the quantified noun phrase occupies in surface syntax.

Contrast this with *Cicero*, which stands for an object (the same object, whatever the sequence), and which is therefore a complete symbol:

(3) ∀s(Ref(*Cicero*, s) = Cicero).

This axiom just says that the referent of *Cicero*, relative to any sequence s, is Cicero. Now perhaps there is a sense in which the *variable* in (3) might

[6] Systems that mix restricted and unrestricted quantifiers are perfectly respectable—indeed, they may be desirable to capture all aspects of the semantics of natural language, especially where quantification over events, times, and places is involved.

[7] See e.g. Davies (1981), Evans (1977, 1980), Higginbotham and May (1981), Neale (1993b), Sainsbury (1990), Wiggins (1980a). I here use "binary" in the sense of Evans and Wiggins (see n. 5).

be construed as *complete-with-respect-to-a-sequence* by virtue of standing for an object in its own relativized way:

(4) $\forall s \forall k(\mathrm{Ref}(x_\mathrm{I}, s) = s_\mathrm{I})$.

But, however you look at it, the way I have set things up neither the English definite description "the king" nor the restricted quantifier $[the_\mathrm{I}: king\ x_\mathrm{I}]$ that binds the variable in (3) is a complete symbol. Given the axioms I have used, the quantifier does not even *purport* to stand for an object, not even when relativized to sequences. There is no interesting sense, then, in which the restricted quantifier treatment of descriptions conflicts with Russell's conception of descriptions as incomplete symbols. It is the element of quantification in "the F is G", "every F is G", and "some F is G" that creates a gap between grammatical form and so-called "logical form".[8] And quantification, whether unrestricted, restricted, or

---

[8] In recent work incorporating part of his (1992b) review, L. Linsky seems to see this in places, but his discussion seems still to be marred by a misunderstanding of Russell's notion of an incomplete symbol. Much of the trouble seems to stem from confusing properties of "the" with properties of "the F", confusing properties of "the F" with properties of $[the_x: Fx]$ (which, unlike "the F", must be connected to an overt variable to do its job), a use–mention confusion that manifests itself in a pervasive equivocation about the meanings of the words "proposition" and "constituent" (on some occurrences "sentence" and "phrase" seem better; on others non-linguistic interpretations seem to be called for; on still others *neither* seems correct), and an equivocation about the meaning of "logical form" (e.g. Linsky says that "Neale argues that Russell's analysis is not the correct logical form" (MS, 13); if, by "the correct logical form", Linsky means the assignation of a quantificational structure with Russell's truth-conditions, then the claim is obviously false; but if he means by it the particular representation of that quantificational structure, with Russell's truth-conditions, within a system of restricted quantification, his claim is trivially true; either way it is uninteresting). Linsky seems to place too much emphasis on Russell's particular notation and not enough on the logical and philosophical ideas behind them, and this seems to blind him to the fact that even the expressions •, ≡ and = occurring in Russell's $\exists x(\forall y(\phi(y) \equiv y=x) \bullet \psi(x))$ are to be analysed away at some point for certain of Russell's purposes, perhaps using | if we take at face value comments in the introduction to the second edition of *Principia Mathematica*.

Linsky argues, correctly, that "Russell's project is committed to his account of definite descriptions as incomplete symbols" (forthcoming, MS, 13). He is quite wrong, however, when he claims that in *Descriptions* I hold that Russell's descriptions are incomplete symbols "simply from the want of a more sophisticated logic" (ibid.). Not only do I not make this claim, I am committed to its negation. Apparently Linsky misunderstands what Russell means by "incomplete symbol", the notation of restricted quantification that I and many others use, and the relationship between the notation of restricted quantification and the particular semantics of generalized quantifiers. The fact that Russell views descriptions as incomplete symbols has nothing to do with the fact that he does not have restricted quantifiers in his system, for the simple reason that a restricted quantifier $[the_x: Fx]$ is just as much an incomplete symbol as Russell's $\imath x Fx$ in systems in which quantifiers do not stand for things, such as in the Tarskian systems I have been using in this book.

binary, can be handled perfectly well while taking denoting phrases to be incomplete symbols.

In view of the need to discuss certain "derived" rules of inference employed by Whitehead and Russell, in this book I use standard logical notation supplemented with the *iota*-operator. But the fact that Russell's theory can be implemented in a system of restricted quantification should quell any fears about the degree of mismatch between logical and grammatical form and also defuse a worry of Gödel's (see Chapter 5) by indicating how Russell's theory can function as a component of a general and systematic theory of quantified noun phrases in natural language.

(Furthermore, as noted above, it is not the restricted quantifier alone, but the combination of the restricted quantifier and a bound variable occupying an argument position that does the work of a natural language description in the language of restricted quantification.) Linsky seems to think that because the restricted quantifier $[the_x: Fx]$ is a syntactic constituent of $[the_x: Fx]\psi$ (in the same way in which the unrestricted $\exists x$ is a constituent of $\exists x\psi$), a semantic theory is somehow *required* to treat it as standing for something. But this is simply not so. It all depends on the overall semantic theory within which an account of restricted quantification is located. Some semanticists view such quantifiers as standing for things; but others—notoriously, Davidson (see Ch. 2)—do not. Perhaps Linsky has something very different in mind from Russell when he uses the phrase "incomplete symbol". As far as I can ascertain, my interpretation of Russell squares with Kaplan's (1972) on matters pertaining to incomplete symbols, logical form, and contextual definition. Why Linsky sees Kaplan and me as taking opposing sides in a fruitless controversy is something of a mystery.

References

ACHINSTEIN, P. (1975), "Causation, Transparency, and Emphasis", *Canadian Journal of Philosophy* 5: 1–23.

—— (1979), "The Causal Relation", in P. A. French, T. E. Uehling, and H. K. Wettstein (eds.), *Midwest Studies in Philosophy, iv: Studies in Metaphysics* (Minneapolis: University of Minnesota Press) 369–86.

ALSTON, W. P. (1996), *A Realist Conception of Truth* (Ithaca, NY: Cornell University Press).

ALTMAN, A., BRADIE, M., and MILLER, D., JR. (1979), "On Doing without Events", *Philosophical Studies*, 36: 301–6.

ANDERSON, A. R., and BELNAP, N. D., JR. (1962), "Tautological Entailment", *Philosophical Studies*, 13: 9–24.

ANSCOMBE, G. E. (1959), *An Introduction to Wittgenstein's "Tractatus"*: (London: Hutchison).

—— (1969), "Causality and Extensionality", *Journal of Philosophy*, 66: 152–9.

ARMSTRONG, D. (1993), "A World of States of Affairs", in J. Tomberlin (ed.), *Philosophical Perspectives*, 7: 429–40.

—— (1997), *A World of States of Affairs* (Cambridge: Cambridge University Press).

AUNE, B. (1985), *Metaphysics: The Elements* (Minneapolis: University of Minnesota Press).

AUSTIN, J. L. (1950), "Truth", *Proceedings of the Aristotelian Society,* suppl. vol. 24: 111–28; repr. in J. O. Urmson and G. J. Warnock (eds.), *Philosophical Papers* (Oxford: Oxford University Press, 1961), 85–101.

—— (1954), "Unfair to Facts", in J. O. Urmson and G. J. Warnock (eds.), *Philosophical Papers* (Oxford: Oxford University Press, 1961), 101–22.

BACH, K. S. (1994), *Thought and Reference* (Oxford: Oxford University Press).

BARWISE, J., and COOPER, R. (1981), "Generalized Quantifiers and Natural Language", *Linguistics and Philosophy*, 4: 159–219.

—— and ETCHEMENDY, J. (1989), *The Liar: An Essay on Truth and Circularity* (Oxford: Clarendon Press).

—— and PERRY, J. (1980), "The Situation Underground", in J. Barwise and I. A. Sag (eds.), *Stanford Working Papers in Linguistics* (Stanford, Calif.), Stanford Cognitive Science Group, 88–101.

234   *References*

BARWISE, J., and PERRY, J. (1981), "Semantic Innocence and Uncompromising Situations", in P. A. French, T. E. Uehling Jr., and H. K. Wettstein (eds.), *Midwest Studies in Philosophy*, vi: *The Foundations of Analytic Philosophy* (Minneapolis: Minnesota University Press), 387–403.

—— (1983), *Situations and Attitudes* (Cambridge, Mass.: MIT Press).

BAYLIS, C. A. (1948), "Facts, Propositions, Exemplification and Truth", *Mind*, 57: 459–79.

—— (1968), "Lewis' Theory of Facts", in P. A. Schilpp (ed.), *The Philosophy of C. I. Lewis* (LaSalle, Ill.: Open Court), 201–222.

BENNETT, A. A., and BAYLIS, C. A. (1939), *Formal Logic: A Modern Introduction* (New York: Prentice-Hall).

BENNETT, J. (1988), *Events and their Names* (New York: Hackett).

BERGMANN, G. 1960: *Meaning and Existence*. Madison: University of Wisconsin.

—— (1992), *New Foundations of Ontology* (Madison: University of Wisconsin Press).

BERNAYS, P. (1946), Review of Gödel's "Russell's Mathematical Logic", *Journal of Symbolic Logic*, 11: 75–9.

BILGRAMI, A. (2000), "Is Truth a Goal of Inquiry? Rorty and Davidson on Truth", in R. Brandom (ed.), *Rorty and his Critics* (Oxford: Blackwell), 242–62.

BLACKBURN, W. (1988), "Wettstein on Definite Descriptions", *Philosophical Studies*, 53: 263–78.

BRANDOM, R. (1994), *Making it Explicit: Reasoning, Representing, and Discursive Commitment* (Cambridge, Mass.: Harvard University Press).

BURGE, T. (1974), "Truth and Singular Terms", *Noûs*, 8: 309–25.

—— (1986a), "Frege on Truth", in L. Haaparanta and J. Hintikka (eds.), *Frege Synthesized* (Dordrecht: Reidel), 97–154.

—— (1986b), "On Davidson's 'Saying That'", in E. LePore (ed.), *Truth and Interpretation* (Oxford: Blackwell), 190–208.

BURKS, A. (1951), "The Logic of Causal Propositions", *Mind*, 60: 363–82.

CARNAP, R. (1937), *The Logical Syntax of Language* (London: Kegan Paul).

—— (1942), *Introduction to Semantics* (Cambridge, Mass.: Harvard University Press).

—— (1947), *Meaning and Necessity.* (Chicago: University of Chicago).

CARTWRIGHT, R. (1968), "Some Remarks on Essentialism", *Noûs*, 2: 229–46.

CHISHOLM, R. (1965), "Query on Substitutivity", *Boston Studies in the Philosophy of Science*, vol. ii (Dordrecht: Reidel), 275–78.

CHURCH, A. (1940), "A Formulation of the Simple Theory of Types", *Journal of Symbolic Logic*, 5: 56–68.

—— (1942), Review of Quine's "Whitehead and the Rise of Modern Logic", *Journal of Symbolic Logic*, 7: 100–1.

—— (1943*a*), Review of Carnap's *Introduction to Semantics*, *Philosophical Review*, 52: 298–304.

—— (1943*b*), Review of Quine's "Notes on Existence and Necessity", *Journal of Symbolic Logic*, 8: 45–7.

—— (1944), *Introduction to Mathematical Logic*, pt. 1 (Princeton: Princeton University Press).

—— (1956), *Introduction to Mathematical Logic* (Princeton: Princeton University Press).

CLARK, E. (1971), "On the Acquisition of the Meaning of 'Before' and 'After'", *Journal of Verbal Learning and Verbal Behavior*, 10: 266–75.

—— (1975), "Facts, Fact-Correlates, and Fact-Surrogates", in P. Welsh (ed.), *Fact, Value, and Perception: Essays in Honor of Charles A. Baylis.* (Durham, NC: Duke University Press).

COOPER, R. (1979), "The Interpretation of Pronouns", in F. Heny and H. Schnelle (eds.), *Syntax and Semantics*, x: *Selections from the Third Gröningen Round Table* (New York: Academic Press), 61–92

CRESSWELL, M. (1973), *Logics and Languages* (London: Methuen).

—— (1975), "Identity and Intensional Objects", *Philosophia*, 5: 47–68.

CUMMINS, R., and GOTTLIEB, D. (1972), "On an Argument for Truth-Functionality", *American Philosophical Quarterly*, 9: 265–9.

DALE, A. J. (1978), "Reference, Truth-Functionality, and Causal Connectives", *Analysis*, 38: 99–106.

DAVIDSON, D. (1969), "True to the Facts", *Journal of Philosophy*, 66: 748–64.

—— (1980), *Essays on Actions and Events* (Oxford: Clarendon Press).

—— (1984), *Inquiries into Truth and Interpretation* (Oxford: Clarendon Press).

—— (1986), "A Coherence Theory of Truth and Knowledge", in E. LePore (ed.), *Truth and Interpretation: Perspectives on the Philosophy of Donald Davidson* (Oxford: Blackwell), 307–19.

—— (1989), "The Myth of the Subjective", in M. Krausz (ed.), *Relativism: Interpretation and Confrontation* (Notre Dame, Ind.: University of Notre Dame Press), 159–72.

—— (1990), "The Structure and Content of Truth", *Journal of Philosophy*, 87: 279–328.

DAVIDSON, D. (1993), "Method and Metaphysics", *Deucalion*, 11: 239–48.

—— (1995), "Pursuit of the Concept of Truth", in P. Leonardi and M. Santambrogio (eds.), *On Quine* (Cambridge: Cambridge University Press), 7–21.

—— (1996), "The Folly of Trying to Define Truth", *Journal of Philosophy*, 93: 263–78.

DAVIDSON, D. (1999a), "Is Truth a Goal of Inquiry?", in U. Zeglen (ed.), *Donald Davidson: Truth, Meaning and Knowledge* (London: Routledge), 17–9.

—— (1999b), "Reply to Gabriel Segal", in U. Zeglen (ed.), *Donald Davidson: Truth, Meaning and Knowledge* (London: Routledge), 57–8.

—— (1999c), "Reply to Stephen Neale", in U. Zeglen (ed.), *Donald Davidson: Truth, Meaning and Knowledge* (London: Routledge), 87–9.

—— (1999d), "Reply to J. J. C. Smart", in L. E. Hahn (ed.), *The Philosophy of Donald Davidson* (Chicago: Open Court), 123–5.

—— (1999e), "Reply to Stephen Neale", in L. E. Hahn (ed.), *The Philosophy of Donald Davidson* (Chicago: Open Court), 667–9.

—— (2000), "Truth Rehabilitated", in B. Brandom (ed.), *Rorty and his Critics* (Oxford: Blackwell), 65–74.

DAVIES, M. (1978), "Weak Necessity and Truth Theories", *Journal of Philosophical Logic*, 7: 15–439.

—— (1981), *Meaning, Quantification, Necessity* (London: Routledge).

DONAHO, S. (1998), "Are Declarative Sentences Representational?", *Mind*, 107: 33–58.

DONNELLAN, K. (1966a), "Reference and Definite Descriptions", *Philosophical Review*, 75, pp. 281–304.

—— (1966b), "Substitution and Reference", *Journal of Philosophy*, 63: 685–8.

—— (1968), "Putting Humpty Dumpty Back Together Again", *Philosophical Review*, 77:

—— (1978), "Speaker Reference, Descriptions, and Anaphora", in P. Cole (ed.), *Syntax and Semantics*, ix: *Pragmatics* (New York: Academic Press), 47–68.

—— (1981), "Presupposition and Intuitions", in P. Cole (ed.), *Radical Pragmatics* (New York: Academic Press), 129–42.

DUCASSE, C. J. (1926), "On the Nature and Observability of the Causal Relation", *Journal of Philosophy*, 23: 57–68.

—— (1940), "Propositions, Opinions, Sentences and Facts", *Journal of Philosophy*, 37: 101–71.

—— (1942), "Is a Fact a True Proposition?—A Reply", *Journal of Philosophy*, 39: 133–5.

—— (1945), "Facts, Truth, and Knowledge", *Philosophy and Phenomenological Research*, 5: 320–32.

ETCHEMENDY, J. (1990), *The Concept of Logical Consequence* (Cambridge, Mass.: Harvard University Press).

EVANS, G. (1977), "Pronouns, Quantifiers and Relative Clauses (I)", *Canadian Journal of Philosophy*, 7: 467–536.

—— (1980), "Pronouns", *Linguistic Inquiry*, 11: 337–62.

—— (1982), *The Varieties of Reference* (Oxford: Clarendon Press).

—— (1985), "Does Tense Logic Rest on a Mistake?", in his *Collected Papers* (Oxford: Clarendon Press), 343–63.

—— and McDowell, J. (1976), "Introduction", in G. Evans and J. McDowell (eds.), *Truth and Meaning: Essays in Semantics* (Oxford: Clarendon Press), vii–xxiii.

Evnine, S. (1991), *Donald Davidson* (Oxford: Blackwell).

Field, H. (1972), "Tarski's Theory of Truth", *Journal of Philosophy*, 69: 347–75; repr. in R. M. Kempson (ed.), *Mental Representations: The Interface between Language and Reality* (Cambridge: Cambridge University Press), 83–110.

Fine, K. (1982), "First-Order Modal Theories III—Facts", *Synthese*, 53: 43–122.

Fitch, G. (1949), "The Problem of the Morning Star and the Evening Star", *Philosophy of Science*, 16: 137–41.

—— (1950), "Attribute and Class", in M. Farber (ed.), *Philosophic Thought in France and the United States* (Buffalo, NY: University of Buffalo Press), 545–63.

Fodor, J. A., and LePore, E. (1992), *Holism: A Shopper's Guide* (Oxford: Blackwell).

Fodor, J. D. and Sag, I. (1982), "Referential and Quantificational Indefinites", *Linguistics and Philosophy*, 5: 355–98.

Føllesdal, D. (1961), "Referential Opacity and Modal Logic", doctoral thesis, Harvard University.

—— (1965), "Quantification into Causal Contexts", *Boston Studies in the Philosophy of Science*, vol. ii (Dordrecht: Reidel), 263–74.

—— (1966), "Referential Opacity and Modal Logic", *Filosofiske Problemer*, vol. xxxii (Oslo: Universitetforslaget).

—— (1967), "Knowledge, Identity, and Existence", *Theoria*, 33: 1–27.

—— (1969), "Quine on Modality", in D. Davidson and J. Hintikka (eds.), *Words and Objections* (Dordrecht: Reidel), 175–85.

—— (1983), "Situation Semantics and the Slingshot", *Erkenntnis*, 19: 91–8.

Foster, J. (1976), "Meaning and Truth Theory", in G. Evans and J. McDowell (eds.), *Truth and Meaning: Essays in Semantics* (Oxford: Clarendon Press), 1–32.

—— (1973), "Extension, Intension and Comprehension", in M. Munitz (ed.), *Logic and Ontology* (New York: New York University Press), 101–31.

—— and Lambert, K. (1967), "On Free Description Theory", *Zeitschrift für mathematische Logik und Grundlagen der Mathematik*, 13: 225–40.

Frege, G. (1879), *Begriffsschrift*, Eng. trans. in J. van Heijenoort (ed.), *From Frege to Gödel* (Cambridge, Mass.: Harvard University Press, 1967).

238   *References*

FREGE, G. (1892), "Über Sinn und Bedeutung", *Zeitschrift für Philosophie und Philosophische Kritik*, 100: 25–50; trans. as "On Sense and Reference", in P. Geach and M. Black (eds.), *Translations from the Philosophical Writings of Gottlob Frege* (Oxford: Blackwell, 1952), 56–78.

—— (1893), *Die Grundgesetze der Arithmetik*, vol i. (Jena: Verlag Hermann Pohle; repr Hildesheim: Georg Olms Verlagsbuchhandlung, 1962); trans. M. Furth as *The Basic Laws of Arithmetic* (Berkeley and Los Angeles: University of California Press, 1964).

—— (1906a), Letter to Husserl, 30 Oct.–1 Nov. 1906, in G. Frege, *Philosophical and Mathematical Correspondence* (Oxford: Blackwell, 1980), 66–70.

—— (1906b), Letter to Husserl, December 9th, 1906, in G. Frege, *Philosophical and Mathematical Correspondence* (Oxford: Blackwell, 1980), 70–1.

—— (1906c), "A Brief Survey of my Logical Doctrines", in G. Frege, *Posthumous Writings* (Oxford: Blackwell, 1979), 197–202.

—— (1919), "Der Gedanke. Eine logische Untersuchung", *Beiträge zur Philosophie des deutschen Idealismus*, vol. i; trans. A. M. and A. Quinton as "The Thought: A Logical Inquiry", *Mind*, 65 (1956), 289–311; repr. in P. F. Strawson (ed.), *Philosophical Logic* (Oxford: Oxford University Press, 1967), pp. 17–38.

GALE, R. (1970), "Strawson's Restricted Theory of Referring", *Philosophical Quarterly*, 20: 162–5.

GANERI, J. (1995), "Contextually Incomplete Descriptions—a New Counterexample to Russell?", *Analysis*, 55: 287–90.

GEACH, P. T. (1972), *Logic Matters* (Berkeley: University of California Press).

GÖDEL, K. (1944), "Russell's Mathematical Logic", in P. A. Schilpp (ed.), *The Philosophy of Bertrand Russell* (Evanston, Ill: Northwestern University Press), 125–53.

—— (1990), *Kurt Gödel, Collected Works,* vol. ii, ed. S. Feferman *et al.* (Oxford: Clarendon Press).

GOTTLIEB, D., and DAVIS, L. (1974), "Extensionality and Singular Causal Sentences", *Philosophical Studies*, 25: 69–72.

GRAFF, D. (2001), "Descriptions as Predicates", *Philosophical Studies*, 102: 1–42.

GRANDY, R. (1972), "A Definition of Truth for Theories with Intensional Definite Description Operators", *Journal of Philosophical Logic*, 1: 137–55.

GRICE, H. P. (1989), *Studies in the Way of Words* (Cambridge, Mass.: Harvard University Press).

GROSSMAN, R. (1983), *The Categorial Structure of the World*, (Bloomington: Indiana University Press).

—— (1992), *The Existence of the World* (London: Routledge).

HALLDÉN, S. (1949), *The Logic of Nonsense* (Uppsala: Uppsala Universitets Arsskrift).

HARMAN, G. (1972), "Deep Structure as Logical Form", in D. Davidson and G. Harman (eds.), *Semantics of Natural Language* (Dordrecht: Reidel), 25–47.

HARRÉ, R., and MADDEN, E. H. (1975), *Causal Powers: A Theory of Natural Necessity* (Oxford: Blackwell).

HERBST, P. (1952), "The Nature of Facts", *Australasian Journal of Philosophy*, 30: 90–116.

HIGGINBOTHAM, J. (1983), "The Logic of Perceptual Reports: An Extensional Alternative to Situation Semantics", *Journal of Philosophy*, 80: 100–27.

—— (1988), "Contexts, Models, and Meanings: A Note on the Data of Semantics", in R. M. Kempson (ed.), *Mental Representations: The Interface between Language and Reality* (Cambridge: Cambridge University Press), 29–48.

—— (1992), "Truth and Understanding", *Philosophical Studies*, 65: 3–16.

—— (1999), "Perceptual Reports Revisited", in R. Stainton (ed.), *Philosophy and Linguistics* (Cambridge, Mass.: MIT Press), 11–33.

HIGGINBOTHAM, J., and MAY, R. (1981), "Questions, Quantifiers and Crossing", *Linguistic Review*, 1: 41–80.

HILBERT, D., and BERNAYS, P. (1934), *Grundlagen der Mathematik*, vol. i (Berlin: Springer; 2nd edn. 1968).

HINTIKKA, J. (1963), "Modes of Modality", *Acta Philosophica Fennica*, 16: 65–82.

—— (1968), "Logic and Philosophy", in R. Klibansky (ed.), *Contemporary Philosophy* (Florence: La Nuova Italia Editrice), 3–30.

—— and KULAS, J. (1985), *Anaphora and Definite Descriptions* (Dordrecht: Reidel).

—— and SANDU, G. (1991), *On the Methodology of Linguistics: A Case Study* (Oxford: Blackwell).

HOCHBERG, H. (1978), "Descriptions, Substitution, and Intentional Contexts", in his *Thought, Fact, and Reference: Origins of Ontology and Logical Atomism* (Minneapolis: University of Minnesota Press).

—— (1984), "Facts and Truth", in his *Logic, Ontology, and Language: Essays on Truth and Reality* (Munich: Philosophia Verlag), 279–95.

HORGAN, T. (1978), "The Case against Events", *Philosophical Review*, 87: 28–47.

—— (1982), "Substitutivity and the Causal Connective", *Philosophical Studies*, 42: 47–52.

HORNSBY, J. (1996), "The Identity Theory of Truth", Presidential Address, *Proceedings of the Aristotelian Society*, 97: 1–24.

HORNSTEIN, N. (1984), *Logic as Grammar* (Cambridge, Mass.: MIT Press).

HUSSERL, E. (1913), *Logische Untersuchungen*, vol. ii, 2nd edn. (Halle: Niemeyer); Eng. trans. J. N. Findlay (London: Routledge & Kegan Paul, 1970).

JOHNSON, H. (1975), "The Meaning of 'Before' and 'After' for Preschool Children", *Journal of Experimental Child Psychology*, 19: 88–99.

KALISH, D., MONTAGUE, R., and MAR, D. (1980), *Logic: Techniques of Formal Reasoning*, 2nd edn. (New York: Harcourt, Brace, Jovanovich).

KANGER, S. (1957), *Provability in Logic* (Stockholm: Almqvist & Wiksill).

KAPLAN, D. (1964), "Foundations of Intensional Logic", Ph.D. thesis, University of California, Los Angeles.

—— (1972), "What is Russell's Theory of Descriptions?", in D. F. Pears (ed.), *Bertrand Russell: A Collection of Critical Essays* (Garden City, NY: Doubleday Anchor), 227–44.

—— (1978), "Dthat", in P. Cole (ed.), *Syntax and Semantics*, ix: *Pragmatics* (New York: Academic Press), 221–43.

—— (1986), "Opacity", in L. E. Hahn and P. A. Schilpp (eds.), *The Philosophy of W. V. Quine* (LaSalle, Ill.: Open Court), 229–89.

—— (1989a), "Demonstratives", in J. Almog, J. Perry, and H. Wettstein (eds.), *Themes from Kaplan* (New York: Oxford University Press), 481–563.

—— (1989b), "Afterthoughts", in J. Almog, J. Perry, and H. Wettstein (eds.), *Themes from Kaplan* (New York: Oxford University Press), 565–614.

KIM, J. (1993), *Supervenience and Mind* (Cambridge: Cambridge University Press).

KÖRNER, S. (1960), *The Philosophy of Mathematics* (London: Hutchison).

KRIPKE, S. A. (1963a), "Semantical Considerations on Modal Logic", *Acta Philosophica Fennica*, 16: 83–94.

—— (1963b), "Semantical Analysis of Modal Logic: I, Normal Modal Propositional Calculi", *Zeitschrift für Mathematische Logik und Grundlagen der Mathematik*, 9: 67–96.

—— (1971), "Identity and Necessity", in M. K. Munitz (ed.), *Identity and Individuation* (New York: New York University Press), 135–64; repr. in S. P. Schwartz (ed.), *Naming, Necessity, and Natural Kinds* (Ithaca, NY: Cornell University Press), 66–101.

—— (1977), "Speaker Reference and Semantic Reference", in P. A. French, T. E. Uehling, and H. K. Wettstein, *Contemporary Perspectives in the Philosophy of Language* (Minneapolis: University of Minnesota Press), 6–27.

—— (1979), "A Puzzle about Belief", in A. Margalit (ed.), *Meaning and Use* (Dordrecht: Reidel), 239–83.

—— (1980), *Naming and Necessity* (Cambridge, Mass.: Harvard University Press).

LAMBERT, K. (1962), "Notes on "E!" III: A Theory of Descriptions", *Philosophical Studies*, 13: 51–8.

—— (1991), "A Theory of Definite Descriptions", in K. Lambert (ed.), *Philosophical Applications of Free Logic* (Oxford: Clarendon Press), 17–27.

LARSON, R. K., and SEGAL, G. (1995), *Knowledge of Meaning: An Introduction to Semantic Theory* (Cambridge, Mass., MIT Press).

LEPORE, E. (1986), "Truth in Meaning", in E. LePore (ed.), *Truth and Interpretation* (Oxford: Blackwell), 3–26.

—— and LOEWER B. (1990), "What Davidson should have Said", in E. Villanueva (ed.), *Information, Semantics and Epistemology* (Oxford: Blackwell), 190–9.

LEVIN, M. (1976), "The Extensionality of Causation and Causal Explanatory Contexts", *Philosophy of Science*, 43: 266–77.

LEWIS, C. I. (1923), "Facts, Systems, and the Unity of the World", *Journal of Philosophy*, 20/6: 141–51; repr. in J. D. Goheen and J. L. Mothershead, Jr. (eds.), *Collected Papers of Clarence Irving Lewis* (Stanford, Calif.: Stanford University Press), 1970, 383–93.

—— (1944), "The Modes of Meaning", *Philosophy and Phenomenological Research*, 4/2 (1943–4), 236–49; repr. in J. D. Goheen and J. L. Mothershead, Jr. (eds.), *Collected Papers of Clarence Irving Lewis* (Stanford, Calif.: Stanford University Press, 1970), 303–16.

—— (1946), *An Analysis of Knowledge and Valuation* (LaSalle, Ill.: Open Court).

—— (1968), "Replies to my Critics", in P. A. Schilpp (ed.), *The Philosophy of C. I. Lewis* (LaSalle, Ill.: Open Court), 653–76.

LEWIS, D. K. (1973), *Counterfactuals* (Oxford: Blackwell).

—— (1975), "Adverbs of Quantification", in E. Keenan (ed.), *Formal Semantics of Natural Language* (Cambridge: Cambridge University Press), 3–15.

—— (1979), "Scorekeeping in a Language Game", *Journal of Philosophical Logic*, 8: 339–59.

LEWIS, D. K. (1985), *The Plurality of Worlds* (Oxford: Blackwell).

LINDSTRÖM, P. (1966), "First-order Predicate Logic with Generalized Quantifiers", *Theoria*, 32: 186–95.

—— (1991), "Critical Study of Jon Barwise and John Perry's *Situations and Attitudes*", *Noûs*, 25: 743–70.

LINSKY, B. (1992a), "A Note on the 'Carving up Content Principle' in Frege's Theory of Sense", *Notre Dame Journal of Formal Logic*, 33: 126–35.

—— (1992b), "The Logical Form of Descriptions", *Dialogue*, 31/4: 677–83.

LINSKY, B. (forthcoming), "Russell's Logical Form, LF and Truth Conditions", in G. Preyer (ed.) *Logical Form* (Oxford: Oxford University Press).

LINSKY L. (1966), "Substitutivity and Descriptions", *Journal of Philosophy*, 63: 677–83.

—— (1977), *Names and Descriptions* (Chicago: University of Chicago Press).

—— (1983), *Oblique Contexts* (Chicago: University of Chicago Press).

LOAR, B. (1976) "Two Theories of Meaning", in G. Evans and J. McDowell (eds.), *Truth and Meaning: Essays in Semantics* (Oxford: Clarendon Press), 138–61.

LOMBARD, B. (1979), "The Extensionality of Causal Contexts: Comments on Rosenberg and Martin", in P. A. French, T. E. Uehling, and H. K. Wettstein (eds.), *Midwest Studies in Philosophy*, iv: *Studies in Metaphysics* (Minneapolis: University of Minnesota Press), 409–15.

LUDLOW, P., and NEALE, S. R. A. (1991), "Indefinite Descriptions: In Defence of Russell", *Linguistics and Philosophy*, 14/2: 171–202.

LYCAN, W. (1974), "The Extensionality of Cause, Space, and Time", *Mind*, 83: 498–511.

—— (1984), *Logical Form in Natural Language* (Cambridge, Mass.: MIT Press).

MCDOWELL, J. (1977), "On the Sense and Reference of a Proper Name", *Mind*, 86: 159–85.

MCGINN, C. (1976), "A Note on the Frege Argument", *Mind*, 85: 422–3.

MACKIE, J. L. (1965), "Causes and Conditions", *American Philosophical Quarterly*, 2: 245–64.

—— (1974), *The Cement of the Universe* (Oxford: Clarendon Press).

MANNING, R. N. (1998), "All Facts Great and Small", *Protosociology*, 11: 18–40.

MARCUS, R. (1947), "The Identity of Individuals in a Strict Functional Calculus of First Order", *Journal of Symbolic Logic*, 12: 12–15.

—— (1948), Review of Smullyan's "Modality and Description", *Journal of Symbolic Logic*, 13: 149–50.

—— (1962), "Modalities and Intensional Languages", *Synthese*, 27: 303–22; repr. in I. M. Copi and J. A. Gould (eds.), *Contemporary Philosophical Logic* (New York: St Martin's Press, 1978), 257–72.

MARGALIT, A. (1984), "Frege and the Slingshot", *Iyyun*, 33: 414–21.

MARTI, G. (1994), "Do Modal Distinctions Collapse in Carnap's System?", *Journal of Philosophical Logic*, 23: 575–93.

MATES, B. (1973), "Descriptions and Reference", *Foundations of Language*, 10: 409–18.

MELLOR, H. (1991), *Matters of Metaphysics* (Cambridge: Cambridge University Press).

—— (1995), *The Facts of Causation* (London: Routledge).
MONTAGUE, R. (1963), "Syntactical Treatments of Modality, with Corollaries on Reflexion Principles and Finite Axiomatizability", *Acta Philosophica Fennica*, 16: 153–68.
—— and KALISH, D. (1959), "'That'", *Philosophical Studies*, 10: 54–61.
MOORE, G. E. (1944), "Russell's 'Theory of Descriptions'", in P. A. Schilpp (ed.), *The Philosophy of Bertrand Russell* (New York: Tudor), 177–225.
—— (1956), *Some Main Problems in Philosophy* (London: Unwin).
MORTON, A. (1969), "Extensional and Non-Truth-Functional Contexts", *Journal of Philosophy*, 66: 159–64.
MOSTOWSKI, A. (1957), "On a Generalization of Quantifiers", *Fundamenta Mathematica*, 44: 12–36.
NEALE, S. R. A. (1988), "Events and Logical Form", *Linguistics and Philosophy*, 11/3: 303–21.
—— (1989), "On *One* as an Anaphor", *Behavioral and Brain Sciences*, 353–4.
—— (1990), *Descriptions* (Cambridge, Mass.: MIT Press).
—— (1993a), "Grammatical Form, Logical Form, and Incomplete Symbols", in A. D. Irvine and G. A. Wedeking (eds.), *Russell and Analytic Philosophy* (Toronto: University of Toronto Press), 97–139.
—— (1993b), "Term Limits", *Philosophical Perspectives*, 7: 89–124.
—— (1995), "The Philosophical Significance of Gödel's Slingshot", *Mind*, 104: 761–825.
—— (1999a), "On Representing", in L. E. Hahn (ed.), *The Philosophy of Donald Davidson* (Chicago: Open Court), 657–66.
—— (1999b), "From Semantics to Ontology", in U. Zeglen (ed.), *Donald Davidson: Truth, Meaning and Knowledge* (London: Routledge) 77–87.
—— (1999c), "Colouring and Composition", in R. Stainton (ed.), *Philosophy and Linguistics* (Cambridge, Mass.: MIT Press), 35–82.
—— (2000a), "On a Milestone of Empiricism", in P. Kotatko and A. Orenstein (eds.), *Knowledge, Language and Logic: Questions for Quine* (Dordrecht: Kluwer), 237–346.
NEALE, S. R. A. and DEVER, J. (1997), "Slingshots and Boomerangs", *Mind*, 106: 143–68.
NEEDHAM, P. (1988), "Causation: Relation or Connective", *Dialectica*, 42: 201–19.
—— (1994), "The Causal Connective", in J. Faye, U. Scheffler, and M. Urchs (eds.), *Logic and Causal Reasoning* (Berlin: Akademie Verlag), 67–89.
OMELYANCHYK, V. (forthcoming), "Constructive Belief and the Slingshot".
OLIVER, A. (1998), "Facts", in E. Craig (ed.), *The Routledge Encyclopaedia of Philosophy*, vol. iii (London: Routledge), 535–7.

244   *References*

OLSON, K. (1987), *An Essay on Facts* (Stanford: CSLI Publications).
OPPY, G. (1997), "The Philosophical Insignificance of Gödel's Slingshot", *Mind*, 106: 121–41.
PAP, A. (1958), "Dispositions, Concepts, and Extensional Logic", in H. Feigl *et al.* (eds.), *Minnesota Studies in the Philosophy of Science* (Minneapolis: University of Minnesota), vol. ii 196–224.
PARSONS, C. (1990), "Introductory Note to [Gödel] 1944", in S. Feferman *et al.* (eds.), *Kurt Gödel, Collected Works*, vol. ii (Oxford: Clarendon Press), 102–18.
PARSONS, T. (1978), "Pronouns as Paraphrases", ms. University of Massachusetts at Amherst.
PATTON, T. E. (1997), "Explaining Referential/Attributive", *Mind*, 106: 245–61.
PERRY, J. (1996), "Evading the Slingshot", in A. Clark *et al.* (eds.), *Philosophy and Cognitive Science* (Dordrecht: Kluwer), 95–114.
POLLOCK, J. (1984), *The Foundations of Philosophical Semantics* (Princeton: Princeton University Press).
PRIOR, A. (1948), "Facts, Propositions and Entailment", *Mind*, 57: 62–8.
—— (1967), "The Correspondence Theory of Truth", in P. Edwards (ed.), *The Encyclopaedia of Philosophy* (New York: MacMillan).
QUESADA, D. (1993), "States of Affairs and the Evolution of Carnap's Semantics", *Logique et Analyse*, 141/2: 149–57.
QUINE, W. V. (1936), "Truth by Convention", in O. H. Lee (ed.), *Philosophical Essays for A. N. Whitehead* (New York: Longmans); repr. rev. in W. V. Quine, *The Ways of Paradox and Other Essays*, 2nd edn., rev. and enlarged (Cambridge, Mass.: Harvard University Press, 1976), 77–106.
—— (1940), *Mathematical Logic* (Cambridge, Mass.: Harvard University Press; rev. 1951).
—— (1941a), "Whitehead and the Rise of Modern Logic", in P. A. Schilpp (ed.), *The Philosophy of Alfred North Whitehead* (Evanston, Ill.: Northwestern University Press), 127–63; repr. in W. V. Quine, *Selected Logic Papers*, enlarged and rev. (Cambridge, Mass.: Harvard University Press), 3–36.
—— (1941b), Review of Russell's *Inquiry into Meaning and Truth*, *Journal of Symbolic Logic*, 6: 29–30.
—— (1943), "Notes on Existence and Necessity", *Journal of Philosophy*, 40: 113–27.
—— (1947), "On the Problem of Interpreting Modal Logic", *Journal of Symbolic Logic*, 12: 43–8.
—— (1953a), "On What There Is", in W. V. Quine, *From a Logical Point of View* (Cambridge, Mass.: Harvard University Press), 1–19; rev. 1961, 1980.

—— (1953*b*), "New Foundations for Mathematical Logic", in W. V. Quine, *From a Logical Point of View*, 80–101.

—— (1953*c*), "Reference and Modality", in W. V. Quine, *From a Logical Point of View*, 139–59.

—— (1953*d*), "Meaning and Inference", in W. V. Quine, *From a Logical Point of View*, 160–7.

—— (1953*e*), "Three Grades of Modal Involvement", *Proceedings of the XIth International Congress of Philosophy*, Brussels 1953, vol. 14 (Amsterdam: North Holland), 65–81; repr. in W. V. Quine, *The Ways of Paradox*, rev. enlarged (Cambridge, Mass.: Howard University Press, 1975), 158–76.

—— (1956), "Quantifiers and Propositional Attitudes", *Journal of Philosophy*, 53: 177–187.

—— (1960), *Word and Object* (Cambridge, Mass.: MIT Press).

—— (1961), "Reference and Modality", rev. in W. V. Quine, *From a Logical Point of View*, 2nd edn. (Cambridge, Mass.: Harvard University Press), 139–59.

—— (1962), "Reply to Professor Marcus", in M. W. Wartofsky (ed.), *Proceedings of the Boston Colloquium for the Philosophy of Science*, (1961–2), 97–104.

—— (1966), "Russell's Ontological Development", *Journal of Philosophy*, 63: 657–67; repr. rev. in his *Theories and Things* (Cambridge, Mass.: Harvard University Press, 1981), 73–85.

—— (1969), "Replies", in D. Davidson and J. Hintikka (eds.), *Words and Objections* (Dordrecht: Reidel), 292–352.

—— (1970), *Philosophy of Logic*, 2nd edn (Cambridge, Mass.: Harvard University Press).

—— (1977), Review of G. Evans and J. McDowell (eds.), *Truth and Meaning*, *Journal of Philosophy*, 74: 225–41.

—— (1980), "Reference and Modality", 2nd rev. version in W. V. Quine, *From a Logical Point of View*, 2nd edn., rev. (New York: Harper & Row), 139–59.

—— (1981), "Five Milestones of Empiricism", in W. V. Quine, *Theories and Things* (Cambridge, Mass.: Harvard University Press), 67–82.

QUINE, W. V. (1982), *Methods of Logic*, 4th edn. (Cambridge, Mass.: Harvard University Press).

—— (2000), "Reply to Neale", in P. Kotatko and A. Orenstein (eds.), *Knowledge, Language and Logic: Questions for Quine* (Dordrecht: Kluwer), 426–7.

RAMSEY, F. P. (1927), "Facts and Propositions", *Aristotelian Society*, suppl. vol. 7: 153–70.

REED, S. (1993), "The Slingshot Argument", *Logique et Analyse*, 143/4: 195–218.

REICHENBACH, H. (1947), *Elements of Symbolic Logic* (New York: Macmillan).

RODRIGUEZ-PEREYRA, G. (1998*a*), "Searle's Correspondence Theory of Truth and the Slingshot", *Philosophical Quarterly*, 48: 513–22.

—— (1998*b*), "Mellor's Facts and Chances of Causation", *Analysis*, 58/3: 175–81.

RORTY, R. (1979), *Philosophy and the Mirror of Nature* (Princeton: Princeton University Press).

—— (1986), "Pragmatism, Davidson and Truth", in E. LePore (ed.), *Truth and Interpretation: Perspectives on the Philosophy of Donald Davidson* (Oxford: Blackwell), 333–53.

—— (1991), *Objectivity, Relativism, and Truth: Philosophical Papers*, vol. i (Cambridge: Cambridge University Press).

—— (1992), "Twenty-Five Years After", in R. Rorty (ed.), *The Linguistic Turn*, 2nd edn (London: Hackett), 371–4.

ROSENBERG, A., and MARTIN, R. (1979), "The Extensionality of Causal Contexts", in P. A. French, T. E. Uehling, and H. K. Wettstein (eds.), *Midwest Studies in Philosophy*, iv: *Studies in Metaphysics*, (Minneapolis: University of Minnesota Press), 401–8.

ROVANE, C. (1984), "The Metaphysics of Interpretation", in E. LePore (ed.), *Truth and Interpretation: Perspectives on the Philosophy of Donald Davidson* (Oxford: Blackwell), 417–29.

RUNDLE, B. (1965), "Modality and Quantification", in R. J. Butler (ed.), *Analytical Philosophy*, 2nd ser. (Oxford: Blackwell), 27–39.

RUSSELL, B. (1903), *The Principles of Mathematics* (London: George Allen & Unwin).

—— (1904), "Letter to Frege", in G. Frege, *Philosophical and Mathematical Correspondence* (Chicago: University of Chicago Press, 1980), 166–70.

—— (1905), "On Denoting", *Mind*, 14: 479–93; repr. in R. C. Marsh (ed.), *Logic and Knowledge* (London: George Allen & Unwin, 1956), 41–56.

—— (1911), "Knowledge by Acquaintance and Knowledge by Description", in his *Mysticism and Logic* (London: George Allen & Unwin, 1917), 152–67.

—— (1912), *The Problems of Philosophy* (Oxford: Oxford University Press).

—— (1918), "The Philosophy of Logical Atomism", in R. C. Marsh (ed.), *Logic and Knowledge* (London: George Allen & Unwin, 1956), 177–281.

—— (1919), *Introduction to Mathematical Philosophy* (London: George Allen & Unwin).

—— (1944), "Reply to Criticisms", in P. A. Schilpp (ed.), *The Philosophy of Bertrand Russell* (New York: Tudor), 681–741.

—— (1959), "Some Replies to Criticisms", in his *My Philosophical Development* (New York: Simon & Schuster), 214–54.

SAINSBURY, R. M. (1979), *Russell* (London: Routledge & Kegan Paul).

—— (1990), *Logical Forms: An Introduction to Philosophical Logic* (Oxford: Blackwell).

—— (1993), "Russell on Names and Communication", in A. D. Irvine and G. A. Wedeking (eds.), *Russell and Analytic Philosophy* (Toronto: University of Toronto Press), 3–21.

SALMON, N. (1981), *Reference and Essence* (Princeton: Princeton University Press).

—— (1982), "Assertion and Incomplete Definite Descriptions", *Philosophical Studies*, 42: 37–45.

—— (1986), *Frege's Puzzle* (Cambridge, Mass.: MIT Press).

—— and SOAMES, S. (1988), "Introduction", in N. Salmon and S. Soames (eds.), *Propositions and Attitudes* (Oxford: Oxford University Press), 1–15.

SCHIFFER, S. (1987), *Remnants of Meaning* (Cambridge, Mass.: MIT Press).

—— (1995), "Descriptions, Indexicals, and Belief Reports: Some Dilemmas (But not the Ones you Expect)", *Mind*, 104: 107–131.

SCHOCK, R. (1968), *Logics without Existence Assumptions* (Stockholm: Almqvist & Wiksell).

SCOTT, D. (1967), "Existence and Description in Formal Logic", in R. Schoenman (ed.), *Bertrand Russell: Philosopher of the Century* (London: Allen & Unwin), 181–200.

SEARLE, J. (1969), *Speech Acts* (Cambridge: Cambridge University Press).

—— (1979), *Expression and Meaning* (Cambridge: Cambridge University Press).

—— (1995), *The Construction of Social Reality* (London: Free Press).

SEARLE, J. (1998), "Truth: A Reconsideration of Strawson's Views", in L. E. Hahn (ed.), *The Philosophy of P. F. Strawson* (Chicago: Open Court), 385–401.

SEGAL, G. (1999), "A Theory of Truth as a Theory of Meaning", in U. Zeglen (ed.), *Donald Davidson: Truth, Meaning and Knowledge* (London: Routledge), 48–56.

SELLARS, W. (1954), "Presupposing", *Philosophical Review*, 63 197–215.

SHARVY, R. (1969), "Things", *The Monist*, 53: 488–504.

—— (1970), "Truth Functionality and Referential Opacity", *Philosophical Studies*, 21: 5–9.

—— (1972), "Three Types of Referential Opacity", *Philosophy of Science*, 39: 153–61.

—— (1973), "Reply to Wideker", *Philosophia*, 3/4: 453–5.

SHORTER, J. M. (1962), "Facts, Logical Atomism and Reduction", *Australasian Journal of Philosophy*, 40: 283–302.

SKYRMS, B. (1981), "Tractarian Nominalism", *Philosophical Studies*, 40: 199–206.

SLEIGH, R. C. (1966), "Note on an Argument of Quine's", *Philosophical Studies*, 17: 91–3.

SLOTE, M. A. (1974), *Metaphysics and Essence* (Oxford: Blackwell).

SMULLYAN, A. F. (1947), Review of Quine's "The Problem of Interpreting Modal Logic", *Journal of Symbolic Logic*, 12: 139–41.

—— (1948), "Modality and Description", *Journal of Symbolic Logic*, 13: 31–7.

SOAMES, S. (1986), "Incomplete Definite Descriptions", *Notre Dame Journal of Formal Logic*, 27: 349–75.

—— (1987), "Direct Reference, Propositional Attitudes, and Semantic Content", *Philosophical Topics*, 15: 47–87.

—— (1988), "Substitutivity", in J. Thomson (ed.), *On Being and Saying: Essays for Richard Cartwright* (Cambridge, Mass.: MIT Press), 99–132.

—— (1992), "Truth, Meaning, and Understanding", *Philosophical Studies*, 65: 17–36.

—— (1994), "Introduction" (to section on Meaning and Truth), in M. Harnish (ed.), *Basic Topics in the Philosophy of Language* (Englewood Cliffs, NJ: Prentice Hall), 493–516.

—— (1999), *Understanding Truth* (New York: Oxford University Press).

SOMMERS, F. (1982), *Logic of Natural Language* (Oxford: Clarendon Press).

—— (1993), "The World, the Facts, and Primary Logic", *Notre Dame Journal of Formal Logic*, 34: 169–182.

SPERBER, D., and WILSON, D. (1986), *Relevance* (Oxford: Blackwell).

SPRIGGE, T. L. S. (1970), *Facts, Words and Beliefs* (New York: Humanities Press).

STALNAKER, R. (1972), "Pragmatics", in D. Davidson and G. Harman (eds.), *Semantics of Natural Language* (Dordrecht: Reidel), 380–97.

STERN, C. (1978), "The Alleged Extensionality of 'Causal Explanatory Concepts' ", *Philosophy of Science*, 45: 614–25.

STRAWSON, P. F. (1950a), "Truth", *Proceedings of the Aristotelian Society*, suppl. vol. 24: 129–56.

——(1950b), "On Referring", *Mind*, 59: 320–44.

—— (1952), *Introduction to Logical Theory* (London: Methuen).

—— (1954), "Reply to Mr Sellars", *Philosophical Review*, 63: 216–31.

—— (1964), "Identifying Reference and Truth-Values", *Theoria*, 30: 96–118.

—— (1972), *Subject and Predicate in Logic and Grammar* (London: Methuen).

—— (1986), "Direct Singular Reference: Intended Reference and Actual Reference", in L. Nagl and R. Heinrich (eds.), *Wo Steht die Analytische Philosophie Heute* (Vienna: Oldenbourg Verlag), 75–81.

TARSKI, A. (1956), *Logic, Semantics, Metamathematics* (Oxford: Clarendon Press).

TAYLOR, B. (1976), "States of Affairs", in G. Evans and J. McDowell (eds.), *Truth and Meaning* (Oxford: Clarendon Press), 263–84.

—— (1980), "Truth-Theory for Indexical Languages", in M. Platts (ed.), *Reference, Truth and Reality* (London: Routledge & Paul): 182–98.

—— (1985), *Modes of Occurrence: Verbs, Adverbs, and Events* (Oxford: Blackwell).

THOMASON, R. (1969), "Modal Logic and Metaphysics", in K. Lambert (ed.), *The Logical Way of Doing Things* (New Haven: Yale University Press), 119–46.

TOOLEY, M. (1997), *Time, Tense, and Causation* (Oxford: Clarendon).

TRAVIS, C. (1973), "Causes, Events and Ontology", *Philosophia*, 3/2–3: 201–46.

TRENHOLME, R. (1975), "Causation and Necessity", *Journal of Philosophy*, 72: 444–65.

VAN BENTHEM, J. (1983), "Determiners and Logic", *Linguistics and Philosophy*, 6: 447–78.

VAN FRAASSEN, B. (1969), "Facts and Tautological Entailments", *Journal of Philosophy*, 66/15: 477–87.

VAN FRAASSEN, B. (1973), "Extension, Intension and Comprehension", in M. Munitz (ed.), *Logic and Ontology* (New York: New York University Press), 101–31.

——and LAMBERT, K. (1967), "On Free Description Theory", *Zeitschrift für mathematische Logik und Grundlagen der Mathematik*, 13: 225–40.

VENDLER, Z. (1967a), "Causal Relations", *Journal of Philosophy*, 64: 704–13.

—— (1967b), *Linguistics in Philosophy* (Ithaca, NY: Cornell University Press).

WAGNER, S. (1986), "California Semantics Meets the Great Fact", *Notre Dame Journal of Formal Logic*, 27: 430–55.

WALLACE, J. (1969), "Propositional Attitudes and Identity", *Journal of Philosophy*, 66: 145–52.

WEDBERG, A. (1966), *Filosofins Historia: Fran Bolzano till Wittgenstein* (Stockholm: Bonniers).

—— (1984), *A History of Philosophy*, iii: *From Bolzano to Wittgenstein* (Oxford: Clarendon).

WEINSTEIN, S. (1974), "Truth and Demonstratives", *Noûs*, 8: 179–84.

WELLS, R. S. (1949), "The Existence of Facts", *Review of Metaphysics*, 3: 1–20.

WESTERSTÅHL, D. (1985), "Determiners and Context Sets", in J. van Benthem and A. ter Meulen (eds.), *Quantifiers in Natural Language* (Dordrecht: Foris), 45–71.

—— (1989), "Quantifiers in Formal and Natural Languages", in D. Gabbay and F. Guenther (eds.), *Handbook of Philosophical Logic*, vol. iv (Dordrecht: Reidel), 1–131.

WETTSTEIN, H. (1981), "Demonstrative Reference and Definite Descriptions", *Philosophical Studies*, 40: 241–57.

WHITEHEAD, A. N., and RUSSELL, B. (1925), *Principia Mathematica*, vol. i, 2nd edn. (Cambridge: Cambridge University Press).

WIDERKER, D. (1973), "A Note on Sharvy", *Philosophia*, 3/4: 449–52.

—— (1983), "The Extensionality Argument", *Noûs*, 17: 457–68.

—— (1985), "Davidson on Singular Causal Sentences", *Erkenntnis*, 23: 223–42.

WIGGINS, D. (1980a), " 'Most' and 'All': Some Comments on a Familiar Programme", in M. Platts (ed.), *Reference, Truth and Reality* (London: Routledge & Kegan Paul), 318–46.

—— (1980b), *Sameness and Substance* (Cambridge, Mass.: Harvard University Press).

WILLIAMSON, J. (1976), "Facts and Truth", *Philosophical Quarterly*, 26: 203–16.

WILSON, G. (1990), "Reference and Pronominal Descriptions", *Journal of Philosophy*, 88: 359–87.

—— (1991), "Reference and Pronominal Descriptions", *Journal of Philsophy*, 88: 359–87.

WILSON, N. L. (1959a), "Substances without Substrata", *Review of Metaphysics*, 12: 521–39.

—— (1959b) *The Concept of Language* (Toronto: University of Toronto Press).

—— (1974), "Facts, Events, and their Identity Conditions", *Philosophical Studies*, 25: 303–21.

WITTGENSTEIN, L. (1921), "Logisch-Philosophische Abhandlung", *Annalen der Naturphilosophie*; trans. by D. F. Pears and B. F. McGuinness as *Tractatus Logico-Philosophicus* (London: Routledge & Kegan Paul, 1961).

YOURGRAU, P. (1987), "Frege on Truth and Reference", *Notre Dame Journal of Formal Logic*, 28: 132–38.

Glossary

A. Principles of Inference

PSME. *Principle of Substitutivity for Material Equivalents*:

$(\phi \equiv \psi)$
$\Sigma(\phi)$
___
$\Sigma(\psi)$.

PSST. *Principle of Substitutivity for Singular Terms*:

$\alpha = \beta$ or: $\Sigma(\alpha)$
$\Sigma(\alpha)$ $\sim\Sigma(\beta)$
___
$\Sigma(\beta)$. $\alpha \neq \beta$

PSLE. *Principle of Substitutivity for Logical Equivalents*:

$\phi \models \dashv \psi$
$\Sigma(\phi)$
___
$\Sigma(\psi)$

EG. *Existential Generalization*:

$\Sigma(x/\alpha)$
___
$\exists x \Sigma(x)$

ι-SUBS. *Iota-Substitution (Principle of Substitutivity for Definite Descriptions)*:

$\iota x\phi = \iota x\psi$ $\iota x\phi = \alpha$ $\iota x\phi = \alpha$
$\Sigma(\iota x\phi)$ $\Sigma(\iota x\phi)$ $\Sigma(\alpha)$
___
$\Sigma(\iota x\psi)$ $\Sigma(\alpha)$ $\Sigma(\iota x\phi)$.

λ-CONV. *Either Lambda-Introduction or Lambda-Elimination*

λ-INTR. *Lambda-Introduction:*

$$\frac{T[\Sigma(x/\alpha)]}{T[(\lambda x \Sigma(x))\alpha]}$$

λ-ELIM. *Lambda-Elimination:*

$$\frac{T[(\lambda x \Sigma(x))\alpha]}{T[\Sigma(x/\alpha)]}$$

ι-CONV: *Either Iota -Introduction or Iota-Elimination*

ι-INTR. *Iota-Introduction:*

$$\frac{T[\Sigma(x/\alpha)]}{T[\alpha=\iota x(x=\alpha \bullet \Sigma(x))]}$$

ι-ELIM. *Iota Elimination:*

$$\frac{T[\alpha=\iota x(x=\alpha \bullet \Sigma(x))]}{T[\Sigma(x/\alpha)].}$$

B. Adaptations from 14 of *Principia Mathematica*

*14.01 $[\iota x\phi]\Sigma(\iota x\phi) =_{df} \exists x(\forall y(\phi(y) \equiv y=x) \bullet \Sigma(x))$

*14.02 $E!\iota x\phi =_{df} \exists x \forall y(\phi(y) \equiv y=x)$

*14.15 $(\iota x\phi=\alpha) \supset \{\Sigma(\iota x\phi) \equiv \Sigma(\alpha)\}$

*14.16 $(\iota x\phi=\iota x\psi) \supset \{\Sigma(\iota x\phi) \equiv \Sigma(\iota x\psi)\}$

*14.18 $E!\iota x\phi \supset \{\forall x\Sigma(x) \supset \Sigma(\iota x\phi)\}$

*14.3 $\forall f [\{\forall p \forall q ((p \equiv q) \supset f(p) \equiv f(q)) \bullet E!\iota x\phi)\} \supset$
         $\{f([\iota x\phi]G\iota x\phi) \equiv [\iota x\phi] f(G\iota x\phi)\}]$

Index